STRENGTH-BASED TEACHING

The Affective Teacher, No Child Left Behind

Tim J. Carman

ScarecrowEducation
Lanham, Maryland • Toronto • Oxford
2005

Published in the United States of America
by ScarecrowEducation
An imprint of The Rowman & Littlefield Publishing Group, Inc.
4501 Forbes Boulevard, Suite 200, Lanham, Maryland 20706
www.scarecroweducation.com

PO Box 317
Oxford
OX2 9RU, UK

British Library Cataloguing in Publication Information Available

Library of Congress Cataloging-in-Publication Data

Carman, Tim, 1947–
  Strength-based teaching : the affective teacher, No Child Left Behind /
Tim J. Carman.
    p. cm.
  Includes bibliographical references.
  ISBN 1-57886-178-0 (pbk. : alk. paper)
  1. Education—Aims and objectives—United States. 2. Educational
accountability—United States. 3. Education—Standards—United States. 4.
Academic achievement—United States. 5. United States. No Child Left
Behind Act of 2001. I. Title.
LA217.2.C38 2005
371.39—dc22

                                                            2004015238

CONTENTS

PREFACE

The American public school system is currently being "forced" (without funding) into a highly rigorous, inflexible, deficiency-based (focus is on weaknesses) system that has important consequences for schools. I am concerned about those consequences while believing strongly in the need to improve the public school system in America. There are several important concepts to understand about this author and book before you begin reading. The primary purpose of this book is to help teachers to make the necessary changes in their classroom to create a "high-performance" environment where the achievement gap no longer exists. When the term *teachers* is used in the text, for our purposes here, it is meant to include certified (licensed) and classified (non-licensed) adults or any other responsible adult who has a stake in the school. I would not be surprised if you were a bit skeptical about the pragmatic nature of expecting that teachers can actually close the achievement gap. Of course, schools can close the achievement gap. It has already been done in every state and region of the nation. The students attending public schools are the most diverse and poor of any cohort group in the past.

Unfortunately, the school community has fallen victim to myths with which schools still struggle. The term *school community* is a broad term meaning everyone who has a stake in school—including but not limited to (depending on your unique situation)—all employees (certified and classified), the family, students, business community, youth groups, law enforcement, board members, and other groups and clubs. As we have just touched on potential, I would like to take a moment to make three themes clear before we begin.

Theme One: This book will debunk several myths that are having damaging impacts on school effectiveness. One of the most prevalent and destructive myths is that poor kids of color cannot be expected to achieve high academic standards. The fact that many school communities still behave as if that myth was true is, in itself, a significant obstacle. I will provide ill-refutable evidence that teachers can and do make a difference in student learning. You will be given enough data to share my belief that individual teachers have a profound influence in student learning, even in schools that are relatively ineffective.

Theme Two: This book will add a practical (can do) perspective to the hopeful picture presented in the research. Equally exciting is the existence of new brain development research that will give you pause and challenge your previous assumptions about poor students of color and their potential for success in school and ultimately in life. This book is written to be used as a focus activity by any school community interested in creating a school improvement plan (SIP) to address academic standards. Within the context of this book such an effort will be called the standards-based school (SBS). Consequently, the book is a training tool and meant to be interactive. Each chapter is built on the previous component (as the experience unfolds, the participants are expected to complete a series of activities and to dialogue about them with colleagues). The activities are intended to ensure that the building blocks of the SBS are mastered as the reading unfolds.

Theme Three: This book recognizes the No Child Left Behind (NCLB) Act, only because your school will, likely, be affected by that federal legislation. I have made no claim that the NCLB Act was written to help (or that it will help) schools close the achievement gap. I have such concerns about NCLB that the intent of the NCLB Act is drawn into question. The No Child Left Behind Act will have an effect on your school, so a portion of this study manual will present the hard data about the consequences of that legislation. I also detail how to prepare the community for any consequences that may occur to your school community as a result of the NCLB Act. To be clear, a brief summary of the book's perspective is provided below.

Serious, clear thinking advocates for closing the achievement gap simply must support the goals of NCLB. High expectations for all students are completely correct as is holding schools more accountable for academic achievement. Parents should be involved in decisions about their child's education. What deeply troubles me are the "impossible to meet" criteria. President Bush's education advisors are highly knowledgeable school people, so I have a difficult time believing that such shoddy work was a mistake or a simple oversight. It bothers me greatly that two of the more influential individuals who are, or have been, long-time education advisors are actively involved in the private "for-profit" school movement. As you know by now, the main vehicle for motivating schools to achieve the "impossible to meet" criteria is sanctions. It troubles me that some of the most respected educational organizations predict that a substantially high percentage of all schools will ultimately be unable to meet annual yearly progress (AYP) as measured by subgroups. The first and most injurious of the sanctions is to give students who do not meet the academic AYP the chance to move to another school at the failing school's expense. First, it is inconceivable! I know of absolutely no research anywhere that has concluded that it is best practice to move the struggling child to a different school or that this is a positive academic intervention. Period. The reason it makes absolutely no sense for the children to be moved is because that particular sanction is not intended to help the student; rather, it is intended to punish the school. The serious shortcoming of NCLB is that schools cannot be muscled into improving. This is why: teachers already are making every effort they can to help their students achieve to NCLB criteria. In addition, when a teacher fails to get the students to the standards, it is one thing. In truth, the teacher sees the failure in the mirror of the child's tear. That is motivation enough. Anything more is not only unnecessary, it is unethical.

1

TEACHING AS A PATRIOTIC PURPOSE

The function of education is to teach one to think intensely and to think critically. Intelligence plus character is the true goal of education.

—Martin Luther King Jr., Nobel Prize winner,
20th-century American civil rights leader

What sculpture is to a block of marble, education is to an human soul.

—Joseph Addison

It has been said that you can't depend on your eyes when your imagination is out of focus. As parents, we use our children's eyes to introduce them first to words, then books, and finally complex ideas and even scary ideas about our world. Caring parents frequently introduce some of life's scariest challenges through folk stories, fairy tales, and fables. The nature of our study is at once both complex and scary. Therefore, it seems only fitting that we as educators undergird our study of the achievement gap with story and metaphor to excite the imagination and strengthen the vision. For these reasons, we introduce the complex and scary realities of teaching in a high stakes No Child Left Behind (NCLB) classroom with the following tale.

THE TALE OF THE EARTH SCHOOL

Once upon a time, long ago, the forest animals wanted to develop a school to help the animal children get ahead in forest life. The parents had high hopes for the school because they believed the school could help the community solve an old problem. For many years, the community elders had observed that all of the little animals were not equally successful in forest life. A particular group of forest animal children always seemed to inherit all of the luck. It was a confusing problem and there just didn't seem to be any real answers so the community just procrastinated about what to do. After much discussion, it seemed unlikely that the same type of animal children would always experience success through luck alone. While the adult animals were respectful and patient, the issue of equity of opportunity had become a point of contention that needed to be addressed. After much discussion and reflective thought the community's elders settled on a strategy that could ensure more equity of opportunity for all of the forest animals. A few of the elders began to point out that some of the forest children had better academic and social skills than others. The community began to believe that if something could be done to ensure that all forest children had access to the same basic academic skills, the community might experience more universal success for all citizens. The community elders began suggesting that a school that recognized the inequity issue and addressed it might be the vehicle through which each little animal child might find success. The elders concluded that the school would be the best vehicle through which all forest children would have a chance to build a solid foundation on which success could rest.

The forest community invited a diverse group of forest animal children to be the first to enroll in the school. The elders agreed to keep an eye on the relative success of two animal children that represented the differences to an obvious degree. The names of the representative animal children were Spike Frog (who generally was thought to be a troubled youth) and Sky Eagle (who was considered a high-performance animal child).

Spike was always getting in trouble and causing problems, so he was thought of as a "shadow kid" because he was the type who just seemed to slip through the cracks, become invisible, and eventually get in trou-

ble and just drop out of school. Sky was perceived to be a high performer with a bright future and therefore he was very excited for school
to begin. Sky was quite popular and his family had the reputation for being strong, brave, and self-reliant. The community treated Sky as if he
was a "sunshine child." It was for that reason the community had high
hopes for Sky Eagle. On the other hand, the community did not think
that Spike Frog was going to have success in school unless something
changed. Actually, Spike somehow knew how the other forest animals
felt and agreed that his future was kind of bleak. Therefore, Spike was
not so excited about having to start school because he had not experienced much success making friends in the neighborhood. After all, how
could the whole community (almost) be wrong about him?

As in many communities, the forest community was divided approximately in half by a creek that ran right down the middle of the valley. In
human communities, the dividing line is sometimes a river, a creek, a
railroad line, a highway, or some other barrier (imaginary or real). In
Happy Falls the dividing line tended to separate the poor or different
animals from the mainstream affluent families. For reasons that no one
could remember, all of the affluent animal families lived north of the
creek, had all of the advantages, and always did well in forest life. On the
contrary, the poor animals who lived on the south side continually
seemed to experience hard times. Sky and the others who lived on the
"right" side of the creek were confident that their success would continue. Those who lived on the wrong side of the creek were less certain
of their success. In modern terminology the animals from the south side
of the tracks would be considered poor and referred to as low-SES,
which is shorthand for lower socioeconomic status. Typically, socioeconomic status is related to the knowledge students bring with them to
school. In people schools, high-SES children typically are affluent
whites of European descent and are more successful academically in
school than low-SES children.

As excitement grew in the community of Happy Falls, the elders reminded each other that the purpose in starting the school was to ensure
success for all of the animal children, at first in school, and then in life.
The village elders all agreed they must monitor the performances of
Spike and Sky to ascertain if the school would be successful in helping
all animal children have an equal chance of success in life.

The community elders asked a wise old owl named Richard to head the project, become the first principal, and appoint a curriculum committee. The curriculum committee studied the issues and decided the curriculum to be delivered to all of the animal children, regardless of background, would be jumping, flying, and swimming.

All of the animals in the forest knew about the economic differences the community elders were discussing but no one could ever figure out what to do about it. The forest animals decided to seek the counsel of wise old Dr. Opossum. They asked Dr. Opossum if he thought the community elders were correct in believing that a school may be a solution to the problem of equity of opportunity. Although Dr. Opossum was somewhat uneasy about the plan, he did agree that the school had a chance to ensure the success of all, thereby creating a bright future for the community. Then everyone could live happily ever after.

The forest animals asked Dr. Opossum why he was uneasy about the idea. Dr. Opossum asked about the differences that seemed to separate the groups. He also asked how long the differences had been a concern and how deep the differences went into the community. The community, with some prodding from Dr. Opossum, agreed the differences went back as far as Father Time himself. They also said the differences like language, money, status, color, and even "religion" went deep. Dr. Opossum, with compassion in his voice and a tear in his eye, explained to the forest people the differences were so old and so deep, the school might not be able to solve all of the problems. He used words like "social dominance" and "interdependent systems." Dr. Opossum explained that social dominance occurred when one group in a community acted to block the advancement of others. The meaning of "interdependent systems" was when institutions worked closely together to eliminate the inequity of opportunity. The forest animals just huddled together expressing confusion and amazement. A spokesperson for the forest animals thanked Dr. Opossum for his knowledge and wisdom and then said, "The community is confused by the terms and complex social issues." Then they asked for a clear explanation and Dr. Opossum pulled it all together. Dr. Opossum wisely explained how he felt the ingrained social problems should be approached and why. In his final statement he said, "When communities are faced with deeply ingrained social problems, there is a tendency to search for a quick and easy solution." Dr. Opossum indicated that single-strategy solutions (like looking for schools to solve the problem) were often quick, simple, and even economical.

Unfortunately, Dr. Opossum indicated that single-option solutions place blame, often obscuring the complexities of both the problem and potential solutions. He praised the forest animals for the courage in attempting to find a solution to the complex community-wide problems of social dominance. After that he predicted the animals would discover what was really needed—a systematic reappraisal of the way the community prepared the animal children to go from birth to being capable adults. Such a school could provide the community with productive citizens that would benefit the whole community. In the final analyses, he indicated that a successful school was a prerequisite to equal opportunity. He emphasized that the school could ensure student success in core academic subjects but, while important, basic academic skills were only part of the solution. Dr. Opossum predicated that Happy Falls would really need a comprehensive and coordinated animal investment strategy for child development and education in the community. The elders just scratched their furry little heads in wonder and expressed their gratitude to Dr. Opossum for his wisdom and counsel. And so, the work that focused on developing the intelligence and character of all the animal children began.

The community of forest animals and the elders agreed they should continue with the school while looking at the more comprehensive approach. Therefore, Mr. Owl recommended the first thing to be done was to elect a school board and set up a curriculum committee. The board would establish school goals to ensure that all of the young were given an equal chance at success in life. The school board also confirmed the appointment of Dr. Owl to be the principal of Happy Falls School. The board and the principal, working together, agreed to endorse the curriculum of jumping, swimming, and flying. The committee felt the students in this school had to demonstrate mastery of each academic content area before they could be promoted or graduated from school. After Dr. Owl reviewed the academic content standards, he turned them over to a regional forest authority for a final review.

Dr. Part T. Pation was very positive about the quality of the curriculum work. But, he told the principal, the curriculum still needed further work. He requested the curriculum committee work with the community to identify the core beliefs (support and philosophy) that the school would need to fulfill their dream (vision) of educating all forest children equitably. When the curriculum committee finished their work, the teachers reported the results to the school board. The teachers reported with pride that they had reached consensus on eight core supports that were universally favored and should, therefore, be used by the whole school community to support the school if necessary. Those beliefs were:

1. Early childhood education (Head Start) was needed to ensure that each baby animal received what the animal child needed—educationally—to get ready for school.
2. Prenatal care for the mother and early childhood medical care were needed to ensure that each baby animal received what was needed—medically—to be ready for school.
3. The school must offer clear and measurable academic curriculum that is relevant and interesting to students and aligned directly to the content standards so students could master jumping, swimming, and flying.
4. To meet the diverse needs of all animal children, the program needed to be culturally competent while still maintaining academic rigor. Further character development was available.
5. High expectations for all animals (no matter the background) must be held and supported by everyone.
6. Capacity-based (strength-based) approaches to teaching and learning must be employed by the Happy Falls schoolteachers and parents. The other significant adults in the lives of the forest children must build on the strengths of the forest children, rather than focusing on their weaknesses.
7. The school community must develop job training and social service support at the school as appropriate for the forest children and their family members.
8. The school community must manifest unconditional love (acceptance) for all students.

It was with great excitement and enthusiasm that Happy Falls Elementary opened its doors to the forest children. Spike Frog was very excited about his experience on the first day of school because he felt valued and academically capable. He was surprised that the school had high expectations for him, and really liked him, as well. Spike could hardly wait to tell his parents about the good feelings he had about school because he knew they would be so pleased and proud of him. Spike reported how much he really loved school. After his first several weeks at school, Spike enthusiastically reported that he was excellent in jumping and swimming, but he was worried about the flying curriculum. "It is so much fun, Mom and Pop," Spike reported excitedly. Spike went on to say, "In school, I really get to do the things I enjoy doing. The best part is that I am invited to do things with which I expect to experience success! I didn't think it was going to be like this at school, but I just truly love this," he shrieked. Spike's parents were amazed because they hadn't really expected things to be going quite that well at school for Spike the frog. Sure, they had agreed to sign a contract with Spike's teacher saying they would support high expectations for Spike, but get real, they never expected anything like this! Therefore, they were not surprised when Spike failed the flying class. From the first day in the flying class Spike knew things were going to be very different for him. Mr. Felix was a highly qualified new flying teacher and quite excited about being hired for this very important vocation at the Happy Falls School. He knew that getting Spike to fly would be a challenge, but the training he had in special and bilingual education had prepared him very well. So, he thought that if he simply applied what he had been taught in teacher preparation school he could easily teach Spike to fly: he would become famous. On the first day of flying class Felix told Spike, "I am going to teach you to fly and I will get rich and you will become famous." Spike wasn't so sure and said, "I can't fly, you idiot! I am a frog, not a canary." Those comments cost Spike a trip to the principal's office. The principal explained, "Any further outbursts, and you will be charged with defying school authority and expelled." In addition, the principal said, "That negative attitude of yours could be a real problem so I am sending you to a 'positive thinking' class." Spike grudgingly went to the positive thinking class and learned about emotions, communication, and self-control, but nothing about flying. When he returned to flying class Mr. Felix saw Spike and he could scarcely control his excitement; Spike could barely control his bladder. Mr. Felix had been advised by the principal that Spike needed an Individual Education Program (IEP) and Mr.

Felix felt confident because in his special education classes he had been taught how to individualize instruction. The pattern, he remembered, was a three-step process: (1) teach the concept; (2) monitor the learner's knowledge and understanding through performance-based assessments and adjust the lesson accordingly; and then (3) re-teach the lesson, focusing on the new or emerging learning needs of the student. Mr. Felix explained the plan to Spike with real enthusiasm. Mr. Felix told Spike he had no reservations, while Spike had heart palpitations. Mr. Felix explained the classroom (flying lab) had fifteen different levels and each successive level was ten feet higher than the last. Each day Spike would be given compassionate and knowledgeable instruction as he began jumping off each of the fifteen levels starting with the lowest and eventually moving to the highest level. Mr. Felix told Spike the flying program was based on performance-based assessment so Spike needed to demonstrate the skill of flying successfully. Spike was told the curriculum committee had decided that flying was a critically important skill for the success of every frog in the forest. Spike went home from school that day feeling defeated and scared out of his mind and already feeling like a failure. After each jump, Mr. Felix would analyze how well Spike flew, isolate the most effective flying techniques, and implement the improved instructional process for the next flight.

By the time Spike reached the highest platform Mr. Felix believed Spike would "surely be able to fly." Spike told his parents the school just wouldn't listen and the school seemed increasingly more hostile. Spike said flying was very scary. So Spike, feeling scared out of his mind, complained that he just couldn't keep himself up in the air and he complained, "If I don't do better, I will fall and be killed." The fear was bad enough, but when all the students laughed and made fun of Spike by saying that when he got on the flying platform, he looked simply hysterical and looked more like a scared little chicken than a frog, Spike just withdrew into himself with embarrassment and shame. This reaction from students was very, very hurtful for Spike and he cried, which only made him look like a bigger "chicken." As Spike related all this to his parents— between sobs—they listened intently and said, "We love you, honey, but hang in there," while quietly wondering to themselves if a frog could actually be taught to fly. "Spike, we know you can do it. If you want to amount to anything in your life, you must pass this class. Okay?" Spike's mom concluded by saying to Spike, "Don't worry, sweetheart, I will stop by the school tomorrow to see how you are doing!"

In the meantime, Sky Eagle experienced little trouble with jumping or flying. However, when it came to swimming, Sky had performed significantly below the class average. He was praised for his high achievement in flying and jumping, and he was held up as an example to all. Sky went to the counselor to see if he could get a schedule change because the little eagle just couldn't get the hang of swimming. The counselor reviewed Sky's cumulative school record and determined that Sky had an excellent academic record and concluded that Sky would meet the swimming standards, so he could drop swimming as soon as Sky could demonstrate treading water. The staff agreed that this "modified curriculum" in swimming was appropriate. They looked at the challenge at hand and after careful review, and with complete confidence in Sky's ability to be successful, determined that birds like Sky didn't really need to swim to live successfully. Rather, birds with Sky's ability and record only really needed to learn how to stay afloat in the unlikely event they ever accidentally tumbled into Sunshine Creek or some other water source in the middle of Happy Falls. Sky was on his way! Sky quickly learned to tread water and easily met the modified swimming standards. Sky was promoted to the next grade with the complete fanfare of a parade. In the forest, Spike felt all the more like a loser. Right before his next flying class, Spike found out about Sky's modified curriculum and asked Sky about his good fortune.

Equally determined to find success, Spike went to his counselor and asked if he could also drop his flying class. The curriculum council met, reviewed Spike's cumulative school record, and determined that flying, "without modification," was an appropriate standard for Spike. The committee was, therefore, unwilling to modify the curriculum to meet the individual needs of Spike. Thinking that Spike would do better if he had more time to concentrate on his weaknesses, the counselor removed Spike from jumping and swimming classes, which gave him twice as much time to work on flying. Spike had always really liked and trusted his counselor and asked her why he didn't get the modified curriculum like Sky. His counselor, who really cared for Spike, said with a tear in her eye, "This is harder for me to say than it is for you to hear, but not everyone can be so naturally blessed with talent as Sky. In our judgment Sky will be successful in life even if he can't swim because flying is such a special skill. Sky can go a long way quickly and safely." Spike thanked his counselor, Mrs. Gold E. Locks, for the response and questioned why this was happening to him. "I still really don't understand why we are different. I can swim at the very bottom of the pond and no one but another frog can even find me." Mrs. Gold E. Locks said, with a tremor in her voice, "Please, Spike, try to understand, dear; Sky is a bird and he can naturally fly so he doesn't need as many basic skills as a frog that can only swim and jump. It isn't too early for you to learn that no one ever promised you that life was fair, because for some, like you, it just isn't fair. I am sorry, Spike, and I will always care for you!"

That decision made Spike so upset he wanted to quit school and never come back. When Spike returned to class the following day he pleaded with Mr. Felix for his life, but his plea fell on deaf ears. He just doesn't understand how important this is, thought Mr. Felix, but I won't let a little bad attitude get in my way.

Mr. Felix decided that all he could do was to be the best teacher he could be. After each jump, Mr. Felix would analyze how well Spike flew, isolate the most effective flying techniques, and implement the improved process on the next flight. Spike pleaded for his life, but again, it fell on deaf ears. He just doesn't understand how important this is, Mr. Felix thought. So with that, Mr. Felix took Spike up to the next level and threw Spike the frog off the ledge and Spike landed with a thud.

The next day (poised for another flying lesson) Spike again pleaded not to be thrown off the cliff. With that, Mr. Felix opened his pocket guide to effective teaching in standards-based classrooms and showed Spike the part that said one must always expect difficulty while learning something for the first time. The pocket guide actually read: Always remember everything is hard before it gets easy. Mr. Felix read it to Spike and Spike just shook his head, completely resigned to his unfortunate fate. And with that, Mr. Felix threw Spike off the cliff. Thud!

The next day, which was the third level, Spike tried a different ploy. Stalling, he asked for a delay in the class until better weather could make flying conditions more favorable. Mr. Felix was ready for him: he produced a timeline and pointed to the third standard and asked, "You don't want to fall behind the schedule, do you?" From his training, Spike knew if he didn't jump today he would have to jump twice tomorrow, so he said, "Okay, let's go," and off the cliff he went. Try as he might, Spike still couldn't fly. And, each landing was less and less pleasant. By the seventh lesson, Spike, accepting his fate, no longer begged for mercy; he simply looked at Mr. Felix and said, "You know you are killing me, don't you?"

Mr. Felix pointed out that Spike's performance was far below exemplary, failing to meet any of the standards he had set for him. With that, Spike said quietly, "There is no chance of survival so just let me step to the edge of the cliff." With that, he leaped off the cliff, taking careful aim at the large jagged rock by the corner of the mountain. Spike went to that great lily pad in the sky.

Mr. Felix was extremely upset that his student had failed to meet a single goal he had set out for him to accomplish. Spike had not only failed to fly, he thought, but he was a little troublemaker. Spike hadn't even learned to steer his flight so he fell like a sack of cement. What was almost worse was that he didn't improve his productivity when Mr. Felix told him to "fly smarter, not harder." The only thing left for Mr. Felix to do was to analyze the process and try to determine where Spike had gone wrong. After much reflection, Mr. Felix smiled and said, "Next time, I'm getting a smarter frog!"

When Spike's mom and pop brought these developments to the attention of the principal, Dr. Owl, he was dismayed because the new school was supposed to be focusing on the core supports and addressing the needs of all students so they could all meet high academic standards. After listening and looking carefully at Spike's cumulative record, Dr. Owl said passionately, "It doesn't have to be this way, because this school should be a place where our children are accepted for who they are and helped to concentrate on what they do well so that each student is successful. In addition, the staff here believes each student should receive unconditional love (from the whole school community) and have a confident and realistic expectation of success. Sadly, it looks like we have fallen into our same old trap." In fact, Spike's counselor, Mrs. Gold E. Locks, said, "It won't be this way from now on. We will do a better job, but only with the help of the family and the community." Then the school, community, and family worked together to create a schedule for others like Spike that not only met their learning needs, but was consistent with the core beliefs of the school. In good time, many like Spike and Sky graduated with honors from school and were recognized as "sunshine kids" and subsequently all the forest animals in the little community of Happy Falls were helped to be even more successful.

WHAT IS THE NO CHILD LEFT BEHIND (NCLB) ACT? APATHY OR CHICANERY?

As we begin to discuss the achievement gap, I hold four assumptions about the readers:

1. You are a teacher or like and respect teachers.
2. You think public schools can and should close the achievement gap.
3. You believe unconditional love in schools is a critically important aspect of successfully "closing the achievement gap."
4. You have read much about NCLB and you are skeptical regarding its pragmatism and purpose, yet open to objective discussions and passionate disagreements.

As a background to this discussion it is important to understand the NCLB Act and the political agenda at play. It is vitally important to also understand the standards-based movement (SBM) and how the two, NCLB and SBM, are different. We begin with a simple overview of the NCLB Act and then turn our attentions to the SBM in the following pages.

The No Child Left Behind Act is a congressional statute spelling out federal education spending for all elementary and secondary public schools. The law that details federal education spending was first approved in 1965 and is regularly authorized by Congress. Well before President George W. Bush signed the current reauthorization bill in January 2002, he started calling it the No Child Left Behind (NCLB) Act to bring attention to the changes in the law. How does it differ from past federal spending laws? The biggest difference is that the federal spending contains sanctions (punishments) for schools that fail to make the academic progress spelled out by Congress. What does it require of schools? The centerpiece of the act is a requirement that public schools have 100% of students performing at grade level by the spring of 2014. How are students measured? Academic progress is measured by the states' reading and math tests. Of great significance is that each school's enrollment is divided into ten specific subgroups along the lines of race, family income, and other factors. Each group must contain at least forty students to be measured. A school meets the NCLB requirement only if each of the subgroups of students makes the academic progress necessary to get 100% of the students at grade level by 2014. If any subgroup fails in either subject, the whole school fails to meet the federal requirement. Are all schools affected? Only schools that receive federal money known as Title I money are at risk of being sanctioned.

All schools will be judged—regardless if they take any Title I money—and the results made public. Schools using Title I money that fail to meet the federal requirements for two consecutive years must offer all students a choice of another school. Schools that fail to meet the federal requirements for three consecutive years must also offer extra tutoring or similar services to low-income students who are performing below grade level.

The story about Spike was used to provide a strong, effective picture of the NCLB Act in its initial application. Spike is not alone: millions of children experience school in much the same way, every day. Many strong parallels were intended. The comparison is not exact, of course, nor should it be, as the interpretation and application of NCLB is uneven, especially during these early years. There are only two things of which we can be certain as it relates to NCLB: (1) it will change over time, and (2) there will be a strong challenge to the purpose, need, and wisdom of said legislation. I am making this commitment to you: I balance a commitment of objectivity and honesty to you, the reader, with respect for American government. Let me make a statement about what this book is and is not. This book is intended as an aid to help policy makers, teachers, and leaders—traditional and nontraditional. The purpose of this book is to help develop high performance standards-based schools (SBSs) in enough quantity—nationwide—to ensure that the needs of all children are met. This book is not intended to be an exclusive focus on the No Child Left Behind Act (NCLB). I believe school administrators, especially teachers and even parents, want to find the secret to closing the achievement gap. Let me hasten to add several important points. There is no secret to closing the achievement gap. It is a devilishly difficult work of the heart. This book provides the school community with all that is necessary. Indeed, it is challenging down to the core, and hundreds, perhaps thousands, of teachers and others have already pulled together and established the mold. The challenge is a test of the will more than skill. The crucial question is, do we really care enough? Nationwide success in closing the achievement gap will require a systematic rethinking of how America prepares a child to get from birth to productivity in America. I have discovered that the necessary prerequisites for accomplishing this shift are already available within our communities. We are among those who already have the caring and compassion to forge ahead. This work at hand can be successfully completed, but each individual must make the journey with heart, soul, and hope in hand. The point that I have been avoiding is that NCLB is more of a hindrance than a help to the journey. It will prove to become a major obstacle to continuing the substantive standards-based reform (SBR) that has been underway in America since 1990.

When I use the term standards-based reform, I am referring to a school where students are expected to demonstrate high academic achievement through performance-based assessments. In a traditional system, graduation or promotion is often based on seat time or the number of credits earned. Student success in an SBS is defined by measured academic achievement when teachers are clear about what they want a student to know or do. Teachers design curricula down from the expected academic outcomes called standards. It is important for high performance standards-based teachers to understand the difference and to be able to self-assess how far they have grown beyond the traditional system. In the following sections, I discuss how SBR is different from the traditional system and mention several of the key differences taken from my 32 years of experience in this field. As I review the major tenets of the two systems, it is amazing to me that the traditional system approach was ever embraced.

Because teaching is a very autonomous endeavor, there is no universal description that adequately addresses all of the many teaching variations in the traditional system. Therefore, while describing the differences in the two systems, my observations necessarily remain at the conceptual level. In a traditional classroom, teachers typically teach until their students reach some arcane saturation point. In a traditional classroom, content standards just seem to quietly and magically emerge as the course content unfolds. In a SBS classroom, however, the academic content standards are made clear to students before instruction begins. Students must learn the content and then demonstrate mastery of the basic skills before moving on. Clear academic standards are important. In my experience, when standards are made clear to students, they find a way to reach them. The students may not meet these extraordinarily high academic standards immediately, but they will meet them in time, especially once the barrier is broken.

Defining the Standards-Based Classroom

In a standards-based classroom (SBC), it is common practice to make standards (academic expectations) clear to students before instruction begins rather than after. It is helpful to ensure that the parents know what the academic expectations are for their student as well. Essentially, then, there are two major differences between the traditional classroom and the SBC:

1. The academic content standards are clearly defined and made known to students before instruction begins.
2. Student achievement (mastery) is determined through a variety of assessments including performance-based assessments at a specified point in time.

In my view there are distinct instructional advantages to such a system. For example, when students understand what the expectations are, they can take more responsibility for their own learning and ultimately for meeting the academic standards. In the SBC students take more responsibility for student learning, and so, also, must leadership teams. Leaders and leadership teams must provide specific supports to ensure the success of the SBC. The specific school supports are discussed at the end of this chapter and the classroom supports are discussed in chapter 2.

As I continue to mention academic standards, I constantly think about a compelling story about the power of barriers. For many years, running a mile in track in less than 4 minutes was an incredible international barrier. Since the beginning of track history, running a mile in less than 4 minutes had never been accomplished, and it seemed impossible to even the world's greatest track athletes. Then in 1954 Roger Bannister broke the 4-minute-mile time barrier. When he broke the time barrier he also broke the mental barrier. Subsequently, after hundreds of years of frustration with the athletes' inability to run a sub-4-minute mile, two other athletes also broke the 4-minute barrier. The point is that when human beings understand a barrier (standard) and believe it can be broken, the likelihood of success is greatly enhanced.

Other advantages of the SBC are as follows:

- Students can progress at their own rate and use learning styles that best match their own needs.
- In classrooms where more learning occurs than teaching, the workload is more equitably delegated to the students.
- In the SBC teachers facilitate learning, and, therefore, meet the individual needs of students more effectively.
- In the high-performance SBC, teachers give students more responsibility by becoming more of a guide on the side, rather than a sage on the stage.

Why Standards Have Had Mixed Support from Teachers

While the SBC has real merit, all too often the standards have been set by policy makers for political reasons, with little viable input from those responsible for implementing them; therefore, the standards are often too high or too numerous. Further, in some cases the test scores required to meet the standard are set too high for many students and schools. The unrealistic rigor of this top-down system, coupled with reduced funding, makes the whole system appear politically motivated. If the standards were universally practical, believable, and fundable the system would have serious merit. Despite these constraints the SBC is a powerful concept that clearly has real potential in helping to close the achievement gap. It is significant to note that parents excitedly support the higher standards until their children fail to meet them. Even with all of these factors many teachers support the SBC but feel they need more information and support to develop an effective SBC. That is precisely where this book comes in. What follows are processes, information, and strategies that can mitigate these kinds of concerns. I agree that teachers need specific types of information, training, and support. Therefore, these first two chapters are intended for the support people, including leaders and leadership teams. The politics of NCLB and the history and purpose of public schools will develop the capacity and generate an understanding of the perspective necessary to maintain high rates of energy and hope. Each chapter includes success strategies designed to provide the necessary support to our teachers. When I use the word teacher, I am describing every adult in the school, both certified (licensed) and classified (nonlicensed). This book is not written to be a passive experience. As you work your way through it, you will find it to be interactive, because the success strategies that appear in the book for teachers and their support people build on each other. It is my hope that you will find this book honest, practical, and helpful as you apply the strategies and information as appropriate to support your work.

The NCLB Act and SBC Are Not the Same

No disrespect intended, but NCLB is a party crasher—late to the party and hoping to mooch a little recognition without any investment. I cannot put my confidence in NCLB and suggest that you remain aloof as well. I have spent the better part of six months studying this issue, while being naively generous in my misgivings and conclusions. I am happy to provide the rationale for my position. The NCLB Act is technically flawed, shoddy in design, selective, and incomplete because it muscles an approach without any honest look at best practices. The Department of Education presents what it calls "research-based reforms" and other "proven methods with proven results" within NCLB. Neither is really, especially relative to some of the key sanctions. The credibility problem here is that unlike the rhetoric around other political issues like greenhouse gases, oil drilling, and SUVs, teachers will come to experience directly the so-called "proven methods with proven results" and they will become deeply disillusioned with the executive branch of government and the federal Department of Education (DOE). To be fair, the NCLB Act does provide a modest number of scraps of helpful information like "Tips for Parents," but in my view, they are aluminum skin, thin in number and research strength. Politics as usual is a poor strategy because you can't fool teachers and parents with an imposter, and it was unnecessarily foolish to try. Carefully crafted work with real honest research-based reforms, coupled to proven results, would be quite helpful and even welcomed. I would scarcely have needed to take well over a year out of my retirement to generate something that would be helpful. The fact is there is no substantive strategy or design in NCLB. Think about it: the NCLB Act was built on reforms already developed and in place in the states. Those reforms vary, rightly, from state to state, but typically there are high academic standards with some form of assessment. The NCLB Act contributes little: no new proven instructional ideas, no helps, no leadership, and no resources—not a thing, except sanctions. If I were evaluating this NCLB suggestion as a university-based learning team project, I would be hard pressed to assign it a "B" without lowering the standards of the university. I am confident that the DOE would not support grade inflation. I return to this topic in more detail later in the chapter where I am quite confident that the facts clearly support the positions taken heretofore. In addition to its coming onto the scene late, I have serious concerns about the motives of NCLB. The NCLB Act has nothing whatsoever to do with the achievement gap.

Nevertheless, I continue my serious look at the NCLB Act. In attempting to complete this work, I have had to take a deep peek into my heart to find a kind of ethereal courage. This book addresses three substantive NCLB issues.

1. The first I call "the politics of eliminating the competition." The first phase of this book examines the purpose and value of the NCLB Act.
2. The second phase of this book (and the actual core purpose) is to assist in closing the achievement gap. During this phase I present important helps including the cardinal principles of closing the achievement gap. In addition, I present the 12 basic structures of a successful SBS. I believe there is an understanding of the processes necessary to be successful. In my experience, education leaders and teachers are not confused, bemused, or even under-enthused; nor are they lacking in courage or strength, will, talent, heart, or happiness. To successfully develop a nation of high-performance SBSs will require a tough minded spirit and a "tough love" approach to children and young adults.

3. The third purpose of this book is to examine the historical purposes for free public schools in America. If that purpose is still viable, then it needs to be communicated to the body politic in America. It could well signal the demise of this republic and with it, the cradle of modern Western culture.

Why Is the Value of the Public School Being Questioned Now?

Standards-based reform cannot ignore the demographic shift America is experiencing. In fact, American society is undergoing some of the most profound economic and demographic transformations in its history, but the social and educational institutions have not kept pace. The significant demographic transition is shifting the United States from an Anglo society rooted in Western culture to a work society characterized by three large racial and ethnic minorities, each of them growing in size. As the white majority declines in population, the achievement gap grows.

It is significant to note that the majority of students in the 21st century are going to be of non-European origin and the majority will be poor.[1] This is a transformational demographic change that is becoming an increasingly difficult challenge for the traditional American institutions. Unless we act swiftly, this nation may jeopardize the survival of America's core values of the inalienable rights of equity, freedom, and justice for all. There is no doubt that standards-based education (SBE) can meet this challenge, and, over time, also close the achievement gap. That is where this book comes in, because it gives the educators, parents, and students the tools they need to meet high academic standards. This is the first step in the elimination of social stratification that schools were innocently perpetrating in the pre-SBE era. This book also provides the reader with the understanding necessary to set up successful standards-based schools (SBSs).

Can NCLB Help Teachers and Principals to Achieve the Goal of Closing the Achievement Gap?

Clearly there is room for improvement in public schools, and it is imperative that those improvements be made. There is no time to deliberate or deny that improvements must be made as soon as possible. Schools must make certain that all students are expected to, and can, achieve rigorous academic standards. In my opinion, sadly, the NCLB Act is not something that teachers, parents, and school leaders can confidently rely on to assist in attaining that laudable goal. Let me be clear; I am committed to the broad goals of NCLB. In my view, those key goals are high standards and high expectations for each student. The act represents an excellent place for us to begin. Beyond that, there are a modest number of viable strengths in the legislation. Several of those positive attributes include:

- Utilizing standards-based curriculum is positive.
- Accountability and reporting are good.
- Parental involvement is also attractive.
- Education has been getting more attention in the media and in politics, which is a plus.
- It is exceptionally important that the spotlight continue to shine on minority achievers.

I recognize that my positions on NCLB will not be viewed favorably by the DOE and the executive branch of the government. The unsupportive positions that I have represent a difference of opinion with regard to President Bush's education agenda, nothing more. I differ with the president on certain issues. I do, however, recognize President Bush as the legitimate leader of America. I realize I have been vocally critical in my position. That position represents the type of freedom in which all citizens should share. I am quite certain of two things regarding the critical positions I have taken heretofore. I believe the president, the DOE, and Bush's cabinet disagree vehemently with the points I have been making. At the same time, I am quite confident that the president supports my choice (as an American citizen) to voice my political differences with the executive branch of government and the Republican Party.

The political differences that I have voiced are specific to the education agenda as articulated by NCLB. Those differences do not necessarily extend beyond this rather narrow concern when the whole spectrum of policy-level positions taken by President Bush and the executive branch of government are considered.

What is true is that NCLB is a liability regarding the achievement of what I consider to be laudable goals. The federal statute creates obstacles for poor students of non-European descent, and even mediocrity for affluent white kids of European descent. Worse yet, I believe the NCLB Act may well threaten the very foundation of this nation because if the law is left unimpeded (and I believe there will be revisions), it has the potential to set the stage for the destruction of the broad-based middle class in America. My thinking is based on a penetrating study of the NCLB Act in conjunction with thirty-five years of teaching and leading school improvement efforts in public schools. In addition, the position I have set forward is also based on the perceptions of people who are in a position to know, namely, the president's political peers in Congress, the work of scholars who have no ax to grind, and further, the actual language of the law itself. The position taken here about the destructive nature of NCLB will stand a serious and comprehensive litmus test. After discussing the relative merits of the NCLB Act in chapter 2, I present a framework that school communities can use to develop successful high-performance SBSs that will, most assuredly, close the achievement gap, eradicate social stratification, and achieve education and social "equity of opportunity" for all. Sound impossible? Roll up your cognitive shirtsleeves and let's get started.

It has been argued that the NCLB Act is a kind of Trojan horse. What is packaged in the NCLB Act is not obvious to the casual glance. What is this perceived crisis really about? Is it failing schools or federal apathy? In my opinion, the most disturbingly disappointing element of the NCLB legislation is that the act has an ulterior motive. By the time you read this work (this was written in the winter of 2003), you will likely already have misgivings about the NCLB legislation. You probably even suspect that something is radically wrong, but you are just not able to put your finger on it. A close look at the many impossible-to-meet and unfunded mandates levied by NCLB clearly details that its purpose has absolutely nothing to do with "closing the achievement gap." I honestly wish that I could report this dark conclusion differently because America's diverse learners and teachers deserve better. I must assume that the executive and legislative branches of government not only were concerned about the perceived failure of public schools, but also were equally concerned about the radical demographic shift that is occurring in America with no feasible solution in sight. I simply wonder how confusion about how to solve the complicated and somewhat interrelated problems of failing schools and the dramatic increase in the numbers of academically diverse students led them to the development of the NCLB Act. I am not suggesting anything sinister at all. It is readily observable to all that this is a very complex issue with no easy solution.

If you don't know where you are going, any road will do!

—The Mad Hatter, *Alice in Wonderland*

On an extraordinarily somber note, I seriously fear that the purpose of NCLB is to destabilize and privatize America's public schools. Be advised that I delve into the key reasons why this attempted takeover is occurring right now. Those comments follow shortly, but first, let me focus on the impact of a corporate takeover of government-sponsored schools. It is my belief that if private for-profit schools replace public schools, the neediest students will likely be the ones that are left out and hurt most immediately and deeply. The National Center for Education Statistics reports that in the fall of 2002 there were 47,222,778 K–12 students enrolled in public schools in America. The competition of the new economy is currently so great that America simply cannot afford to waste any of its precious human resources. Many of the academically diverse kids are already in school and those children do not have time for corporate America to get it right. It is quite possible, even likely, that the private for-profit schools will become the turf of the perceived elite and people of privilege. Eventually, after vouchers and tax credits take hold, I predict that America will have two school systems. I predict there will be one well-funded for-profit school system for the children of wealthy parents of European descent and another (less able school) for everyone else—typically poor white children and others of non-European descent.

The consequences of having two separate school systems should be clear to everyone. I fear this disturbing dilemma has—in the long range—potential to eliminate the working "middle class" American, creating a new class system (affluent whites versus poor white people and other poor people of color and of non-European descent). A study of the public schools in America makes it clear that America's schools served to at least create the illusion of equal opportunity. The free public school is not without problems; nevertheless, having one school system for all citizens has for more than 200 years of American history established the fact that liberty and equity of opportunity remain the "dominant patriotic themes" in America. Can a private school system generate literally overnight a system that can effectively educate 47 million highly diverse students? I question if private schools have either the capacity or the will to assume responsibility for the compulsory education of nearly one-half million children and young adults. Time is not a trivial issue, but rather a huge significant obstacle to the conversion of the current school system to an alternate capable of educating the diversity of all groups. It would be nice if America had a decade like the one President Kennedy established when he gave his inauguration speech with the words, "I think it should become a goal of America, before the end of this decade, to put a person on the moon and return them safely again to earth." A school system as large and diverse as the one in America is certainly not a rocket program, but the children simply do not have the ten years given the race to the moon. It clearly presents significant challenges. It would be a fair statement to say that children would have half the time (five years) as a rocket. That is about the time it takes an average student to finish one of three components (elementary, middle, and high school) of the American school system.

In my view, the transition to a private for-profit school would have at the most—arguably—five years to make the successful transition to a high-performance school system capable of meeting the needs of all students as advertised in the brags. A private system with no staff, no facilities, no instructional materials, and no history with the families in question would struggle mightily to gain the trust of people who have a long (and sometimes deep) mistrust of big business. It is difficult to believe that a big corporate system with no history of nurturing positive, trusting relationships of any kind will easily—if at all—win the trust of poor minority families with whom a trust gap exists so wide that it could only be viewed as a cavernous breach at best. The private for-profit schools could probably serve the affluent students of European descent because it is, at least in part, the political persuasion of their parents that is spearheading this movement. Ironically, that is the group with which public schools are currently most successful. It is not as if the private for-profit schools have been remarkably successful to date. Nor can it be said that the trust and respect of leadership expertise in corporate America is at an all-time high in spite of what Chester Finn had to say in a 1998 issue of the *Wall Street Journal*. Chester Finn said, "The school system can't reform itself. . . . You've had your chance. We warned you. We gave you the Nation at Risk over twenty years ago. Nothing has changed. It's time to apply American business expertise to education."[2] Mr. Finn, an executive with Whittle, has embarrassingly failed to notice the crisis of confidence in corporate America as defined by the post-Enron economy. Every time there is another greedy executive stealing or lying, public confidence takes a negative turn as evidenced since the leadership debacle that is currently defining corporate America. Is the expertise Mr. Finn speaks of defined by the unethical scandals and leadership fiascos typified with companies like Enron, Tyco, Global Crossing, ImClone, WorldCom, and the scores of dotcoms that went belly-up because their officers didn't have a clue as to how to provide inspired, visionary leadership? And is it educational leaders who, according to Mr. Finn, need to turn to "business expertise"? Really, I wonder. I suggest a good lesson in character development popularized by public schools as a way to still educate the whole child in the shadow of the obsession with academic excellence to the detriment of educational humanity. I once heard Arthur Combs say during an institute to teachers, "Education is not suffering so much from a lack of efficiency as from a lack of humanity."[3] Having Combs make that astute observation compels me to add that corporate America is not suffering so much from a lack of prosperity as it is from a lack of parsimony. Agree or otherwise, think about it while you consider the following:

> Teachers, who educate children, deserve more honor than parents, who merely gave them birth; for the latter provided them mere life, while the former ensured a good life.
>
> —Aristotle

To complete the task I set out for myself in writing this book I present ideas that are certainly complex if not controversial. In my view, there are several core reasons for what Gerald Bracey called a NCLB setup. And, even more disappointingly, it is why I call it the resegrega-

tion of schools. I believe this is happening primarily for reasons of elitism, greed, preference, and status of a few who may not be able to either hold onto their status or earn it without help. I am, of course, disappointed by what are such selfish and shallow motives and absolutely
shocked by such avarice. Most citizens want to think well of their government, so I recognize that the truth about some elements of our government (radical conservatives) is shocking and hard for many to believe. It is especially difficult for teachers to believe such things because
teachers come to their vocation for reasons of the heart. With so much
goodness at play, I believe it is hard for teachers to believe that anything
as diabolical as what you are about to read could possibly be true. In addition, and even more tragically, some children will get hurt. I believe
teachers' political beliefs are defined by the "Pollyanna syndrome."
Therefore, when it comes to children, teachers tend to resist elements
that represent the worst. Nonetheless, facts are facts.

> Facts are stubborn things, and what ever may be our wishes, our in-
> clinations or the dictates of our passions, they cannot alter the state
> of facts and evidence.
>
> —John Adams (1770)[4]

Deception on a grandiose scale is actually quite common in the annals
of history. In fact, historically, intelligent people were routinely duped.
Over the years, for example, there have been a number of scientific ex-
peditions to Scotland to prove the existence of the Loch Ness monster
(Nessy to the scientists and overnight proprietors). While, arguably, no
hard evidence to prove its existence has really ever surfaced, many in
Scotland choose to believe in the fable of Nessy, the friendly monster of
the loch—just the same.

Unfortunately, duping routinely makes the news. I am always amused
that many intelligent people persist in believing in such "possible" illu-
sions as unidentified flying objects (UFOs) or the infamous Sasquatch
(Bigfoot) reportedly foraging for food in the remote regions of the northwest United States and Canada. Please don't be angry if my last comment
describes you. Rather, just be reminded that some people are more easily
deceived than others. And, it probably has much more to do with the de-
ceptive liar than the naive listener. A particularly amusing fable common

in schools is that students are much more unruly when it is the time of the full moon. In this case such deception is generally harmless, as have been the others. Perhaps you have even heard of it yourself, or naively, you are a believer as well. I have frequently heard otherwise intelligent people make the same assertion—certainly not you, of course—that the crazies come out during the full moon. Who really knows? Nevertheless, it is sometimes difficult to admit that one has been duped. Sometimes people are quite gullible and easily taken advantage of by charlatans of any kind and type. People in the business of deception know well that battling disbelief is difficult. As John Burroughs once said, "It is always easier to believe than to deny. Our minds are naturally affirmative."[5] Adolf Hitler said it this way, "The great masses of the people . . . will more easily fall victims to a big lie than a small one."[6] The point is that the more we come to trust our government, the more likely it is that a lie will go unquestioned. In other words, people can be fooled by a government. In fact, educators are probably a rather easy lot to fool because we want to believe the best about the government.

I must tell you that I am afflicted by the same Pollyanna attitude that I have just accused teachers of having. There was a strong part of me that wanted to gloss over the sad truth presented here. The point is that the unhappy truth about government and corporate America is hard to believe because I am sure you want to believe the best. Therefore, I had to choose to either be honest with you, or to gloss over serious issues and just move on. The fact is clear: this book is primarily not about NCLB, but about what we will discover about what it takes and how difficult it is to get academically diverse students to reach the standards. I will not vacillate; therefore, you can count on my most objective truth about this and all other matters as I know it. You should know that my decision to pursue this information honestly, or otherwise, turned on a discussion that I had with a public school teacher in Helena, Montana, which is where I started teaching more than 30 years ago. I am extremely proud to say the teacher in question is my sister (a highly regarded teacher in the school and district with a last name different from mine). When I was first thinking about this project I started to talk with my teaching sister about the difficulties of the project. She said, "Don't gloss over the tough situations because some of these students pose an unbelievable challenge." Her reaction quickly reminded me that it is important to believe that all kids can meet the standards, but just not necessarily in the same way or at the same rate. It is also unlikely that anyone could guarantee that every child will meet the academic standards and can be helped to develop to their maximum potential.

As noted earlier, I wrote with as much honesty as possible. That is my commitment to you. If something doesn't strike you as being realistic or true, it is not because I failed in my commitment. Rather, you can presume that you have detected an error. Since this book is written primarily for teachers I feel I have a profound responsibility to be both accurate and complete.

As I noted earlier, this chapter now explores why government-sponsored public schools are under such a serious and constant attack at this particular time. This is a complex area to address because the reasons for this attack on public education are, at least, disappointing if not disheartening and are even more despicable because the rationale for the NCLB Act has, in my opinion, absolutely nothing to do with high standards for all students. I do not claim that what follows are exhaustive reasons for such a brash attack on public schools. A major reason for this attack is related to the agenda of the radical conservatives. President George W. Bush, like his father and President Reagan as well, ran on a platform favoring smaller government. The strategy used during the first years of President George W. Bush's administration was to set the stage for corporate America to assume responsibilities that have been heretofore the state government's responsibility. In plain words, President Bush wanted to outsource hundreds of thousands of government jobs to private corporations. He wants, in other words, to get the government out of government.[7] And, apparently, that means that education as well as other areas of government responsibility need to be outsourced and shut down. The sleight of hand here is that viewing education as government is atypical. Technically, I suppose that public schools are an arm of local government. As a practical matter, however, few in education see schools in that light. This is primarily because local control is democratically exercised through locally elected school boards. In fact, as a leader in executive management positions at the local level, I often heard the comment that school elections were the final vestige of democracy in America. Sadly, I have to agree. My personal experience with this growing phenomenon is as follows: recently I was at a social activity discussing education funding (probably complaining about it) when someone (probably a friend) in our community called me an "educrat." I was quite surprised because it was the first time in more than 20 years that the term was used in reference to me as a school administrator (at the time, superintendent).

Another key reason for the current attack is not really a surprise, but it is even more disappointing and disheartening than the first reason, and it is that certain affluent, white, upper-middle-class parents want to maintain a place of rank and privilege for their children. I was equally disheartened to learn that this phenomenon goes back in history. Just after the release of the NCLB Act, the Applied Research Center made the following point: "One way of looking at the history of education is to see how wealthy people and businesses shaped the schools to contain and control poor people and turn them into useful workers and consumers. That's why rich people are willing to support public schools with their tax dollars."[8] In an earlier time, businesspeople and their supporters were not shy about saying so directly. Horace Mann, Massachusetts's first state superintendent of schools, told business owners in the 1940s they would get better workers if they paid for public education. Workers who had been to school were distinguished by their "docility and quickness for applying themselves to work, personal cleanliness and fidelity in the performance of their duties, not by their ability to read and do math."[9] In a compelling discussion of this very issue, in 1990, sociologist Barbara Ehrenreich wrote a pithy analysis of social and economic anxieties that were haunting current upper-middle-class Americans—anxieties she called the "fear of falling" syndrome. "College professors . . . business executives and other privileged Americans," according to Ehrenreich, ". . . have become politically conservative because they fear that their own children may not attain, as adults, their parents' affluence."[10] That emerging sociological concept was underscored for me when I was reviewing the work of Jeannie Oakes and Amy Stuart Wells (scholars out of UCLA). In my opinion, Jeannie Oakes is the foremost authority on tracking (the sorting of students by perceived ability) in America. Her work has led her to a place where she is interested in the "detracking" of high schools in America. Accordingly, detracking led Oakes and Wells to a teacher working in a middle school gifted education program. The teacher was offering challenge courses for all groups of students, and to her surprise, the parents severely criticized her for not offering their children separate enrichment classes. The teacher, while talking about the experience with Dr. Oakes, reportedly said, "They didn't ask, 'what are our kids learning in your classes?' I found that really dismaying . . . I'm dealing more with their egos than with what their kids really need educationally."[11] The reform implications and issues of social stratification are amazingly complex. Of course! Dr. Oakes sees it this way: "The battle was ostensibly fought over which kids—gifted or not gifted, according to which definition—would have access to which teacher and which curriculum. . . . At risk for the families of high-track students is the entire system of meritocracy on which they base their privileged positions in society."[12]

In my study, a final reason for the attack is also troublesome but not unexpected. Since about 1990 there has been a work in progress between the executive branch of government and business tycoons to transition public schools to private, for-profit schools. This is too tangled a story to unravel easily. The story begins late in the presidential term of President George H. W. Bush. Let's get a start by talking about two powerful forces that came together just prior to 1990. The first force is Whittle Communications. The second force is the executive branch of the government. In 1990, America 2000 was announced. One could think of America 2000 as the precursor to NCLB. President Bush and his secretary of education, Lamar Alexander, had serious misgivings about the quality of the public school system in America. Together, Alexander and Chester Finn, who worked in the Nixon White House and later was a major policy maker in the Department of Education under Reagan, took a very active roll in the drafting of America 2000. America 2000—like NCLB—was simply a vehicle, according to Richard Jaeger, with which to "divert public funds to private schools."[13] The key vehicle in America 2000 was to subtly funnel public money to fund private schools by working through goal two of America 2000, which called for "establishing 525 one of a kind high-performance schools." Those schools were designed to compete with and to eventually replace public schools across America. The strategy stated, "We will unleash America's creative genius to invent and establish a new generation of public schools, one by one, community by community. These will be the best schools in the world, schools that will enable their students to reach the national goals, to achieve a quantum leap. . . ." The plan was to bring 525 of these schools into existence by 1996. To establish "America's best schools, America's business leaders will establish . . . the New American Schools Corporation that will reward contracts (in 1992) to a number of Research and Development (R and D) teams. . . . Each school was to be awarded one million dollars to help defray 'start-up costs.'"[14] The plan called for Congress to provide at least 150 to 200 million dollars to jump-start the R and D teams.[15] Edison Schools, whose parent company was Whittle Communications, was headquartered in Knoxville, Tennessee. Referring to his "New American Schools," Chris Whittle's plan even echoed some of the same rhetoric in America 2000. How did Whittle know about the details of America 2000? Secretary of education Alexander was a close personal friend of Chris Whittle. Therefore, Alexander asked Whittle and Chester Finn (who by now worked for Edison) to help in the design of America 2000. Whittle, of course, took advantage of the invitation to help Edison Schools prepare to meet what Whittle anticipated to be a significant profit when America 2000 generated a need for hundreds of superior private schools.

That, then, is the first piece of the puzzle. In summary, in 1990 two powerful forces created a dubious alliance between America's corporate interests and the White House. The initial corporate entity was Whittle of Edison Schools and the White House entity was America 2000 (President Bush's education plan). Very shortly after America 2000 was announced, Whittle announced his intentions to expand Channel One (his first attempt to be involved in public education) by establishing the Edison Project. To make the idea profitable, Whittle needed Alexander and Bush to push vouchers through Congress. The plan that the government and Whittle made was an alliance designed to make the transition to private (for-profit) schools. Whittle believed his Edison Schools could be the vehicle. The project was loftily projecting 200 schools by 1996 and 1,000 to be ready by the year 2000. He projected the cost at one billion dollars to create the prototype and another two billion dollars to ramp it up nationally. Whittle thought he would be in a position to cash in on the investment by having the necessary schools available for a federal tax voucher subsidy, perfectly on schedule with the implementation of

America 2000. His written plan even resembled the America 2000 blueprint to create 525 experimental schools.

As a result of President Bush's first term election—the election of 1988—a charter school movement got off to a running start. To make it all come together financially, Whittle needed Bush and Alexander to push their school voucher plan through Congress. To Whittle's shock, Bush was defeated in the 1992 general election in spite of the success of Desert Storm. Bill Clinton was not in favor of the privatization of public schools, thereby stifling the alliance. Whittle's scheme was all but over, at least as far as Clinton's administration was concerned. This was a very serious fiscal setback for Edison Schools. The investment in the Edison prototype had been made. And, with the defeat of Bush and the corresponding death of America 2000, Edison Schools appeared to be dead.

How do the individuals fit into this alliance and how did each individual profit? When Whittle Communications was headquartered in Knoxville, Tennessee, Lamar Alexander was the governor, before he became Bush's top education advisor. Although Alexander was not an actual partner in Whittle Communications, while governor of Tennessee he was, however, involved in the Whittle empire by serving on the Whittle board and serving as a consultant for a fee of $125,000. In addition, Alexander bought $10,000 worth of stock in Whittle Communications. At the end of his gubernatorial term, and before assuming the position of president of the University of Tennessee, Lamar transferred the stock to his wife's name. For some reason, she also wrote a check for more of the same stock. Whittle never cashed the checks. Nevertheless, Whittle bought the stock back for a tidy sum of $330,000.[16] Nonetheless, in contrast, what Whittle projected as the quality of his Edison Schools was, at best, mixed. In fact, the Philadelphia arm of the Edison Schools was harshly criticized. Whittle was forced to take a step back because the Edison Project, without the federal monopoly and subsidy, was not deemed to be profitable. The economic pressures were stifling for Whittle Communications. Chris Whittle was forced to seek paying customers through the use of his friends. Whittle again relied on his old friend and secretary of education Lamar Alexander. Tom Ridge knew Alexander because they had met in gubernatorial circles as Ridge was the governor of Pennsylvania. Consequently, Alexander convinced Governor Ridge to superimpose the Edison Project on the Philadelphia schools.[17]

The grand plan of the Edison Project was to "invent" and open 200 schools by 1996. The overall success the Edison Project had in raising test scores (including those in Philadelphia) was, at best, mixed. The dozen schools (at most) that Edison listed as having positive academic trends terminated their contracts.[18] Consequently, Edison Schools struggled to keep out of receivership. In fact, Edison posted its first quarterly profit in its twelve years of existence for the quarter that ended June 30, 2003. Edison had been at the center of public debates (nationally) about for-profit private education. Disappointments with some big contracts and complaints about their performance helped Edison's price per share to drop. Alarmingly, shares that sold for as much as $38.75 in February sold for as little as $0.14 in October of 2003. At the time of the aforementioned fiscal forecast, Edison was operating 130 full-year schools and 200 summer schools. Finally, on Wednesday, November 12, 2003, the Edison shareholders agreed to a management-led merger. The merger took the company private, halting a roller-coaster ride for the investors in the school management company. Sixty-six percent of the 68 million voters approved the merger at a meeting in New York. Shareholders were offered a paltry $1.76 per share, less than 10% of the $18.00 per share Edison sold it for when it went public in 1999.[19] Whittle envisioned that a private company could run schools more efficiently and effectively than the current system of local government. The spotty success of Edison Schools flew in the face of the vision of excellence for for-profit schools. For a brief time in the early 1990s, it appeared as if Edison Schools, Inc., was in a unique and powerful position to just step in and provide a viable and respected alternative to public schools. The unilateral ability of Edison Schools to provide the needed alternative to free public schools significantly diminished when Edison Schools shareholders approved the management-led merger deal to take the company private. Edison may not represent the single most likely alternative to free public schools, but the alliance that Whittle made with the Bush White House created an awareness of a possible marketplace that could reduce taxes while improving the quality of education. Chris Whittle and Edison Schools made an impact in that they created the momentum necessary to make for-profit education a viable alternative. The main elements of Edison Schools were as follows:

- There is a heightened public awareness of alternatives to free public school.
- Political groups have emerged with strong views on the privatization issue, including Reason Public Policy Intstitue, which is a think tank promoting choice, competition, and a dynamic market economy as the foundation for human dignity and progress. Several other groups opposed to the privatization of schools have emerged to keep this issue before the people. They include the Alliance for Excellent Education and Expose Racism and Advance School Excellence (ERASE), which is concerned about "critical racial dynamics at work in public schools."[20]
- Department of Education (DOE) officials admitted that the department is being "ideologically driven" by NCLB. One DOE career staffer quipped, "That NCLB should be renamed: NCL-B.S."[21]
- The focus on high academic standards had become a single-minded universal obsession.
- The public is increasingly voicing that private for-profit schools are more responsive and accountable than free public schools. "Education privatization is better than the status quo because it introduces accountability into the system. An education provider like Edison has a contract with actual requirements for performance. . . . That's the point, and it shows privatization works better than the status quo."[22]

Chris Whittle found that developing profitable private schools was more challenging than had been anticipated. Whittle, however, did succeed in creating acute public awareness of private for-profit schools as viable alternatives to free public schools. In addition, advocacy and support groups have also emerged from the Edison legacy. The fundamentally important fact is that private for-profit schools are lurking on the scene waiting to fill in for public schools that presumably are not meeting the grade. One must conclude that Whittle created a concept that in the mind of a growing number of people who believe, for the first time, that there is finally an option to the monopoly of government-sponsored schools.

PERCEPTIONS AND FINAL THOUGHTS ON
PRIVATE FOR-PROFIT SCHOOLS

When I began the deep look into the claims that NCLB was nothing more than an attempt to destabilize and privatize American schools, I heard Gerald Bracey present his view during July 2003, in a seminar. Following his presentation, I was convinced, along with the majority of the group, that Bracey's position simply could not be accurate. I agreed with the conclusion of the group. I thought there had to be a better explanation of the impossible-to-meet criteria imbedded within the NCLB Act. The reasons for my skepticism centered largely on a strong desire to believe the best of my (our) government. Additionally, I knew public schools were struggling with declining public support. And, finally, one could not dispute the evidence of a failing school system, such as that dropout numbers were up, graduation rates were down, school violence was up, and academic achievement was down. I left the Institute on the Development of Educational Achievement (IDEA) week-long fellows program with a troubled heart. Simply said, I did not know what to believe, so I decided to have dinner with Dr. Bracey that evening, which was a typical opportunity at the IDEA fellows program. The conversation quickly turned again to the "hidden" purpose of NCLB. In short order the proof began to add up once again. I could not think of a way to refute the evidence being presented, especially as it related to President George H. W. Bush's education agenda entitled America 2000. The scheming and profiteering of people whom I admired, like Lamar Alexander, President Bush himself, and others, was disappointing. I left dinner more confused than before. I tried to think through why I was having such feelings of skepticism. I realized that I had hoped NCLB would give standards-based education (SBE) a presidential endorsement. At this time, I was about a quarter of the way through a book that I was writing to help teachers develop an effective standards-based classroom (SBC). As a result, I decided I would have to look into the education privatization matter for myself. I started by looking into Edison Schools. In November 2003, I was reading in the *Miami Herald* about Whittle's attempt to orchestrate an Edison Schools merger when I happened onto the following matter-of-fact comment: under the plan, Whittle would own only 3.73% of a company that was founded to execute the transition from public to private status.[23] I was amazed at how matter-of-factly the Miami community was being told about the planned destruction of one of America's strongest and most stable institutions—public schools. Then I happened onto a website named *Corp Watch* whose intended purpose is to hold corporations accountable. My mouth dropped at the opening sentence: "The 2002–2003 Profiles of For-Profit Education Management Companies released today . . . finds that large education management organizations (EMOs) dominate the industry." I was surprised to find that for-profit education had already grown into an industry large enough that it was being tracked by a corporation watch group. The website reported further, "The report found that 47 management companies operate in 24 states and the District of Columbia, enrolling some 190,000 students." I was still stubbornly trying to verify if Gerald Bracey was correct in his assertion that NCLB was really an attempt to destabilize and privatize public schools. Therefore, I began to look again, and in short order I found there were research groups founded to help facilitate a dialogue between the education community, policy makers, and the public at large about "school-house commercialism." "The Commercialism in Education Research Unit . . . is the only academic research center dedicated to school-house commercialism."[24] With just one more look, I found an advocacy group pushing for "education privatization." Lisa Snell, writing for the Reason Public Policy Institute, argued that "education privatization is better than the status quo. It introduces some accountability into the system. An education service provider, like Edison, has a contract with actual requirements for performance. And when they fail to meet some of those performance measures everyone hears about it and some districts or schools cancel their contracts. That's the point, and it shows privatization works better than the status quo."[25] As I read about Reason, I saw mention of the Association of Educational Parishioners and Providers Conference. Apparently there were several owners and CEOs of for-profit management companies in attendance to showcase their programs.

As can be easily seen, I am somewhat surprised at the speed with which the transition from public to private status is obviously moving forward. There is a large number of education management companies (EMCs), enough at least to generate the creation of research groups founded to facilitate dialogue. Further, there are advocacy groups surfacing to push for

privatization. Theoretically, this transition has been strong enough to generate conferences where members of associations meet to explore mutu-
ally beneficial programs and positions. What gives me pause is not that a
corporate entity can get organized so quickly but rather the fact that so
many people got involved with this experiment so quickly. It is a clear and
sobering testimony to just how far the trust in traditional government-
sponsored education has fallen. The people to whom I have been referring, those who were anxious to look at alternatives, clearly see the public
school system as unresponsive because it was built on a foundation of tradition and recidivism. The public sees the traditional school system (TSS)
as unresponsive. One must admit that the TSS has been difficult to
change. The protagonists are not making their worries personal as they
complain about the traditional school system. I predict they will return to
the traditional system in earnest when the SBS is in place. The younger
the students, the less resistant they are to change.

EDUCATION AS A MORAL PURPOSE

In the post-NCLB era, discourse about education in the national media
has risen to a deafening crescendo. Missing the forest for the trees, the
leading story on the education beat often ignores the massive inflow of immigrants, which has had massive impacts on our economic, social, political, and educational systems. To date, American institutions have been isolated from each other, which has generated renewed inequity and racial
(ethnic) stratification. This is not the first large immigration that institutions have had to accommodate. In general, historically schools have been
able to meet the needs of diverse immigrants. The fact is that schools were
effective in accommodating the thousands of immigrants that flooded the
"new world" before and after the Revolutionary War. Schools were so successful that the Founding Fathers made education available, free of
charge, to a larger group of people, for a longer period of time. It is critically important for schools to improve to such a degree that no children
will be left behind. To do anything less would be unpatriotic.

   Do not assume that because I have made that comment that I am necessarily a supporter of the NCLB Act, because that would be entirely incorrect. There are just too many concerns for me to feel comfortable. I do

not support NCLB at the simplest level for the exact same reasons announced by the National Education Association (NEA): because it focuses
on punishments rather than assistance. It is true, however, that America
has a genuine national crisis. More and more, America is becoming divided into two nations: one with children who read and one with those
who don't; one with children who dream and one whose children don't.
That type of division has, of course, appeared at other times in American
history. The slavery issue was so divisive and irresolvable that it led to war.
While speaking to the Institute of Arts and Science in New York (1896) regarding the segregation and freedom of blacks, Booker T. Washington
made a foreboding comment when he said, "My friends, there is no mistake; you must help us to raise our character of civilization or yours will be
lowered. Can you make your intelligence affect us the same way our ignorance affects you?"[26] Washington's point was that the two cultures were inextricably woven together. With the advantage of hindsight, it is clear that
Washington's flash of brilliance is no less true today than it was in 1886.
When you listen to the typical political pundits discussing America's foreign policy in Iraq, especially after the fall and capture of Saddam Hus-
sein, it is commonplace to hear the debate regarding the relative advisa-
bility of "nation building" in a foreign land. The key perspective is that we
cannot seed something in a foreign land that has been lost at home. The
perspective that must be valued is that America is still in need of nation
building in our own homeland. What this great nation has to share is the
hope of freedom built on the strong economic foundation of diversity. It is
absolutely imperative that free public schools be left to the job of creating
a hope of freedom for all. Heretofore, I have suggested that free public
schools are as relevant today as they were in Jefferson's day. I believe that
the NCLB Act was written and enacted by the Republicans to both destabilize and privatize public schools. I believe that to be an egregious error
in judgment that will disallow the United States to make full utilization of
the rich and powerful diversity represented by the non-Western, non-
white culture that is currently locked out of mainstream America.

Where Does the Public Stand on SBE versus NCLB?

At a conceptual level most educators are committed to the success of
all students, and are angry at the injustices their students have to endure.

Teachers are already motivated, so the issue is not a matter of "will"; rather, it is a matter of which school improvement framework is most effective. Parents need to understand and support the schools' efforts to ensure success. For these reasons I explore how parents see a traditional SBE reform effort as opposed to the NCLB Act. First, where does the public stand on the NCLB Act, which was passed by a strong majority of both houses and was heralded as a watershed piece of legislation in an attempt to improve public schools? The strong bipartisan support of NCLB belies the growing controversy among many educational and community leaders and policy makers over the act's landmark requirements, sanctions, and lack of funding. Yet over the racket and confusion it has been difficult to hear from the public regarding SBE versus the NCLB Act. I summarize the two most complete and objective reports available at this writing.

The first was designed to go beyond phone polls, surveys, and other snapshot techniques. To create real dialogue, the Mid-Continent Regional Educational Laboratory (McREL) launched a national dialogue on SBE with support from the U.S. DOE. McREL conducted large focus groups that represented a broad crosssection of the public.[27] First, please be reminded that SBE and NCLB are not the same thing; the differences were delineated earlier in this chapter. In my opinion the core differences are that the SBE laws have been enacted at the local level with more involvement. The level of participation, however, was not ideal in every case. The point is that local efforts remain more accessible and responsive than the centralized, federally mandated NCLB Act. In addition, local SBE reforms generate student data to make improvements in the instructional program. The NCLB Act uses the data to levy sanctions that become increasingly harsh. Many in your community probably support the local school's efforts to improve and do not want to have to relocate their child to a "more successful" school. The tensions between the decentralized local reform effort and the centralized federal mandates will in time become a base of support for these efforts. Therefore, the focus question should be: What can be done to recruit support of the community in the locally controlled SBE reform? To initiate thinking about a short-term course of action, we will look at how the public feels about the NCLB Act and how that information can be use to create solid support for the school and its certified and paraprofessional staff.

The information that was generated by McREL sheds some light on the issue of public support. The report found that "over one-half (53%) wanted to continue standards as planned. This was opposed to only slightly over one-third (34%) who wanted standards to continue, with adjustments. Only two percent wanted to undo standards. Only eleven percent says their child's school requires them to take too many standardized tests."[28] I would suggest that this particular data collection project demonstrates the public's strong support for continuing the SBE reform. The results of the perceptual data presented below will be used to form a possible approach to what will likely be public concern as NCLB sanctions begin to name thousands of schools "in need of improvement."

During the early moments of McREL's focus group process the data were not particularly helpful, but as people discussed the issues further, important nuances emerged and they are presented below as five key themes:

1. Standards are meaningless without tests, but accountability should be based on more than just test scores. The public is suspect of using test scores.
2. Accountability makes schools more responsive to parents and communities, not outside officials.
3. Parents and students are a crucial yet often missing part of most accountability systems.
4. The biggest problems with the public schools have little to do with standards or academics. Parents keenly believe this.
5. People in urban areas were generally less satisfied with and less supportive of their schools than people in non-urban areas.[29] As an educator in an urban school, you have more work to do than those working in the non-urban environment.

Each spring a highly reputable professional organization, Phi Delta Kappan (PDK), collaborates with the Center on Education Policy to publish and release the PDK poll on the public's attitudes toward public education. The results of the 2003 poll are interesting and helpful as we begin to plan a response to the NCLB backlash. The following are key results of the 2003 poll.

- The public sees itself as uninformed on NCLB, with 69% saying they lack information needed to say whether their impression of the act is favorable or unfavorable. It is fair to say that after one year, the public doesn't feel they know enough to say they either support NCLB or oppose it.
- A total of 84% of respondents believe decisions regarding what should be taught in the public school should be made at the state level (22%) or by the local board (61%). One might conclude this since there is a wide belief that NCLB is another unfunded mandate from the DOE. Eighty-four percent believe the job a school is doing should be measured on the basis of improvement shown by students.
- The public is concerned about getting and keeping good teachers, thinks salaries are too low, and is willing to see higher salaries paid to teachers teaching in more challenging situations.
- The public continues to believe that closing the achievement gap between white students and black and Hispanic students is important but believes the gap is unrelated to the quality of schooling.
- The public has high regard for public schools and wants needed improvement to come through those schools. The public has little interest in seeking alternatives.[30]

Have You Been AYP'd?

Annual Yearly Progress or AYP has quickly become "education-ese" coming into existence with the NCLB Act. All schools must achieve annual yearly progress (AYP) in student academic achievement. By 2014 all schools must meet or exceed math and reading standards. AYP is a contrived score that represents the trajectory of improvement all students and schools must meet annually to meet the standards in 2014. While only Title I schools that don't meet their AYP are subject to federal sanctions, all schools that are not successful are listed, generating sharp questions from the community.

No one really knows how many schools did not meet AYP in the first year (2003). Certainly hundreds of schools (probably more) were unsuccessful but some states were hit especially hard. Florida, with 87% of its schools falling short, was a state that was much less than successful.

One of the major reasons schools do not meet AYP is because of all the subgroups (defined by race, ethnicity, income, disability, or English speaking ability) that are part of the formula. The outcome has been at once confusing and surprising. In one instance in Florida, Governor Jeb Bush said that a Gulfport school did so well academically that the school was eligible for a bonus check of about $40,000. But Jeb's brother George disagreed with him and said in opposition that the school did so poorly that parents could pull their children out. Which Bush is right?[31] How do you handle it when your school is reported "in need of improvement"? Later in this book I provide tips giving you strategies to use to combat the negativeness of the NCLB Act. Let us focus on several key conclusions that are helpful to us. The public does not feel they are informed enough to conclude that NCLB is either favorable or unfavorable. The public overwhelmingly feels that the federal DOE should not mandate what should be taught, because there is strong agreement (83%) that curriculum issues should be determined at the local level. The public strongly feels (83%) that the effectiveness of a school should be based on how well the students are doing. The public is concerned about the quality of teachers, and the public is willing to pay higher salaries to retain more effective teachers. The public wants high quality schools yet they are not willing to consider alternatives to the current structure.

Summary of PDK Public Poll Relative to NCLB versus SBE

The key finding for our purposes here is that while the public has questions about SBE they support it far more than the NCLB Act because the public favors local control and is simultaneously suspicious of centralized federal control. The key, yet subtle, opinion is that the public wants schools to improve and also to be more responsive to the community. For example, when asked about SBE, the public generally supported the idea of having high academic standards along with more than one assessment to measure student success. The public does not feel the same way about NCLB, and they are skeptical and suspicious because they do not feel well informed. The public is concerned about getting and keeping good teachers, while they still overwhelmingly believe, however, that their local school is doing a good job. The public likes accountability and feels that schools should be measured by how well their students perform on academic tests. The public continues to believe that closing the achievement gap is important but that key school improvement decisions should be made at the local level. In my opinion, the public strongly opposes the privatization of public schools. They do not think it would be in the best interests of American democracy. In my opinion, the key points to be derived from the data are critically important in beginning to plan how to respond to potential school communities' backlash to NCLB outcomes.

LEADERSHIP TEAM: PLANNING AND COMMUNICATION PRECEDE ACTION

Needless to say, it is a prudent assumption to realize that your school community will be disturbed when the NCLB results are released. In my opinion, during these times of public admonition it is extremely important for the leader or leadership team to become advocates for the school's academic program. Even so, as we continue to pursue standards-based school improvement, these thoughts still most certainly apply and make good sense. Public opinion has been used to make the following response suggestions. The public opinion data revealed several powerful truths for us to consider. Firstly, the public is skeptical of schools in general, but they feel their local school is doing a good job. The NCLB Act has been painful to absorb within the school community and the public does not feel they have adequate information to make an informed judgment about the relative value of NCLB for their neighborhood school. If your school is on the "need to improve" list, it will most assuredly stimulate cognitive dissidence. In other words, what your public will be hearing will be incongruent with what they already know and believe about the school. Secondly, the public favors local control. The more important the issue is to the public, the more the public wants to see the decision made locally. These two truths have been consistent in the polling data since long before the NCLB Act was enacted and before America 2000 as well. Beyond those data, the public likes accountability as defined by student academic achievement. The public thinks students and adults should be actively involved in the improvement effort. These findings are good news because they provide a clear direction for schools to initiate planning and can easily predict increased public concern about the community school when the next data are released. I have studied the public's opinion about NCLB and have used those perceptions to provide school leaders with a blueprint to consider as each begins planning the school's response to a probable negative reaction. Now the tips! The pivotal strategies are threefold:

1. Demonstrate that the school is committed to improvement and is responsive to the community through standards reform.
2. Drive a wedge between your local effort and the NCLB Act—the two are *not* the same.
3. And finally and most importantly, make it a matter of educational equity and freedom to pursue the benefits of life in America for all children and young adults no matter the category as defined in NCLB (race/ethnicity, poverty, handicap condition, English speaking ability).

The following action points are intended to give school leaders, either informal or formal, a general direction, but must, of course, be adapted to the community. I leave you with a simple acronym that will serve you well in the planning process. The acronym is *SUCCESS*! Your tips to the success strategy are as follows.

Support: It is wise to anticipate a negative backlash when the NCLB results are released this coming cycle. You have background information about the politics and purpose behind NCLB. Be reminded that many people support the goals of NCLB. Any response on your part should take that point into consideration. I doubt in most cases it would be helpful to initiate a conversation about the politics of NCLB because it may appear as if you are defensive and unsupportive of accountability and holding students to high academic standards. Rather, it is prudent to agree with your public and support accountability as measured by academic achievement. Do not be defensive about test results. Rather, explain what the results mean and how the teachers are using the information to help their students to improve. It is prudent to focus on continuous improvement rather than the cut score of NCLB. Remember that the cut score is a single imprint reflecting the outcome for one student at a precise point in time. Rather, show the school community how students are improving, and then involve the school community in the school improvement process. The public is already suspicious and skeptical of the federal DOE and is not supportive of centralized control, especially at their school site. Involve the leaders in an effort to find out more. And then, demonstrate your support for the academic program by beginning to align the curriculum and also to generate staff development activities that will help support teachers and the aligned curriculum.

Understand: Help the community to understand that closing the achievement gap is a highly complex issue. Agree that educational equity is very important. Consequently, creating it will require a comprehensive community effort. The important point is that there is no quick fix and serious solutions will take integrated interagency cooperation. Academically diverse learners (social stratification) are a challenge for all of America's agencies, both public and private, and those agencies will have to be part of the solution.

Communicate: Begin discussions with your school community directly and start early. Involve your key communicators in this process. Key communicators are a group that has credibility and represent the significant interests in the community. They should be representative of interests like the press, police, youth groups, youth ministers, local businesses, students, and their parents. To find out who your key communicators are, ask those in the people traffic. To give you a possible direction, I like to use what I call the three *b*s: beauticians, barbers, bartenders, and the like. For more information on this idea, check Success Strategies at the end of this chapter.

Comprehensive: America has undergone profound economic and demographic transformations. America is in the process of a transformational shift from a culture defined by affluent whites of European descent to a culture defined by nonaffluent people of color of non-European descent. The social dimensions of this transformation of American culture are challenging for all of America's institutions. As has been discussed, this is a social issue about power and social dominance and it must be addressed with interdependent systems. In my opinion, it has always been true that if school improvement is left just to the educators, then schools just do not improve. Teaching a child, like raising one, is a partnership. Single teachers struggle no less than single parents. Therefore, closing the achievement gap is a value shared by educators and non-educators alike. However, the social dislocation of this transformation has created complex sociological shifts that are difficult to achieve because of a long continuum of needs. All of the American institutions are as chaotically confused as schools. The community must understand and support that the response must be team-oriented, comprehensive, and cohesive. In other words, to create educational equity, the nation, state, district, and school need to create a comprehensive and interactive strategy of human investment that reestablishes the process whereby children mature from birth to adulthood. This strategy must include early childhood development, including physical, emotional, social, and academic growth and development to such a degree that the child becomes a productive member of American culture.

Expectations: It has been said and written that what you do speaks so loudly they can't hear what you say. The whole school community must set clear, high academic expectations. The first step is to create high expectations for the adults who in turn create them for children and young adults. I am describing a kind of self-confidence or efficacy (potency, belief in self). The only successful way to teach "self-efficacy" is to begin with the self (model it). Ensure that the school community is willing to create and capable of creating high expectations for itself, and then for the students. We must first develop an adequate skill set for the parents and other significant others (adults) so they can be in a position to help. The school community would then be in a position to develop and coordinate the interagency support for students.

Safe and Wholesome Culture: When Arthur Combs presented his paper "Concept of Human Potential and the School" he said, "Education is suffering not so much from a lack of efficiency as from a lack of humanity."[32] Therefore, the whole school must create a safe, wholesome, and nurturing environment. The first effort is to create a safe, nurturing environment for adults, and they in turn create it for students. This single-minded movement to create this environment has had the net effect of causing fear and anxiety at all levels. There is no question that public education is being challenged from a variety of constituent levels including federal, state, and local levels. During this time of accountability, uncertainty, and doubt, public education needs empathy, strong support, and teacher leadership. It is quite clear that public education is at the center of a volatile debate that is only likely to get worse. Public skepticism, rebuke, and scrutiny are likely to be constant companions of schools. Student performance is being portrayed as unacceptably poor. It is prudent to recognize that NCLB mandates will likely portray student performance as poor and getting worse. The NCLB Act will reinforce the view that schools are foible and unconcerned. Obviously these attacks are creating, and will continue to create, dread and consternation. That feeling of fear and insecurity must be answered with a strong message of acceptance and respect.

The NCLB Act has apparently assumed that the playing field is level. In other words, it has recently been assumed that all students come to school equally ready to learn. It is also assumed that students learn in the same general way and rate.

These twin assumptions are seriously flawed, yet they continue to drive (consciously or not) the political decisions that have been made centrally and in relative isolation from the field. Simply said, all students do not come to school equally ready to learn, nor do all students learn in the same way or at the same rate. The students that do *not* come to school ready to learn are students we have been referring to as academically diverse in this book. These students—whatever they are called—see the school as threatening and hostile. The academically diverse student experiences fear (emotional) because these particular students do not have confidence they will satisfy the academic standards. Fear and anxiety are the by-products when students believe they will disappoint their families, friends, and selves, and these emotions are painful and humiliating. High academic standards are injurious not because they are high, but because school communities pursue them by looking at the deficiencies of—in this order—first the students, then the teachers, then the families, and finally the schools and ultimately the whole community. In other words, it is part of our Western culture to look at what is wrong rather than at the strengths of the individuals and the communities involved in the education process. This is an important point. The real tragedy is not that each student doesn't have enough strengths; it is, rather, that schools fail to use the strengths they have. Ben Franklin referred to wasted strengths as "sundials in the shade." The academically diverse students do not enjoy drawing attention to themselves, and, therefore, they purposely hide their "sundials in the shade."[33]

Standards are problematic because they assume standardization (sameness) and students are not the same. Worse, standards assume that all students come to school ready to learn. Deteriorating further, standards assume that all kids learn in the same way and at the same rate. The typical question is, "What has to be fixed?" How do we ensure the success of all children or young adults, middle and high school age? We do not ask what are the talents or strengths of these children (or teachers, or parents, or schools, or communities), and how best can we use these talents to ensure success. The deficiency-based approach causes fear in the student, their teachers, and the parents.

Succeed: I am strongly persuaded that the work you have already accomplished in your school must continue. As of this writing, the NCLB Act has not been revised. However, no matter what happens at the national level in the near future, the politics of NCLB will change due to pressure from the local level.

Just think of it, what kind of school could we create if we put our instructional genius to work to find ways to challenge children without threatening them? With this new understanding of child potential, we now understand that poor children of non-European descent become school failures and social malcontents, not because of the will of God, but because of the lack of the will of man.

It is often said that in the new world economy, achievement is highly valued. To compete in the world economy, workers are judged not so much by what they are but by what they do. In justification, it is argued that the global economy has no need for unskilled or even skilled workers. The world, it is often said, will pay more for information and ideas than it will for manufactured products. Therefore, the global economy is demanding knowledge workers. Under this kind of pressure grows the demand for a person who is able to produce knowledge more readily than products. That pressure comes to bear on teachers, who instinctively resist because teachers understand that a child must know they are valued not because of what they can produce but because of who they are. Ultimately, however, the task of freeing our classrooms and students of fear rests with the individual teacher. Bonarc Overstreet said it well when he remarked, "What children need more than anything else, for their own good and for the good of society, is the privilege of growing up with parents and teachers whose interpersonal relations are not distorted by fear."[34] The key to developing a successful, high-performance learning environment for all students is for the teacher to develop strong individual relationships with each student. High-performance teachers must believe there is no power in position, only relationships. We all have heard it called "tough love." The Greeks had enough insight to realize there are many kinds of love. In their wisdom, the Greeks called one kind of love "agape," which meant wonder and amazement or being wide open to possibility.[35]

The formula for teaching fear, then, is simple. Create an atmosphere in which achievement is valued over personal worth, and in which the opinion of others is more important than the opinion of self. The formula for self-acceptance is also simple. Create an atmosphere in which freedom is valued over force, in which realistic evaluation is more important than scapegoating, and in which psychological maturity is more important than pedantry.[36] The vehicle for creating a safe, wholesome, familial environment for children is trust. Trust is the lubrication that generates growth. Unconditional love is the emotional glue that solidifies a nurturing relationship that generates the foundation for community building. The formula is Trust (T) $\times$ Unconditional Love (UL) = growth squared (G^2). I have used a formula to visually express love, and then growth multiplies. The critically important point is that trust is the lubrication that generates the condition for success. Trust creates a kind of wholesomeness for the academically deficient child that says we care about you. Further, it is a statement that we believe in you and have confidence to risk failure to achieve academic excellence. Establish trust and the foundation for success has been set down—$T \times UL = G^2$. Trust is built on a solid foundation of strong relationships. The teachers must be given permission to build strong personal, yet professional, relationships with their students. Relationships and trust are the vehicles through which a safe and wholesome environment must be nurtured to erode the fear that is rampant, especially in the shadow of NCLB. The adults in the school community ideally must work together to establish the safe and nurturing environment for students. It is important for leaders to know that the adults cannot create a trusting and safe environment while they simultaneously experience fear. The teachers and other adults must experience a safe and nurturing environment so they can generate the same for the students.

SUMMARY

The story about Spike is provided to give you a place to start in developing a clearer picture of the NCLB Act in its initial application. Spike is not alone, as millions of students experience school with the same level of success as Spike. The purpose of this book is to help teachers and school leaders close the achievement gap. It is not intended as an exclusive action against the NCLB Act. The NCLB Act is seen as a hindrance rather than a help. I urge teachers and schools to understand the requirements of NCLB, but above all continue the pursuit of standards-based classrooms (SBCs). The NCLB Act and the SBC are not the same.

The two main criteria of the SBC are:

1. The academic content standards are clearly defined and made known to students before instruction begins.
2. Student achievement (mastery) is determined through the use of a variety of assessments including performance-based assessments at a specific point in time.

The academic standards are high but once students understand what the academic expectations are they will meet them more readily. Standards were typically developed by policy makers in relative isolation from teachers. The NCLB Act is technically flawed; therefore, the act is less than helpful in helping teachers close the achievement gap. Besides questioning the use of research-based improvement strategies, I have concerns about the motives that are driving the NCLB Act. The United States is experiencing a significant demographic shift that is having challenging effects on all of America's institutions (not just education). The demographic shift is defined as follows: the majority of students in the 21st century are going to be from poor families of non-European descent, as opposed to the previous majority who were the children of affluent whites of privilege and status. Unless schools act quickly, it is unlikely that the new majority of non-white children will experience equity, freedom, and justice for all. I strongly support high academic expectations for all children. In my opinion, the real purpose of the NCLB Act is the destabilization and privatization of public schools. There are education alternatives to public schools that are waiting for a chance to drive public schools to close. Government-sponsored schools now educate a little more than 47 million students annually. Corporate-sponsored schools like the Edison Schools have not met with much success to date. In fact, the Edison project ran into both academic and fiscal challenges to such a degree that it was sold, and for a much-reduced cost per share. There have been a variety of high-ranking education officials in both Bush administrations that have actively supported the NCLB Act and getting government out of the education business. The NCLB Act was not an effort in isolation. President George H. W. Bush supported legislation entitled America 2000. America 2000 was a precursor to NCLB, but President Bush's defeat by Bill Clinton brought about an end to that effort. Chris Whittle and the Edison Schools made an impact by creating the inertia to make private for-profit education a viable corporate interest. Support for private, for-profit alternatives to government-run schools is clearly on the increase. A number of groups have emerged with strong support of for-profit schools. One such group is Reason Public Policy Institute, which is a public policy think tank promoting choice, competition, and market share economic approaches. In addition, other advocacy and support groups have also emerged from the Edison legacy.

America's Founding Fathers supported free schools because they believed schools helped to integrate the immigrant into Colonial America. While America is experiencing some of the most numerous immigration in history, the integration purpose of schooling has been all but lost. America continues to experience what has been termed a growing national crisis. The public supports SBE. They want high standards for all and schools that are responsive to the wishes of the public. Parents and students want to be more involved in the schools' SBC movement. The public wants local control of the curriculum. Accountability is good because it make schools more responsive to their communities. According to the public, the biggest problems with public schools have little to do with standards.

The public does not understand the NCLB Act well enough to have an opinion on whether it is a good thing or otherwise. The public wants local control of the curriculum. The public is less supportive of schools in urban areas than in suburban areas. The public is suspicious of federal involvement in schools.

This chapter concludes with tips for leaders regarding an action plan for their communities. The tips to success are framed by the acronym SUCCESS. The seven tips are as follows:

- *Support*: earn the informed support of your community.
- *Understand*: help the community to understand your interest in closing the achievement gap through SBR.
- *Communicate*: begin discussions with your community directly and early.
- *Comprehensive*: inform your community of the demographic shift that is occurring in America and communicate the need for comprehensive interagency cooperation.
- *Expectations*: involve the community and the teachers in creating high academic expectations.
- *Safe and Wholesome Culture*: ensure that students, parents, and teachers alike feel emotionally safe at school.
- *Succeed*: commit to the academic success of all students.

QUESTIONS FOR DELIBERATION

1. Were Sky and Spike treated differently? And, if so, how? And why?

2. In your opinion, do all children come to school equally ready to learn? If not, why is that a problem?

3. Should schools create equitable access to academic development? If so, how did the animal people of Happy Falls try to address the issue of equity of opportunity?

4. In your opinion, did the Happy Falls community succeed in bringing equity of opportunity to all children? Why or why not?

5. To meet the diverse needs of students do you think the curriculum should be modified while maintaining academic rigor? Why or why not?

6. There were seven actions (tips) schools were encouraged to pursue. In your opinion, which was the most important and why?

7. What is the most important difference between "shadow" and "sunshine" kids?

8. Do you think it should be a school responsibility to solve the equity of opportunity issue? Why or why not?

NOTES

1. Karen Lambourne and Maxine Baca Zinn, "Education, Race, and Family: Issues for the 1990s," Julian Samora Research Institute, http://www.jsri.msu.edu/RandS/research/wps/wp16.html, [accessed 22 Dec. 2003].

2. Quoted in Gerald Bracey, "No Child Left Behind Act: A Plan for the Destruction of Public Education, Just Say No," (paper presented at the Development of Public Education [IDEA] Fellows Program, Denver, Colo., 2003), 5–6.

3. Arthur W. Combs, "Concept of Human Potential and the School," (paper presented at the annual meeting of Montana's Association for Supervision and Curriculum Development, Missoula, Mont., March 1978), 1.

4. Quoted in David C. Berliner and Bruce J. Biddle, *The Manufactured Crisis*, (Reading, Mass.: Addison-Wesley Publishing Company, 1995), 5.

5. Quoted in Berliner and Biddle., *Manufactured Crisis*, 8.

6. Quoted in Berliner and Biddle, *Manufactured Crisis*, 8.

7. Quoted in Bracey, "No Child Left Behind Act: A Plan for the Destruction of Public Education, Just Say No," 1.

8. Applied Research Center, "Public Schools in the United States: Some History," 2003, http://www.arc.org/erase/j_history.html, [accessed 22 Nov. 2003], 2.

9. Quoted in Applied Research Center, "Public Schools in the United States: Some History," 2.

10. Barbara Ehrenreich, *Fear of Falling: The Inner Life of the Middle Class*, (New York: Pantheon, 1989), 6.

11. Jeannie Oakes and Amy Stuart Wells, "Detracking for High Student Achievement," *Educational Leadership* 55, 4. March 1998, http://wilsontxt.hwwilson.com/pdffull/03461/LBEI1/LZB.pdf, [accessed 12 Nov. 2003], 6.

12. Oakes and Wells, "Detracking for High Student Achievement," 4.

13. Quoted in Berliner and Biddle, *Manufactured Crisis*, 148.

14. *America 2000: An Education Strategy*, SOURCEBOOK (Washington, D.C.: U.S. Department of Education Press, 1991), 25, 27.

15. *America 2000: An Education Strategy*, 27.

16. Bracey, "No Child Left Behind Act: A Plan for the Destruction of Public Education, Just Say No," 6.

17. Bracey, "No Child Left Behind Act: A Plan for the Destruction of Public Education, Just Say No," 7.

18. Bracey, "No Child Left Behind Act: A Plan for the Destruction of Public Education, Just Say No," 6

19. Beth Demain Reigber, Associated Press, "Edison Schools Shareholders Approve Buyout to Take Company Private," *Miami Herald*, 12 Nov. 2003, http://www.miami.com/mld/miamiherald/business/7245618.htm?lc, [accessed 15 Nov. 2003].

20. Lisa Snell, "School Choice, Education Privatization: What's the Difference?" Reason Public Policy Institute, http://www.rppi.org/charterschools.html, [accessed 12 Dec. 2003].

21. Gerald W. Bracey, "13th Bracey Report on the Condition of Public Education," *Education News*, Oct. 2003, http://www.educationnews.org/13th-bracey-report-on-the-condition.htm,, [accessed 11 Dec. 2003].

22. Lisa Snell, "School Choice, Education Privatization: What's the Difference?" Reason Public Policy Institute, http://www.rppi.org/charterschools.html, [accessed 12 Dec. 2003].

23. Beth Demain Reigber, Associated Press, "Edison Schools Shareholders Approve Buyout to Take Company Private," 2.

24. Tali Woodward, "Edison's Failing Grade: Investors and School Districts Are Ditching the Country's Leading Public Education Privatizer," *Corp Watch*, 20 June 2002, http://www.corpwatch.org/issues/PID.jsp?articleid=2688, [accessed 5 Dec. 2003].

25. Snell, "School Choice, Education Privatization: What's the Difference?" 2.

26. Booker T. Washington, "Democracy and Education," address in New York on 30 Sept. 1896, http://teachingamericanhistory.org/library/index.asp?document=57, [accessed 6 Dec. 2003], 1.

27. Bryan Goodwin, "Digging Deeper: Where Does the Public Stand on Standards-Based Education?" Mid-Continent Regional Educational Laboratory (McREL), *Issues Brief*, July 2003, http://www.mcrel.org/topics/productDetail.asp?productID=141, [accessed 3 Nov. 2003], 2.

28. Bryan Goodwin, "Digging Deeper: Where Does the Public Stand on Standards-Based Education?" 2.

29. Bryan Goodwin, "Digging Deeper: Where Does the Public Stand on Standards-Based Education?" 5.

30. Quoted in Susan Castillo, *Oregon Superintendent's Update* #23, 28 Aug. 2003, http://www.ode.state.or.us/superintendent/update/, [accessed 9 Sept. 2003], 2.

31. Jonathon Steinhoff, "No Child Left Behind Inflicts Curse on Public Schools," *Oregonian*, 5 Oct. 2003, 2(B).

32. Arthur W. Combs, "Concept of Human Potential and the School," 1.

33. Marcus Buckingham and Donald O. Clifton, *Now Discover Your Strengths*, (New York: The Free Press, 2001), 12.

34. Quoted in Donald J. Rogers, "How to Teach Fear," in *Four Psychologies Applied to Education*, Thomas B. Roberts, ed., (New York: Schenkman Publishing Company, 1975), 30.

35. *Webster's New Riverside Dictionary, 11th Edition*, revised, (New York: Houghton Mifflin Company, 1996) 15.

36. Rogers, "How to Teach Fear," 31.

2

FROM VALUED ALLY TO
VACANT VAGABOND:
UNDERSTANDING THE ROAD BACK

It is the supreme art of the teacher to awaken joy in creative expression and knowledge.

—Albert Einstein

Education is light; lack of it is darkness.

—Russian proverb

I have a hunch that after reading the previous chapter regarding the NCLB Act you are frustrated and wondering how schools in America fell out of favor so quickly. The answer to the question is that the fall of education was precipitous yet steady. Public education most assuredly will rebound from the current position of disfavor. I know that educators are committed to making a comeback all across America and I hope this experience will help you on your way.

I guarantee that a comeback for your school is not only possible but predictable. I am persuaded that it would make no sense to make that journey without an understanding of both the rise and the untimely fall from favor of public schools. Through the discerning lens of understanding, a pathway to success can be created. I am significantly persuaded that the pathway must be lined with the wisdom of understanding. A wise

man once said, "Seek first to understand, and then to be understood."
The following blithe story was written by a fellow educator, John Taylor,
superintendent of schools for the Lancaster County School District.[1] The
story is a lighthearted way of moving beyond NCLB to the substance of
the work at hand.

The Best Dentist—"Absolutely" the Best Dentist

My dentist is great! He sends me reminders so I don't forget checkups.
He uses the latest techniques based on research. He never hurts me, and
I've got all my teeth, so when I ran into him the other day, I was eager to
see if he'd heard about the new state program. I knew he'd think it was
great. "Did you hear about the new state program to measure effectiveness of dentists with their young patients?" I asked.

"No," he said. He didn't seem too thrilled. "How will they do that?"

"It's quite simple," I said. "They will just count the number of cavities
each patient has at age 10, 14, and 18 and average that to determine a dentist's rating. Dentists will be rated as Excellent, Good, Average, Below Average, and Unsatisfactory. That way parents will know who the best dentists
are. It will also encourage the less effective dentists to get better," I said.
"Poor dentists who don't improve could lose their licenses to practice."

"That's terrible," he said.

"What? That's not a good attitude," I said. "Don't you think we should
try to improve children's dental health in this state?"

"Sure I do," he said, "but that's not a fair way to determine who is prac-
ticing good dentistry."

"Why not?" I asked. "It makes perfect sense to me."

"Well, it's so obvious," he said. "Don't you see that dentists don't all
work with the same clientele; so much depends on things we can't control? For example," he said, "I work in a rural area with a high percentage
of patients from deprived homes, while some of my colleagues work in up-
per middle class neighborhoods. Many of the parents I work with don't
bring their children to see me until there is some kind of problem and I
don't get to do much preventive work. Also," he said, "many of the parents
I serve let their kids eat way too much candy from an early age, unlike
more educated parents who understand the relationship between sugar
and decay. To top it all off," he added, "so many of my clients have well
water which is untreated and has no fluoride in it. Do you have any idea
how much difference early use of fluoride can make?"

"It sounds like you're making excuses," I said. I couldn't believe my
dentist would be so defensive. He does a great job.

"I am not!" he said. "My best patients are as good as anyone's, my work is as good as anyone's, but my average cavity count is going to be higher than a lot of other dentists because I chose to work where I am needed most."

"Don't get touchy," I said.

"Touchy?" he said. His face had turned red and from the way he was clenching and unclenching his jaws, I was afraid he was going to damage his teeth.

"Try furious. In a system like this, I will end up being rated average, below average, or worse. My more educated patients who see these ratings may believe this so-called rating actually is a measure of my ability and proficiency as a dentist. They may leave me, and I'll be left with only the neediest patients. And my cavity average score will get even worse. On top of that, how will I attract good dental hygienists and other excellent dentists to my practice if it is labeled below average?"

"I think you are overreacting," I said. "'Complaining, excuse making, and stonewalling won't improve dental health. . . . I am quoting from a leading member of the DOC," I noted.

"What's the DOC?" he asked.

"It's the Dental Oversight Committee," I said, "a group made up of mostly laypersons to make sure dentistry in this state gets improved."

"Spare me," he said. "I can't believe this. Reasonable people won't buy it," he said hopefully.

The program sounded reasonable to me, so I asked, "How else would you measure good dentistry?"

"Come watch me work," he said. "Observe my processes."

"That's too complicated and time consuming," I said. "Cavities are the bottom line, and you can't argue with the bottom line, it's an absolute measure."

"That's what I'm afraid my parents and prospective patients will think. This can't be happening," he said despairingly.

"Now, now," I said, "don't despair. The state will help you some."

"How?" he said.

"If you're rated poorly, they'll send a dentist who is rated excellent to help straighten you out," I said brightly.

"You mean," he said, "they'll send a dentist with a wealthy clientele to show me how to work on severe juvenile dental problems with which I have probably had much more experience? Big help."

"There you go again," I said. "You aren't acting professionally at all."

"You don't get it," he said. "Doing this would be like grading schools and teachers on an average score on a test of children's progress without regard to influences outside the school, the home, the community served, and stuff like that. Why would they do something so unfair to dentists? No one would ever think of doing that to schools."

I just shook my head sadly, but he had brightened.

"I'm going to write my representatives and senator," he said. "I'll use the school analogy—surely they will see the point."

He walked off with that look of hope mixed with fear and suppressed anger that I see in the mirror so often lately.[1]

The point of the story is that you cannot be distracted by outside pressures from doing the good work you are already doing. From the time of the founding of America's public schools in the late 1700s, schools rose to almost mystical heights in the 1950s and then fell to dark lows in the latter part of the 20th century. You would not be reading this book if you were not interested in finding the road back for your school. The process of finding the road back is a process that will take time. Please see figure 2.1. There are five steps or phases to this process:

1. Step 1, or phase 1, is adult development.
2. Step 2, or phase 2, is high adult expectations.
3. Step 3, or phase 3, is community development.
4. Step 4, or phase 4, is youth development.
5. Step 5, or phase 5, is academic development.

The success of the school in America has always been inextricably linked to the greatness of the country at large. That is a profound concept clearly supported by the nation's sacred documents and history. What has happened to that sacred bond? What led to the development of a school system so exceptional that it was, for a time, not only the envy of every nation on earth, but also believed to be the cradle of the greatest nation? How did such a system fall out of favor so suddenly? The accountability movement (including NCLB) has surfaced these questions regarding the purpose and effectiveness of compulsory public education. The purpose of this section is to articulate the value of free public schooling in a historical context. The focus question is: What purpose have public schools served both historically as well as in contemporary

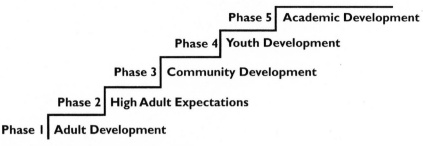

Figure 2.1.   Sequencing the Road Back

America? And do the same conditions warrant a continued effort or can private alternatives be created to improve on the relative success of America's schools? It is universally understood that public schools in America have played a meaningful role in both historical and contemporary America. The purpose of free and equal access to public schools in America has been chiseled into the following values that I call core values of American life. The public school was developed to:

- Sustain the principles of democracy.
- Knit diverse populations into the fabric of a common culture.
- Perpetuate the core principles of democracy and American capitalism.

This brief survey makes no claim at being a definitive account of the purpose of the public school in America, but it provides a place to start.

THE PAST IS DEAD; LONG LIVE THE PAST!

History provides a unique and valuable perspective. An account of things past allows one to see broad themes that reoccur in the present and continue into the future. History does not, of course, repeat itself exactly, but events and issues of the past do have a tendency to reappear, albeit in a slightly different form. The broad themes underscored here suggest that from the Founding Fathers to the leaders of contemporary America education has been valued because education sustained the principles of democracy, weaved diverse populations into a common culture, and helped perpetuate the core principles of democracy and American capitalism. First, I examine the historical purpose of free public education and then look at what has changed so that today's national leaders seem to scorn the role of public schools in modern day America. Axioms of history are truths that emerge from the past and must serve as the foundation for the return of public education to prominence in America. Consider the following historical axioms below.

- Axiom 1: The Founding Fathers intended that public education support the core principles of America.
- Axiom 2: Successful public schools precede the common culture in America.
- Axiom 3: Public support for schools is preceded by successful schools.
- Axiom 4: Education has sustained freedom and equity.
- Axiom 5: Education harnesses the power of diversity in American culture.
- Axiom 6: The public will not pay more for the same.
- Axiom 7: Schools must earn support by becoming successful.
- Axiom 8: Student success in school precedes freedom, equity, and success in life.
- Axiom 9: A connection with the wider environment is critical for finding the way back.
- Axiom 10: Education is a legally binding hope.
- Axiom 11: Poor kids of color are caustic casualties of a primordial myth.
- Axiom 12: Standards-based reform (SBR) is the true hope for the future.

As I discuss each axiom in more detail please make a determination as to how each could be used to return your school to prominence.

Axiom 1: The Founding Fathers intended that public education support the core principles of life in America. It has been said that the quintessence of political traditions of equality, liberty, and justice for all are the core concepts that separate America's form of government from other, less evolved forms of government. The Founding Fathers had a profoundly strong belief that all children should have access to a quality education. Yet, there was a growing concern about the diversity of people immigrating to the colonies. The Founding Fathers believed in free education for all because they believed that school would strengthen citizenship by enhancing the core principles of equality, freedom, and justice for all. Those who wrote the U.S. Constitution believed that schools were necessary to enhance the core beliefs of equality, justice, and freedom for all. That belief was noticed and admired by some of the world's intellectuals of the day. For instance, Alexis de Tocqueville typified that admiration when he noted, "Education in a democracy must be an apprenticeship in liberty."[2] Throughout the course of U. S. history, some of our greatest leaders have voiced a profound belief that democracy and education walk hand in hand. John Kennedy said it this way, "Liberty without learning is always in peril and learning without liberty is always in vain."[3] The key point here is that America's leaders, until just recently, believed that education should play a major role in ensuring that the young experiment of democracy would grow into full maturity. Further, immediately after the American Revolution (1775–1783) the founders of the United States argued that education was essential for the prosperity and survival of the new nation. Thomas Jefferson, author of the Declaration of Independence, proposed that America give a high priority to a "crusade against ignorance."[4] Jefferson was not alone in his belief that education was essential for the prosperity and survival of the new nation. In fact, as early as 1647, the General Court of the Massachusetts Bay Company decreed that every town of 50 families should have an elementary school and that every town with 100 families should have a Latin school. The support of free and equitable schooling evolved to such a degree that by 1779 Thomas Jefferson proposed a two-track educational system, with different tracks for, in his words, the "laboring and the learned."[5] In 1785 the Continental Congress created a law that surveyed the Northwest Territory, creating townships and ensuring that a portion of each township be reserved for a school.[6] At approximately the same time (1790), the Pennsylvania state constitution called for free public education for poor children only, expecting rich parents to pay their own way.[7] As early as 1817, Boston created a system of free public schools, then in 1837 Massachusetts passed a law making all grades of public school open to all pupils free of charge.[8] The Founding Fathers believed that democracy in America would become an example to others as a beacon of light.[9]

Axiom 2: Successful schools precede the common culture in America.
America's noble experiment—universal education for all citizens—is a
cornerstone of American democracy. Universal education was highly
valued by the Founding Fathers, at least in part because they saw education as a way to bring diverse people together under one government.
By the time of the American Revolution, the colonial population had
reached approximately 2.5 million people of diversity. Black slaves, for
example, constituted roughly 22% of the total—more than 500,000 people. About 250,000 were Scots-Irish and approximately 200,000 were
Germans. Protestants formed the overwhelming majority of people, although approximately 25,000 were Roman Catholics, and about 1,000
Jews also lived in the colonies.[10] Just before and after the American Revolution, about 15,000 lowland Scots settled in North America. Just after
the French Revolution several thousand French men and women who
had opposed the French Revolution made their way to America as well.
By the 1830s, another 150,000 immigrants, mostly from Northern Ire-
land and England, immigrated to the Americas. Alarm was expressed
about the growing numbers of diverse immigrants and how the group as
a whole might affect the emerging yet delicate democracy. Therefore, in
1789 President John Adams and Congress passed four laws intended to
slow the rate of immigration to provide adequate time for schools to
properly integrate immigrants into American culture.[11] Americans had
such confidence in the integrating power of education that they not only
provided more years of schooling, but also provided schooling to a larger
percentage of the population than had the countries the immigrants
were coming from. In fact, Thomas Jefferson was one of the first American leaders to suggest creating a system of free schools for everyone
that would be publicly supported through taxes.[12] American education
was used to help assimilate diverse immigrants into the popular culture
so they would join and strengthen the new nation. The assimilation of
immigrants was so potent that Henry Ward Beecher wrote that school
was "the stomachs of the country in which all people that come to us are
assimilated within a generation. When a lion eats an ox, the lion does not
become the ox but the ox becomes the lion."[13]

*Axiom 3: Public support for schools is preceded by successful
schools.* At the heart of the American dream there's a simple bargain:
if you work hard and play by the rules, America will give you an op-

portunity to build a better future. Thomas Jefferson, one of the key Founding Fathers and author of the Declaration of Independence, argued that education was essential for the prosperity and survival of the new nation.[14] A plank in the 1888 national Republican platform said it this way: "The free school is the promoter of that intelligence which is to preserve us as a free nation; therefore, the state or nation, or both combined, should support free institutions of learning sufficient to afford to every child growing up in the land the opportunity of a good common school education."[15] Some even put education on par with the core principles of freedom and justice. In 1888, James Bruce wrote, "Education ought, no doubt, to enlighten a man; but the educated classes speaking generally, are the property holding classes and the possession of property does more to make a man timid than education does to make him hopeful. . . . In the less educated man a certain simplicity and openness of mind go some way to compensate for the lack of knowledge. He is more apt to be influenced by the authority of leaders; but as, at least in England and America, he is generally shrewd enough to discern between a great man and a demagogue; this is more a gain than loss."[16] In a letter accepting the Republican nomination in 1880, James Garfield said it this way: "Next in importance to freedom and justice is popular education, without which neither freedom nor justice can permanently be maintained."[17] Not surprisingly, there were those that thought that education would ensure the continued success of the great American experiment in democracy. This was a thought that was voiced in America even before America had free compulsory education for all. In a letter to John Adams in 1821 Thomas Jefferson made the point, "And even should the clouds of barbarism and despotism again obscure the science and liberties of Europe, this country remains to preserve and restore light and liberty to them."[18]

From the genesis of America, the leaders and others have assigned a number of exigent roles to the common school in America. In a simplified form, the Founding Fathers thought schools would be able to assume the role of "the keeper of democracy." It was believed that schools would help sustain the principles of democracy by weaving the diverse immigrant population into a unified culture, and perpetuate the principles found in the Constitution. I realize that this point, to some, may seem far afield from the implications of NCLB. The point is crucially important, however. Many credible educators including Gerald Bracey contend that NCLB "is a grand scheme of the school privatizers. No Child Left Behind sets up public schools for the final knockdown."[19] If so, what type of system would fulfill the roles deemed so important by America's Founding Fathers? Could the for-profit schools (e.g., Sylvan Learning Centers, Edison Schools, Whittle, or Bennett) fulfill the need? If so, would the families of failing students be interested in them and, if so, could they afford the cost of private (for-profit) placement? The children who theoretically will be left behind in school come from poor minority families, which are without the resources to pay for private school placement. It is doubtful that either private schools or private programs could accept the role of "keeper of democracy."

Axiom 4: Education has sustained freedom and equity. Freedom and equity were rare in the world before the American Revolution. Many of the early colonists migrated from Europe to the New World so they could live in freedom and have equity of opportunity. Freedom and equity did not come easily, nor were those rights sustained without great sacrifices. America's early leaders believed that the free public school would help to stabilize the great American experiment in democracy. In fact, the democratic tenet that rights are inalienable was taken from one of the greatest speeches in American history. In the Gettysburg Address, President Lincoln highlighted liberty as one of the core beliefs that led to both the American Revolution and also to the Civil War. During the Civil War, in the Battle of Gettysburg, one of the bloodiest battles in all of American history, liberty as a core value was tested beyond reality. The sacrifice for liberty at Gettysburg was unparalleled in U.S. history to that time. Specifically, at Gettysburg 158,000 men died in just a few minutes of bloody combat. The battle at Gettysburg was so hard fought that about one in three soldiers (approximately 32.3% of the total of the two armies) was killed by several volleys lasting only minutes each but spread over several days. I emphasize the egregious death count because these soldiers died protecting the core beliefs of liberty and equality of all people. America fights wars for freedom and equity abroad and at home, but has always relied on the schools to keep those core values alive. Franklin Roosevelt said it with power when he said, "The gains of education are never really lost. Books may be burned and cities sacked, but truth, like the yearning for freedom, lives in the hearts of humble men."[20]

Axiom 5: Education harnesses the power of diversity in American culture. The demographic concerns that challenge America are nothing new. America is a nation of diversity and, in my opinion, diversity may well be the reason America stands as a successful symbol of wealth and tolerance to the rest of the world. There is no question that increased diversity and poverty have been taxing on American institutions. People who were no more courageous or intelligent than school people today have successfully responded to such challenges previously in American history. I am persuaded that today's demographics are not dramatically changed. It seems there are more similarities to our history than differences. For example, immigration rates during the Revolutionary War are comparable to today's rates. Certainly the global economy and resurgence in ethnic pride have increased rather than decreased the need to socialize immigrants to life in the American culture. It is clearly understood that the increasing diversity has generated challenges for education as it has for all of America's institutions. It appears there is, arguably, one significant difference and it is that the Founding Fathers and the people of early America looked to public schools for a solution to diversity, while contemporary America seems to see public schools as part of the problem.

When the achievement gap is mentioned, I hear comments about how schools are failing, rather than what potential schools have to unlock the core values of freedom (from poverty) and equity (of opportunity). As has been noted, preserving and solidifying freedom from poverty and equity of opportunity have been important roles of America's public schools since the time of the American Revolution. I am considerably concerned because if public schools fail, the poor may well be sealed off from equity of opportunity and freedom from poverty, which is a violation of trust with our sacred documents. Low socioeconomic status (SES) kids (which is a fancy way of saying poor kids) will tragically be denied the hope of a better life. The salient point is that we need to wake up to what NCLB really represents and move past the limiting effects of NCLB. The issues around the act are not about strategies of improving schools through free market competition, tax credits, or vouchers, but rather about equal access to America's wealth for children that come from poor families. To say it succinctly, the achievement gap is not about race;

it is about political and economic power. Further, it is a challenge to our schools' ability to clearly meet the emotional, social, and academic needs of their students. As early as 1788, Thomas Jefferson seemed to have a foreboding glimpse into America's future when he wrote, "The natural progress of things is for liberty to yield and government to gain ground."[21] I have been persuaded that American schools can and will return to the basics of serving diverse children so well that affluence will be unlocked for all Americans. I believe that NCLB represents a public policy that has drifted far afield from the core values that once galvanized America to action. The core values of equity of opportunity and freedom from poverty are so deeply knit into the fabric of America's culture that those ideals have lengthened the shadow of America as a great nation. This book explores standards-based reform (SBR) as substitute for NCLB as the vehicle for advancing the cause of freedom and equity through educational excellence. Let us begin to understand how SBR has the potential for success that will support the core values of freedom and equity. The NCLB Act is, of course, disguised as SBR with the purpose of closing the achievement gap. It has been noted that the NCLB Act is an imposter. Nevertheless, it is the responsibility of each concerned adult to ensure that the school community understands and is committed to using the act as an impetus to move ahead for what is right for both children and America.

Axiom 6: The public will not pay more for the same. It is quite clear that public education is at the center of a volatile debate that is only likely to get worse. Public skepticism, rebuke, and scrutiny are likely to be constant companions of teachers for years to come. Student performance is portrayed as low and getting worse. Schools seem to lack direction almost to the point of vertigo. Yet schools are built on a foundation of tradition and recidivism. Many high-placed education critics such as Chester V. Finn suggest that "the school system has proven it is an ossified government monopoly that can't reform itself." In fact, that was the exact statement made by Finn, the undersecretary of education (for President Reagan), in the *Wall Street Journal* when he said, "You've had your chance. We warned you. We gave you the Nation at Risk over 20 years ago. Nothing has changed. It's time to apply American business expertise to education."[22] I am always both confused and surprised that some officials expect schools to use corporate America as an example of efficient yet effective organizations. Certainly there are some good examples from which we all could learn. But the arrogance of Mr. Finn's comment flies in the face of repeated examples of corporate scandals and apparent incompetence, including Enron, Tyco, Global Crossing, ImClone, WorldCom, and hundreds of other companies that have adjusted their accounting reports to falsify records to inflate the value of the company to justify enormous payouts to company officials, resulting in the loss of retirement benefits for scores of employees. Beyond the ethical violations of lying for personal gain, there have been myriad dotcoms that failed because their officers didn't have any idea of how to run a business.[23] This is not a criticism that has been lost on the forces opposing privatization. I fully realize the reform statute underscored herein (NCLB) received strong bipartisan support in Congress and has some faltering support from some of education's traditional critics. It is further recognized that schools are perceived to resent the proposed and largely unfunded statute and appear apathetic toward reform. That reaction is a poor measure of the thousands of dedicated teachers and other adults who strive to serve America's children in some amazingly hostile conditions. It must be said that the approach used to generate the necessary improvement appears to have been selected to ensure the absolute failure of the proposed outcome. Any graduate student in business administration would predict poor "transfer" rates when unfunded transformational changes are developed in isolation and then superimposed on people who are emotionally exhausted and feeling quite undervalued. An important note on perspective: it has been my experience that schools have done very well for many students, but not all. Many educators recognize the concerns and still have, understandably, become emotionally hardened and skeptical from years of criticism and isolation. On balance, it must be noted that public education has made tremendous strides in the 20th century. It is because of these advances that America leads the world in the percentage of children who attend school and the percentage that go on to college. Credit these improvements to two important factors. First, Americans have been generous in their support of public schools through increased taxes, volunteerism, and understanding. Second, schools have made valiant attempts to keep pace with a culture that is changing at light speed. The reader can be certain, as am I, that the same effort will again emerge from schools and, in fact, would have been more readily forthcoming if schools had been more actively involved in the design process.

Axiom 7: Schools must earn support by becoming successful. A wise person once commented, "There is no short cut to any place worth going." That admonition could not be truer, particularly with regard to community support and the understanding and support of teachers. The reader represents a broad spectrum force and it is essential for you, whether you are a teacher, school leader, parent, or student, to understand and support teachers if high academic achievement for each child is to be achieved. I necessarily make a few points intended to enhance community understanding and support among the caring forces of education.

Please understand that a teacher works for reasons of the heart. As such, it hurts when the work of a teacher is marginalized (sometimes innocently enough) by an important official of government or a community member. Teachers teach who they are. It is impossible for them to do less. Teaching is a very private, even intimate and personal, experience usually executed in privacy from other adults. Even how a teacher approaches instruction is personal. Teachers tend to model their teaching after one of their own much-loved teachers, often the teacher who initially inspired them to become a teacher. Even more personal, teachers tend to select teaching strategies that were personally most effective for them when they were students. What teachers do in their own classrooms is, in reality, the very personification of who they are as people. When the work of a teacher is marginalized, it is taken personally, because it is, in fact, personal.

At this most intimate level the personal exposure is intense with emotional risk. I do not believe that is true for any other worker in America except, arguably, the parent. I am persuaded this is the reason why teachers feel so misunderstood. Then add to that the equally intimate nature of each individual student. When an adult teacher fails in private it is one thing, but teachers tend to see their own failure in the mirror of a child's (or family's) tears. Each child is extraordinarily complex and immensely valuable and each comes to school with unparalleled hope and trust in their teachers. Understand that behind each sterile content standard there is a whole child and teacher. Let me gnarl my way to an explanation of what that means. It is into this delicate mix of human beings that we inject a high-risk, inflexible, high-stakes testing system that some have designed to function as a sanction for failure. Certainly it must be understood that when people are threatened and intimidated by hostile circumstances, optimum performance is unlikely for either the student or the teacher. It is the responsibility of all parents, students, and educators to ensure that the value of a child is not placed at risk for the purpose of intimidating a school into higher performance. Not only is it unethical, it is unnecessary. The hope in a child's eyes is motivation enough. Even in this type of environment (potentially hostile), I know that teachers will commit to SBR for reasons of the heart, and most assuredly will move forward with dedication and compassion to create an instructional environment that is safe, wholesome, and nurturing for children. The point is, behind each high academic standard there is the humanness of two people: the whole student and a whole teacher. Working with today's broad mix of children is extremely complex. Obviously, every classroom is a microcosm of the community from which the children come (good and ill). Teachers must intuitively and automatically adjust to the social complexities of the community including issues such as elitism, indifference, inhumaneness, ethnocentricity, sexism, favoritism, and friendship. In a flash of less than a nanosecond, while continuing with the academic content, the teacher will simultaneously and subliminally discipline a student with a look or gesture while encouraging and reinforcing another with a smile or wink. All of this communication is expected, understood, and appreciated by students. This complex interaction goes on thousands of times a day because students are at least as sophisticated as a computer, with one complicating detail: children have feelings that are constantly changing for reasons usually invisible and expressed as emotional pain that is completely unpredictable. Complicating the emotional challenges are other complex variables like hunger, health, hygiene, and abandonment. Phenomenally, all of the interaction with a child typically occurs without the teacher ever losing touch with the student who is reciting. Is every teacher as magnificent as the one we have just admired? No, of course not. But every school has at least one, and whenever disrespect is administered (albeit frequently unintended) to one, it is administered to all. Ironically, the situation is much like that when a teacher is unfair or unkind with an undeserving child. The point is simple but essentially important: some teachers have become cynical and unresponsive for reasons that by now should be obvious to all. It is true that public schools have been unsuccessful with too many students (certainly not all) and schools can do better. And that is where the very essence of this book comes in. It reveals several truths essential in the support of a teacher in a standards-based classroom (SBC).

Axiom 8: Student success in school precedes freedom, equity, and success in life. Public schools can do better and they, in general, know how. Beginning in chapter 3, this book serves as a reminder of the skill set teachers have, but which has become hard to sustain without the understanding and support of the community. The next step is readily understood but agonizingly difficult to execute over time. Through a combination of unconditional love and soul-wrenching hard work, I believe teachers can and will get more of their students to attain, even master, high academic standards. I say much more on that point in subsequent pages. This particular chapter is intended to remind the school community of its responsibility, with the instructional detail following in chapter 5. Now, for all of you high-performance readers, please do not jump ahead (in school you are labeled as having attention deficit hyperactivity disorder [ADHD]). Instead, let's focus. It is necessary to keep the whole team together as we gird our learned loins and move forward with objectivity and understanding. Stephen Covey once wrote, "Seek first to understand, and then to be understood."[24] I am sure you must realize by now that there are no easy ways to avoid the soul-wrenching work ahead.

You have already been reminded that there is no shortcut to any place worth going, so let's get started. It is my hope that from this dialogue will trickle out ideas that will work for you and your program.

Axiom 9: A connection with the wider environment is critical for finding the way back. Clearly, schools need to get better if our young adults are to remain successful in a brutally competitive international marketplace where intellectual capital is now as valuable as investment capital. In the SBS, simply trying harder is no longer good enough, either for school personnel or for schools. For the first time, effort is not the issue. Student success as measured by the standards is what matters. There can be no doubt that the challenge ahead is daunting, but the SBS is this country's and your community's best chance of making the transformational improvements that are necessary. I predict that the SBS will succeed mightily, but only if the human dimension is given adequate attention along with or slightly ahead of the productivity dimension. The culture of a school is of great significance because the ultimate benefactor is children. If adults are treated with disregard, what can be expected for the children? If teachers are valued and treated with dignity and respect in school, wide expectation has been set and modeled.

Recognize that when top-down strategies impose higher expectations and simultaneously reduce resources, one should expect a negative effect. Then, to impose those requirements on schools with disingenuous promises of adequate resources is putting the children of this nation at risk. The pragmatic issue for your leader or leadership team (LT) is that those kinds of mindless steps have already been taken, so it is up to you to grow hope. Always remember that a leader is a dealer in hope. Teachers will, I predict, move ahead anyway with unconditional love and support from the leader or LT and the community, because teachers initiate with their heart. It must be recognized and voiced that schools need to become much more accountable than has been the case until just recently. Even for the richest nation in the world the billions spent on education in America is a staggering sum. Clearly, the investment is a good one but accountability must be a part of the process. To effectively move from where schools are today to where they need to go requires a brief look at how public schools arrived in this current place. It is a storied journey full of success and hope. It is because of the monumentally successful past that now our critical friends seem to expect the impossible. A wise person once cautioned against building castles in the sky; first, he advised, build on a solid foundation. That is what we will do.

> Teachers are expected to reach unattainable goals, with inadequate tools. The miracle is that sometimes they accomplish the impossible task.
>
> —Halm G. Ginor

Axiom 10: Education is a legally binding hope. Prior to the launch of Sputnik, schools in America were secure, confident, and seldom challenged. Until that time schools were valued and viewed as the vehicle through which all citizens could develop a foundation of success in life.

School is so much a part of life in the United States that compulsory attendance laws were written and passed to require school attendance of
all children between the ages of 7 and 16. Further, school attendance
was viewed as important to ensure that all people have equal access to
wealth. In the context of American life, the concept of school is defined
by the U.S. Constitution and the U.S. Supreme Court as wealth (i.e.,
property). Amendment V of the United States Constitution guarantees
that no person shall be deprived by the federal government of life, liberty, or property, without the due process of law.[25] That guarantee found
in the Constitution was extended to education by the Supreme Court in
Gross v. Lopez. In this 1975 case, the court found a property interest in
education, clearly linking education to wealth and status.[26] By law in
America, education is equated to wealth as a property right. Arguably,
then, school success guarantees all citizens a right to wealth and status.
Sadly, America has yet to achieve the legal precedent established in
Gross v. Lopez. The average educator was, of course, not even remotely
aware that such staggering hope had been hung on the schoolhouse
door by the Supreme Court in 1975. It was in the shadow of that procla-
mation of hope that the very foundation of the institution of public
school began to shake. The institutional quaking came as suddenly and
surprisingly as a thief in the night.

The seeds of school failure were planted as public schools in the
United States entered the post–World War II era, when the principles
of equity and freedom were zealously supported by the American people, and schools were given a sense of well-being and importance. It was
a proud time to be a teacher. All of that changed in the 1990s when most
states created rigid accountability measures called standards-based education (SBE), all of which predated NCLB. Some of the unreasonable
expectations that are seen today exist not so much because of the inept-
ness of the school, but rather because of the incredible success of the
school system and the incredible optimism rampant in post–World War
II America. And this is why: after the war, Americans were overly opti-
mistic about life in the United States, while much of the rest of the
world was suffering through the physical annihilation of the world's
structures. Starvation and illness were rampant. In the United States,
however, employment was high, the economy was good, and Americans
were safe and warm. Resources were adequate to meet the needs of the

poor and elderly, which by today's standards were miniscule. America was a booming success. I am persuaded that the public felt education was the secret to America's unlimited wealth, success, and power. The educators were, of course, only vaguely aware of this phenomenon, and certainly did not resist the positive attention. The years that followed World War II were unique in American history. These years generated not only a booming economy, but also an incredible expansion of public education. During this very period, enrollment in America's public schools increased by 50% or more and American colleges and universities more than doubled their capacities. As I said at the beginning of this chapter, at the end of this period America had an educational system that was the envy of the world because of the opportunities it offered to a much expanded range of Americans.[27] It is ironic that while more people were coming to participate in the educational system, criticism was on the rise. During the 1950s and 1960s the school system, in spite of the growing criticism, had a difficult time expanding rapidly enough to meet the apparent need. At one time in the late 1950s, the rate of growth of public schools was so rapid that a new school of 500 elementary students was required each Monday morning.[28] Resources, while increasing, did not keep absolute pace with the burgeoning enrollments. Seventy percent of the elementary schools in this country had no libraries; many of these schools had an average of one half of a book per child.[29] Expansion did bring with it some problems that remain, at least in part, unresolved yet today. After all these years, it is easy for us to diminish the strains such tremendous expansion brought to bear on schools. A common stressor was that teachers were frequently aware that they were beginning to teach more and more students that were less and less motivated. Unfortunately, many of these new problems for schools proved difficult to resolve. These expansion-related problems increased sharply beginning in the 1970s and steadily increased through the end of the century. Most of these issues remain unresolved and have grown steadily worse.

Axiom 11: Poor kids of color are caustic casualties of a primordial myth. I had just started teaching in the 1960s and remember the fuss that was made when the Soviet Union surprised the world and beat the United States with the first man-made space satellite. On October 4, 1957, the Russian Sputnik with cosmonaut Yuri Gagarin successfully entered space first, well ahead of the United States. This highly publicized event trumpeted that the Communist system was ahead in the Cold War. How could the space race possibly affect public schools? While the two may seem disconnected, they are very much interrelated because the public and political officials were caught up in the hysteria about the perceived omnipotence of public schools.

The fact that the Soviet Union had beaten the United States by having the first satellite in space came as a sudden shock to American citizens because America did not feel challenged on any front, especially a technological one, largely for demographic, not educational, reasons. Before that event, the United States enjoyed the largest monopoly of power in contemporary world history. During the years immediately following World War II, the United States had the most powerful military and manufacturing system in the world. The competing systems in the Western world had been destroyed during the war. The United States had unilateral possession of the world's most powerful weapon (i.e., the atomic bomb). Further, the U.S. factory system was untarnished by bombing and therefore functioning at peak capacity while saturation bombing had left the rest of Europe and Asia with little to no production capacity. Therefore, from 1945 to 1949 the United States had a powerful military and industrial advantage over all of our traditional enemies like no other nation in modern history. Times were good and public opinion apparently gave too much credit for the success to schools.

The United States seemed to be in complete control. In 1949, all of that ended suddenly when China unexpectedly fell to Communism, and suddenly the Soviet Union also got the atomic bomb. With the Soviet Union and China together, suddenly and precipitously two-thirds of the world's population was Communist, and now the Communists (perceived to be a mortal enemy of the United States) also had the most feared weapon in history—the atomic bomb. The sudden and unexpected shift in the balance of power created paranoia not seen at any other time in history. The Cold War was just beginning and the global competition of the 1950s was just emerging, leaving the American people feeling unnaturally vulnerable. Joseph McCarthy, the junior senator from Wisconsin, exploited this fear for political gain by naming scores of respected U.S. citizens as Communists or Communist sympathizers.

The rabid paranoia seemed to run wild almost overnight. Happily, the extreme paranoia began to subside as the McCarthy hearings began to wind down in the late 1950s.

Then, when the Soviet Union beat the United States with the first space flight in 1957, there was paranoia and concern expressed anew. Sputnik threatened the national interest of America even more than when the Soviet Union broke America's atomic monopoly in 1949. This event rocked the very essence of American security because it suddenly became apparent that the Soviet Union could now build rockets powerful enough to propel, in just minutes, a nuclear device into the heart of America. After having such a distinct advantage from 1945 to 1949, it was a shock for Americans to see the Communist world suddenly and unexpectedly catch up (in just 4 short years). Presumably, the American leaders began to look for reasons why the United States was not able to press their post–World War II advantages further. There was great concern expressed about how foreign nations could catch up to the United States so quickly. It became apparent that America's tradition of being number one was facing very stiff competition. What had gone wrong, particularly in the areas of science, technology, and education? Naturally, the school system came under close scrutiny. Predictably, it was that concern that led Congress to commission a massive study of education to determine if there was a problem with the public school system. James Coleman was the chief investigator of what has since been called the Coleman Report. This study was a landmark of incredible significance for several reasons. It may come as a surprise to some to know that up until that time teaching had not been systematically studied in a scientific way. That is not to say that excellent teaching was nonexistent in schools; rather, it suggests that little was known about the definition of good teaching. What was good teaching? The findings of the Coleman Report were shocking in that it concluded that the major differences in student achievement was a function of factors over which schools have little control. After collecting and analyzing data from approximately 600,000 students and 60,000 teachers in more than 4,000 schools, Coleman and his colleagues concluded that the quality of a school (not teachers) accounts for only about 10 to 12% of the variance in student achievement. That finding was shocking for teachers and came as a demoralizing bombshell. If schools have little influence on student achievement, why even try? I am persuaded that the Coleman Report is still having an effect on the beliefs about academic potential of low-SES students. If the school only accounts for about 10% of the difference in student achievement, what makes up for the other 90%? According to the Coleman Report, the differences are factors like a student's natural ability, motivation level, socioeconomic status (SES), and home environment. An esteemed Harvard researcher, Christopher Jenks, confirmed the findings in his landmark book entitled *Inequality: A Reassessment of the Effects of Family and School in America.*[30] Happily, I must hasten to add that the findings of Coleman and Jenks were not entirely accurate because they were looking at average school-wide effects and simply did not account for the tremendous variation from teacher to teacher within each school. Nevertheless, these were discouraging findings for schools as immigration into urban America was on the rise. Public schools were beginning to show the strain that was only amplified with the additional migration of a multitude of low-SES Americans who also migrated to the cities in search of better jobs. Fortunately, schools can now be comforted to know that studies of good teaching clearly conclude that good teachers have a profound effect on student achievement (more so, than any other factor), even in schools that perform poorly.[31] I am persuaded that the seeds of the current crisis of confidence in schools were planted for two significant reasons: the impact of the Coleman Report, coupled with the massive expansion of schools, created challenges that have yet to be solved. In spite of its fallacies, the Coleman Report was not good news to teachers. If schools didn't really matter, why even try? I was just beginning to teach at the time the Coleman Report was first released. I did not hear about the Coleman Report at school, but I did in graduate school (in great depth). Nor did I personally make the connection between the bad news of the Coleman Report and the wonderings of teachers in search of how they could be more effective. I do remember wondering, however, about all of the innovative programs that just seemed to emerge overnight. In my intermediate school, suddenly one person was hired to coordinate a district-wide career education program and another to coordinate "interaction analysis." Beyond those two programs, I was also involved in modular scheduling, open concept learning, the new social studies, economics in society, and the student-centered curriculum, to name just a few. I am not suggesting that all of the aforementioned programs had a negative effect on student learning. I do believe, however, that the emphasis shifted away from rigorous academic content during that time.

The Coleman Report was a radical departure from traditional thinking about schooling. Essentially the study concluded (and Congress apparently agreed) that schools didn't make as much difference as SES (meaning the economic and education level of the family). In my personal experience, the impact of the Coleman Report was demoralizing and the effect continues. The message was confusing for teachers. On one hand teachers felt the importance of their work because the school was attracting a much-expanded range of students, while important school officials were simultaneously communicating that the school accounts for only about 10% of the variance in student achievement.[32] The Coleman Report was limiting for schools because it suggested that schools were not as efficacious as family background. I fear that the shadow of that limiting feeling is still with us. I must repeat that much scientific evidence clearly demonstrates that individual teachers have a profound effect on student achievement, even in a poor school. In fact, the single most important variable in the success of the school is the teacher. Finally, Robert Marzano, Debra J. Pickering, and Jane Pollack summarized his classroom research by commenting, "The myth that teachers do not make a difference in student learning has been refuted."[33] The departure of research from the effects of schools signaled the birth of a new approach to accountability. Prior to the Coleman Report, research on school improvement efforts focused primarily on what went into the schooling effort (processes). Coleman, however, focused his study on how much the children were learning (academic results). In short, Coleman focused less on what teachers taught and more on what students learned. And that is precisely where the standards-based movement (SBM) came from. As I have said previously, the SBS is better for students, and where it has been in use academic achievement is improving.

Looking at the SBM from the public-policy perspective, which I was honored to do as an advisor to the Oregon state school board, I have seen irrefutable statewide evidence of steady academic gains through the use of the SBS. It quite clearly shows the achievement gap has not yet been bridged in Oregon or this nation. Yet, I am confident that if Oregon and

America stay the course we will succeed in creating educational equity for all. The singularly important point is that I know firsthand that the SBS has generated better results in student learning. I believe you know this also.

Axiom 12: Standards-based reform (SBR) is the true hope for the future. Your school is already moving ahead and there is no time to be distracted. To the next point, the history of SBR has been presented to clearly demonstrate that the current SBM found its genesis of disillusionment in the aftermath of the Coleman Report, rather than the complete collapse and failure of the current public school system. I am completely persuaded that this point is critically important so that the heart-driven teachers will understand that the accountability emphasis of the SBM is an outgrowth of a much earlier time, rather than a response to the failure of just the contemporary public school system. I believe that schools in general have improved, but the improvement has been made amid a sharp decline in resources. This brings another key point to my study of why we should remain motivated and understand that the public, above all else, supports each teacher as an individual and a professional. The purse strings of government are tight everywhere. Please do not conclude that the shortage of resources means a lack of support for your school. The evidence clearly shows that while the vast majority of parents may wonder about the quality of schools in their neighboring communities, they are simultaneously experiencing satisfaction with the education of their own children in the local schools. The point is there is no more money. That, of course, is a relative statement. Arguably, resources are limited even in the wealthiest nation in the history of the world. My personal strong opinion is that the public will simply not pay more for the same level of service. When your school is at that place where no child is left behind, the money will become forthcoming. Until then, please understand that schools are not being given the same high priority as they were when the National Defense Education Act was passed in 1958. That fact is unrelated to the quality of schools at that time.

Rather, in the 1950s there was a sassy surging of confidence in all of America's institutions, including schools. The new confidence was, arguably, stimulated more by the surging mood of America than by either the institutions or the public school system itself. The economically rich years of post–World War II America created a mood of hope and optimism that also had an effect on how schools were viewed by the public.

That isn't to say there were not good schools that deserved that kind of laudatory recognition. Rather, as a whole, schools are significantly stronger today than they were 50 years ago. In my opinion, schools were not as good in the 1950s as they were portrayed to be; nor are schools as weak today as they are being portrayed. Simply said, schools are better today because we know more about good teaching today than we did in the 1950s. We are just now, for example, beginning to understand the workings of the brain in relationship to learning. Further, we are just beginning to understand what happens in a child's brain or psyche to cause learning.

I am not one of those who believe that one can improve the political standing of schools by attacking our funding competitors. I believe that America exists in an increasingly dangerous world where America needs to defend its people against enemies. For me, it is not an issue of all or nothing, but reasonable balance. Are you aware of America's amazing stealth technology? The F117 Nighthawk is an attack bomber so elusive it cannot be detected by radar. Certainly, this particular technology has, happily, saved the lives of innumerable pilots flying missions in the defense of America. I was stunned to hear that it cost $6.5 billion to develop such a sophisticated weapon. While the $6.5 billion cost makes no sense to me, what is more at issue is that a military official would actually comment that $6.5 billion was nothing to develop such a marvelous weapon. The issue is not the extreme cost (legitimate or not) of developing a technologically superior weapon system, or gun platform as it is sometimes called, but that America (with its vast wealth) can afford a superior military industrial machine—the best in the world. The issue is not just about defense, but it must also be about the human cost of such priorities. The strongest military in the world comes with the cost of having the poorest children in the world and a health-care system with increasingly limited access. Clearly, we will not solve the devilishly difficult dilemma of the cost of defense. I will simply let one of the greatest generals in American history, and also one of the most popular presidents, conclude with the following foreboding reminder. General Eisenhower warned America of the consequences of improper prioritization. He said, "Every gun that is made, every warship launched, every rocket fired signals the final sense of theft from those that hunger and are not fed, those that are cold and not clothed. The world in arms is not spending money alone. It's spending the sweat of laborers, the genius of scientists, and the hopes of its children."[34] When a president or other official ridicules public schools while simultaneously funding stealth gun platforms and cutting education, we recognize it as bully-based reform rhetoric. The positive in that realization is that we can be comforted (not distracted) in knowing that we are conserving our energy and resources for the comeback.

THE NATIONAL DEFENSE EDUCATION ACT

The National Defense Education Act (NDEA) was a response to an era of paranoia and America's perceived failure in the space race. To experience the mood of the Congress as it deliberated the priority of education, please notice the title of the legislation. The NDEA increased federal funding for schools.[35] Presumably, Congress concluded that with more money, the quality of education would improve. Unfortunately, the desired quality was not defined until much later, when the definitions of effectiveness first emerged through the Elementary and Secondary Education Act (ESEA) rather than through the NDEA.

Please notice that, in retrospect, the current funding crisis was brought on through a lack of definition about what America wanted from its schools. As has been noted, after World War II public schools were perceived to be the best hope for the economic salvation of the individual and prosperity of America. Arguably, it was believed that education could create a level playing field ensuring equitable educational opportunities. However, schools standing alone cannot create a cultural plateau that ensures a level playing field, so the idea of a level playing field was, and is, a false assumption. Much has been learned in the last 50 years about what it will take to give every child in America a highly desirable equality of educational opportunity. Some extraordinary, individual teachers and some schools will be successful without anything more. Institution-wide, I believe that hope is unrealistic. We cannot hope ourselves into being better. And this is why: policy makers simply do not have a clear vision of excellence for all public schools and all children. The key to this contrived school crisis then is to clearly establish what we want our schools to accomplish and what it will cost, and then make it a priority. The final step is to fund and measure the "vision." I am powerfully persuaded that this is what the federal and state policy leaders must accomplish for schools. Schools cannot, however, wait because the children are too important. There are approximately 48 million children nationwide that simply do not have the luxury of waiting. Children cannot, of course, repeat childhood. Nothing changes for teachers. They will continue to function at their highest level possible. I am confident in saying that because I have never met a teacher who would willingly leave a child behind. Schools must use the impetus of this time to push forward to their limits. I believe if that happens, support will follow. And, in the meantime, a generation of children (approximately 48 million) will not be left behind.

THE SEEDS OF FAILURE BEGIN TO SPROUT: THE FALL FROM GRACE

The purpose of this short review is to clearly demonstrate that the rejection educators feel today is not as much about the American school system at this moment in history as it is about disillusionment. This disillusionment was brought about when hopes for schools exceeded the capabilities of schools and the resources that were available to support them.

During the 1960s and 1970s, two powerful forces coalesced at the schoolhouse door. Some of the unresolved problems of earlier years surfaced again, but this time with more force. This time, schools were unable to adapt quickly enough to satisfy the emerging concerns as public confidence continued to decline, creating a confidence barrier. What follows is a short review of how schools came to be in the middle of those two powerful forces.

Vision and Caring Precede Accountability in Education

During the post–World War II years, many of America's poor families began a migration to urban America in search of jobs. That migration, coupled with heightened immigration, forced public schools to rapidly expand their capacity. Be reminded that this unprecedented expansion of schools brought a much broader range of students into the schoolhouse. The curriculum was changed to meet the emerging need of the more academically diverse student.

Initially it wasn't immediately recognized that there was a relationship between resources spent and the effects of school. Remember, at that time there was an erroneous assertion that schools really didn't make a difference. In fact, President Richard Nixon (a Republican) was the first presidential voice that articulated the connection between resources spent and student learning. As we get more education for the dollar, Nixon stated in 1970, "I will ask Congress to supply many more dollars for education."[36] By the middle of the 1990s, President George H. W. Bush introduced America 2000, which was a federal strategy to create "better, more accountable schools."[37] In this way the seeds of the accountability movement were planted deeply into the foundation of public schools. Urban educators longed for real answers to the suspected fallacies reported in the Coleman Report. Happily, urban educators found the answers in the firms of Ron Edmonds, B. Rosenshine, W. B. Brookover, and other researchers in the educational field. In my view, these forlorn few produced a kind of theomorphic work clearly establishing that some schools were more effective than others precisely because of the instructional variables that effective schools chose to emphasize. Recognize that this was contrary to the thinking of intellectuals of that day. Confidently, Ron Edmonds elected to fly in the face of the highly trumpeted Coleman Report. In time, the Association for Effective Schools, an association that conducts school surveys, raised enough questions that other scholars began to challenge the report as well. Finally, in 1986, after reviewing hundreds of studies done in the 1970s, Jere Brophy and Thomas Good officially, and at long last, refuted Coleman's myth of the unequivocal effect of SES on academic achievement. Therefore, I will always think of Ron Edmonds as the founder of the effective school movement, which was precursor to the SBS movement. His singularly profound contribution was generating the understanding that schools are not equally effective. Simply said, some schools were better than others because of what the teachers were doing in those schools. It wasn't long until schools were being pressured to improve their results.

Why Have Schools Been Slow to Improve?

The repeated discussions about academic standards, performance-based assessments, vision building, funding levels, and leadership all have become so voluminous it is mind-numbing. Unfortunately, the effective school movement sparked very little of substance and once again left teachers feeling devalued, depreciated, and dubious, with public skepticism on the increase. When schools were not able to meet the (arguably) unrealistic expectations in postwar America, disdain quickly followed disillusionment. For many families, a good education was still the only way for their children to gain admittance to material success and the good life in America.

If anything else could go wrong, America was just entering a recession. Rather than having increased funding for expansion, schools were forced to make program cuts. Pressures without resources made for uneasy tensions between schools and poor parents of color. It is easy to understand how poor families of non-European descent experienced frustration when it appeared as if their children were being cheated out of the promise of equity of opportunity. To these families, the white students seemed to be having their needs met nicely. These social issues were national in nature and very complex. Schools were controlled locally, of course, so it was difficult for the local school boards to grasp the complex national issue and they did not appear overly motivated to address the problems at hand. Additionally, it doesn't appear there was much local support for raising taxes to solve problems that were brought on by unwanted community growth and school expansion. Most schools were supported though local property taxes and communities were unwilling to raise the taxes of the existing residents to support expanded schools for the newcomers. As a result, schools were caught without the resources they needed, which caused teachers and administrators to appear callous and insensitive to such problems. Nationally, rather than locally, the capabilities of schools fell into question and schools themselves into disregard. Adding to the uneasy tension and lack of trust was the emergence of perplexing social problems characteristic of a capitalistic democracy. These problems included an uneven distribution of wealth; recent stagnation of the economy; growing racial, ethnic, religious, and linguistic diversity in America; prejudice toward Americans of color; the "ghettoization" of America's cities; violence and drugs; the aging of the population; and the restructuring of the workplace. Such problems are quite common to a democracy in a global marketplace, but proved to be more acute in America than in other Western nations.

In addition, some of the time-tested structures and instructional approaches began to cause problems that didn't seem to exist in earlier times. These structures included age-graded classrooms, heavy stress on public competition, tracking systems, regressive student management programs, inequitable response to community complaints, the impersonal bureaucratization of large schools and systems, quasi-independent and autonomous local control of schools, pressures from private schools, the acceptance of too many tasks for schools, incredible variations in the funding of schools, and a belief that all students come to school equally ready to learn.

In my opinion, it is no wonder that many teachers seemed to view reform with only a casual interest. Without a doubt, some teachers were slow to make reforms because they felt confident their own classroom program was working well for their students. Besides, pressure was only coming from the parents of current students and parental participation was mixed, at best. Simply said, the Coleman Report appeared ludicrously flawed about school effects. Teachers had learned from personal experience that what they were doing in their classrooms was working and making a difference for their students. Therefore the research appeared to be laughable and was taken without serious merit. Skepticism about research is another holdover that can be problematic for contemporary SBSs.

SUMMARY

It is understood that teachers are doing everything they can to close the achievement gap and conclude a school comeback. That process is unlikely to move at Mach speed because there are readiness issues that need to be understood and resolved. The successful effort will take time. The rich tradition of public school education in America presents the astute observer with several historical truths (axioms) on which we can build. The standards-based movement has certainly underscored the importance of academic basic skills. Few would argue that basic academic skills are of central importance to schools. The recent academic emphasis could possibly obscure the importance that schools have played in enhancing and integrating the core principles of government and economics into the cultural fabric of American life. Such things as character education and the responsibilities of citizenship are not a stretch from the historical purpose of school. The roots of public school seem to have been forgotten in the fray to improve. It is up to the teachers to become the keepers of Jefferson's vision. Jefferson and Madison (two of the Founding Fathers) in their wisdom established those roots and was viewed schools as a cornerstone in America's noble experiment in democracy. Universal education for all children was a bold experiment and was viewed as a keystone in the structure of democracy. By the time of the American Revolution, the colonial population included approximately 2.5 million people of diversity. Universal education was the vehicle through which the Founding Fathers sought to bring the diverse group of people in the colonies under the Constitution and democratic rule. Throughout history, public support for universal education was readily forthcoming to such a degree that some even put education on par with the core principles of freedom and justice. Some even thought that education would ensure the success of America, even in the shadow of two world wars and the economic collapse of the Great Depression. The historical support for education collapsed in post–World War II America. The public will, undoubtedly, support universal education again. This integration of history will require that schools earn public support by becoming effective with all children. The public is naturally inclined to support public schools, but schools are attempting to earn that support in erroneous ways. Educators will not acquire the much-needed support by complaining about the kids and simultaneously asking for more money. America is in the midst of a demographic shift away from the culture that has been dominated by affluent whites. Public schools are needed now more than ever to ensure the continuance of the common culture of the broad-based middle class. Public schools must create schools where all (not just affluent white kids) can achieve the American dream. There is, once again, as it was in Colonial America, a solemn challenge before public schools to harness the power of America's rich diversity. As we gird our loins for that effort it is foolhardy to believe that the public will willingly fund that effort up front. It may not be fair, but it is something to most surely expect. It is widely recognized that the lack of freedom and equity of opportunity for the poor of color is a deep cancer eating into the moral fiber of America. Public schools must succeed in creating a level playing field for all of America's children. This battle is as significant as any foreign war since World War II. Student success in school precedes success in life. Education is a legally binding hope that has fallen to public schools. It is significant that poor kids of color have been casualties of a primordial myth that was created by the federally commissioned Coleman Report and perpetuated by the U.S. Department of Education. There is no time to be distracted by the NCLB Act. Rather, there is too much to do to build on the foundation that already exists in your school.

QUESTIONS FOR DELIBERATION

The activation of planning has two steps: (1) answer the six questions formulated for you below, and (2) begin to keep a record of your responses when discussing your thinking with colleagues as time permits.

Ideally for your students your thinking will generate a journal regarding the ideas you would consider incorporating into your instructional repertoire or ideas you are willing to share with other staff (with appropriate support). It is recommended that the journals be combined into your standards-based school improvement plan (SIP).

1. Do you remember what motivated you to work in schools? Do you still hold those beliefs?

2. What steps can be taken immediately to begin to build a base of support with the public in your service area?

3. In your school is there a need to socialize students into successful living in your community? What steps could be taken to initiate that process?

4. Do you personally believe that America's promise of freedom and equity of opportunity can be fulfilled through your school? How should your school begin? What support will you need and how will you get that support?

5. Is your greater community satisfied with the academic strength of your program? Are your parents satisfied? Students? Business leaders?

How important is their support? Is it possible for you to gain that support today? How should you proceed?

6. Do you believe that all students should achieve high academic standards? Why or why not? Has the importance of basic academic skills been obscured by any other priorities?

NOTES

1. John Taylor, Superintendent of Schools for the Lancaster County School District, "The Best Dentist—'Absolutely' the Best Dentist," e-mail to author, 15 Dec. 2003.

2. Raymond V. Hand, ed., *American Quotations*, (New York: Random House, 1989), 9.

3. Hand, ed., *American Quotations*, 9.

4. Quoted in Facing History and Ourselves, "Teaching is a craft...Adolescents are our future," 22 Oct. 2003, http://www.facinghistory.org/facing/fhao2.nsf/main/about+us, [accessed 7 Nov. 2003].

5. Quoted in "Public Education in the United States," *Microsoft Encarta Online Encyclopedia 2003*, http://encarta.msn.com/encyclopedia_7615714941 Public_Education_in_the_United_States.... [accessed 4 Nov. 2003], 2.

6. Applied Research Center, "Historical Timeline of Public Education in the US," http://www.arc.org/erase/timeline.html, [accessed 24 Nov. 2003], 2.

7. Applied Research Center, "Historical Timeline of Public Education in the US," [accessed 10 Nov. 2003], 1.

8. Applied Research Center, "Historical Timeline of Public Education in the United States," [accessed 10 Nov. 2003], 2.

9. "Historical Timeline of Public Education in the United States," *Microsoft Encarta Online Encyclopedia 2003*, 4 Nov. 2003, http://encarta.msn.com/encnet/refpages [accessed 10 Nov. 2003].

10. "Immigration," *Microsoft Encarta Online Encyclopedia 2003*, http://Encarta.msn.com/encyclopedia_761566973/immigration.html, [accessed 15 Oct. 2003], 10.

11. "Immigration," 10.

12 "Public Education in the United States," [accessed 12 Nov. 2003], 2.

13. Quoted in Jordan Friedlander, "History of Education in the 19th Century," Historic Documents, Abstract, http://www.bigredboots.com/map.htm, [accessed 15 Oct. 2003].

14. Hand, ed., *American Quotations*, 204.

15. Hand, ed., *American Quotations*, 205.

16. Hand, ed., *American Quotations*, 337.

17. Hand, ed., *American Quotations*, 2.

18. Quoted in David Berliner and Bruce J. Biddle, *The Manufactured Crisis*, (Reading, Mass.: Addison-Wesley Publishing, 1995), 215.

19. Bracey, Gerald. "No Child Left Behind Act: A Plan for the Destruction of Public Education, Just Say No," (paper presented at the Development of Public Education [IDEA] Fellows Program, Denver, Colo., 2003) 10.

20. Hand, ed., *American Quotations*, 210.

21. Quoted in Hand, ed., *American Quotations*, 337.

22. Quoted in Bracey, "No Child Left Behind Act: A Plan for the Destruction of Public Education, Just Say No," 6.

23. Bracey, "No Child Left Behind Act: A Plan for the Destruction of Public Education, Just Say No," 6.

24. Stephen Covey, *The Seven Habits of Highly Effective People*, (New York: Simon and Schuster, 1989), 235.

25. "Compulsory Attendance," *Indiana State Department of Education*, 3 Oct. 2003, http://indstate.edu/iseas/cmps-atd1, [accessed 3 Oct. 2003].

26. "Compulsory Attendance," *Indiana State Department of Education*, [accessed 2 Oct. 2003].

27. Berliner and Biddle, *Manufactured Crisis*, 129.

28. John I. Goodlad, *A Place Called School*, (New York: McGraw-Hill, 1984), 12.

29. Goodlad, *A Place Called School*, 12.

30. Quoted in Robert J. Marzano, Debra J. Pickering, and Jane E. Pollock, *Classroom Instruction That Works*, (Alexandria, Va.: Association for Supervision and Curriculum Development, 2001), 2.

31. Marzano et al., *Classroom Instruction That Works*, 3.

32. Marzano et al., *Classroom Instruction That Works*, 1.

33. Marzano et al., *Classroom Instruction That Works*, 3.

34. Quoted in Gerald Celente, *Trends 2000*, (New York: Warner Books, 1998), 217.

35. "National Defense Education Act," *Columbia Encyclopedia*, Sixth Edition, 2001, 1.

36. Quoted in *America 2000: An Education Strategy*, SOURCEBOOK (Washington, D.C.: U.S. Department of Education Press, 1991), 21.

37. *America 2000: An Education Strategy*, 27.

3

GROWTH AS A MORAL RESPONSIBILITY

What lies behind us and what lies before us are tiny matters compared to what lies within us.

—Oliver Wendell Holmes

By learning you will teach, by teaching you will learn.

—Latin proverb

I am not one who believes the primary way to close the achievement gap is to focus on the technology of teaching. Teaching strategies are an important consideration, of course, but they pale in contrast to the need for each teacher to look within him- or herself for the directions. I am completely persuaded that the functional solutions or next steps are already within each teacher and educational leader. I use the phrase "next steps" to communicate improvement through building on your strengths. You are the expert: there is no one on earth who understands your strengths and the learning needs of your students like you understand them. Therefore, the next steps must come from within you! You must have confidence in yourself—you must believe. In this chapter, I describe the powerful inner belief of personal efficacy. Do not, therefore, expect this book to dictate a standardized approach because it would be much less than successful, plus that concept is entirely foreign to the thesis of this book. First, you must begin with personal efficacy. The dictionary defines efficacy as "capability of producing a desired effect." I believe that my use of the word here is much more powerful than that wimpy definition. Therefore, I define efficacy as potency. Potency is a mighty, even mystical, ability to have a positive effect. Potency is drawn from who you are. Efficacy requires you to trust your own instincts, experiences, and each other. Ralph Waldo Emerson penned it this way in his essay on self-reliance: "Trust thyself: every heart vibrates to that iron string."[1] Stephen Covey introduced the concept of the inside-out approach, which means start with self first.[2] The most powerful motivation for teachers is to be doing something for their students, and we must utilize that motivational tool to effect change. A wise person once asserted, "There are two bequests we can give our children—one is for roots and the other is wings."[3]

I believe in giving wings by achieving unity—oneness—with ourselves, colleagues, parents, and students. Teamwork is the most sophisticated work that can be done. Efficacy and teamwork are needed to build a foundation for the vision of public schools in America. The inside-out way means that your work begins with yourself. You must begin by believing in your own efficacy. I am significantly persuaded that as a teacher you make a difference every day that you interact with your students. No human kindness is ever given in vain, because every good experience given to a child is given forever. You are not alone because children can also be taught to help. The following story is about a helping perspective and making a difference. Children are the bedrock of our effort to improve schools.

The Gift of Empathy

At a fundraising dinner for a school that serves learning-disabled children, the father of one of the school's students delivered a speech that would never be forgotten by all who attended.

After extolling the school and its dedicated staff, he offered a question.

"Everything God does is done with perfection. Yet, my son, Shay, cannot learn things as other children do. He cannot understand things as other children do. Where is God's plan reflected in my son?"

The audience was stilled by the query. The father continued. "I believe," the father answered, "that when God brings a child like Shay into the world, an opportunity to realize the Divine Plan presents itself. And it comes in the way people treat that child."

Then, he told the following story: Shay and his father had walked past a park where some boys Shay knew were playing baseball. Shay asked, "Do you think they will let me play?" Shay's father knew that most boys would not want him on their team. But the father understood that if his son were allowed to play it would give him a much-needed sense of belonging.

Shay's father approached one of the boys on the field and asked if Shay could play. The boy looked around for guidance from his teammates. Getting none, he took matters into his own hands and said, "We are losing by six runs, and the game is in the eighth inning. I guess he can be on our team and we'll try to put him up to bat in the ninth inning." In the bottom of the eighth inning, Shay's team scored a few runs but was still behind— by three!

At the top of the ninth inning, Shay put on a glove and played in the outfield. Although no hits came his way, he was obviously ecstatic just to be on the field, grinning from ear to ear as his father waved to him from the stands.

In the bottom of the ninth inning, Shay's team scored again. Now, with two outs and the bases loaded, the potential winning run was on base. Shay was scheduled to be the next at bat. Would the team actually let Shay bat at this juncture and give away their chance to win the game?

Surprisingly, Shay was given the bat. Everyone knew that a hit was all but impossible because Shay didn't even know how to hold the bat properly, much less connect with the ball. However, as Shay stepped up to the plate, the pitcher moved a few steps to lob the ball softly so Shay could at least be able to make contact. The first pitch came and Shay swung clumsily and missed.

The pitcher again took a few steps forward to toss the ball softly toward Shay. As the pitch came in, Shay swung at the ball and hit a slow ground ball to the pitcher. The pitcher picked up the soft grounder and could easily have thrown the ball to the first baseman. Shay would have been out and that would have been the game.

Instead, the pitcher took the ball and threw it on a high arc to right field, far beyond reach of the first baseman. Everyone started yelling, "Shay, run to first. Run to first." Never in his life had Shay ever made it to first base. He scampered down the baseline, wide-eyed and startled.

Everyone yelled, "Run to second, run to second!" By the time Shay was rounding first base, the right fielder had the ball. He could have thrown the ball to the second baseman for a tag. But the right fielder understood what the pitcher's intentions had been, so he threw the ball high and far over the third baseman's head. Shay ran toward second base as the runners ahead of him deliriously circled the bases toward home.

As Shay reached second base, the opposing shortstop ran to him, turned him in the direction of third base, and shouted, "Run to third!" As Shay rounded third, the boys from both teams were screaming, "Shay! Run home!" Shay ran home, stepped on home plate and was cheered as the hero, for hitting a grand slam and winning the game for his team.

"That day," said the father softly with tears now rolling down his face, "the boys from both teams helped bring a piece of the Divine Plan into this world."

TEAMWORK AND UNDERSTANDING
PRECEDE SCHOOL REFORM

The story represents a perspective on empathy that some would say is history and no longer a functional component of children today. It doesn't have to be that way. Therefore, we should harness the spirit of the child to make the classrooms more inviting and accepting. See the team-building activities in Appendix B. Almost through an accident of history, the organization of schools isolates teachers from other teachers, and all of the adults in the school from the whole of the school community. Unfortunately, teachers have had to get used to working alone. The isolation of the conventional school culture does not tend to encourage the teaching professional to look to the outside for help. It is called conventional for a reason. It is easier! Nor have there been staff development funds that encourage the search for such outside expertise. Therefore, teachers quite naturally struggle mightily, and usually alone, to develop their program and have a corresponding commitment to that program. Without a shared vision of instructional excellence, any new idea comes as an unwelcome addition to the existing program, which already has strong support. The culture of a teacher was, and still is, one of isolation over cooperation and of individualism over teamwork. Effective teamwork stimulates shared efficacy. Unhappily, teachers work in isolation and therefore are somewhat slow to detect a failing curriculum. Typically, curriculum gaps or overlaps are nearly impossible to detect at only the classroom level.

There has been little hard evidence presented that individual classroom programs are failing. Teachers are in constant communication with parents and easily ascertain that parents of their students strongly support their neighborhood school and child's classroom program. Distant public officials may express concerns about a school, unaware and unconcerned that the parents are quite satisfied. The harsh reality is that parents of children attending a school are more likely to find another school in trouble rather than their own school. The lack of objective data was confusing and raised little reason for alarm. Teachers simply did not see the need to make individual program changes because of concerns that were voiced far from their individual classrooms. In the 1960s, concerns about access, equity, and international competition in the space race were distant concerns—if concerns at all—for the typical teacher. Nevertheless, the debate itself had a destructively damaging effect on the professional self-esteem of educators. A defense mechanism born in skepticism from hurt.

> [A]nd nothing to look backward to with pride, and nothing to look forward to, with hope.
>
> —Robert Frost, "The Death of the Hired Man," *North of Boston*[4]

Prior to this time, the culture in a traditional American school was calm, secure, and seldom challenged. Most teachers were quite unaware of the mounting dark clouds of disdain and disillusionment that were bearing down on public schools. Prior to that time schools enjoyed a strong reputation. Schools had been widely accepted and supported. All of that changed quickly and dramatically during the 1960s, when the politics of the Cold War and rapid expansion of diversity generated dissatisfaction— even hostility. The long-held approaches to schooling, once so highly regarded, were suddenly being challenged from new directions. Government began to superimpose incredibly high academic standards on schools and also tended to be less supportive. This abandonment was sudden, severe, and scurrilous. The searching and dissatisfaction continued with some variation until it all exploded during the 1990s, first with the accountability movement of SBR and, second, with the NCLB Act.

Currently, public education is being challenged by a variety of forces voicing dissatisfaction. During this time of accountability, uncertainty, and doubt, public education certainly needs strong, effective teaching. Public skepticism, rebuke, and scrutiny are likely to be constant companions of teachers for years to come. Student performance is viewed as low and getting worse. In 1983—for the first time in the history of American schools—admonition of complete dissatisfaction began in earnest. That year could be remembered as the year of the reports. No fewer than eight reports of national significance were released, accompanied by dozens of similar reports released regionally. The most significant of those reports was the Nation at Risk report issued by the National Commission on Excellence in Education in April 1983. In a poignant description of failing schools, the report argued, "If an unfriendly foreign power had attempted to impose on America the mediocre educational performance that exists today, we might well have viewed it as an act of war," and it goes on to say we have in effect "been committing an act of unthinking, unilateral educational disarmament."[5] The report, which is highly critical of public schools, includes recommendations that fall into categories reminiscent of recommendations made at the very turn of the 20th century. The recommendations, while made with words that educators perceived to be hostile, were not new. In fact, the "five new basics," as they were called, surprisingly are not all that different from those that were advocated by the Committee of Ten in 1893. This Committee of Ten was appointed at the National Educational Association (NEA) at Saratoga on July 9, 1892, as a task force to determine academic levels for schools. The point is that the recommendations never seem to change; consequently, neither have schools. In fact, schools are built on a foundation of tradition and recidivism. This resistance to change is not entirely new. In fact, in the late 1960s Carl Rogers observed, "Can the system as a whole, the most traditional of our time . . . come to grips with the real problem of modern life? Or will it continue to be shackled by the retrogression, added to its own traditionalism?"[6] Teachers and school administrators are already committed to leaving no child behind. The challenge is not a matter of will because there is ample motivation, but the teachers' needs are unlike anything in the past. There is an abundance of criticism and a real shortage of support for teachers. As the traditional school continues to make the transformational changes inherent in moving to the SBS, roles are changing as well. These are the roles of support for teachers, to be provided by leaders and parents, and also for students, to be provided by the adults in the school.

THE SEVEN PILLARS OF CAPACITY-BASED SUPPORT

As schools are pressured by inflexible high-stakes assessments and declining resources, the culture of teachers has been exposed to long periods of stress and rejection. Therefore, we have failed to provide the kind of support necessary to ensure the success of the transformation to the SBS. I use the word "framework" to define necessary structural changes required. I am told when carpenters build a building they also begin by building a framework. The framework in turn supports the rest of the structure. The framework alone is not strong enough to provide the needed support, so carpenters build weight-bearing walls into the structure. The supports have been changing and for our purposes here I call these important supports "pillars." In figure 3.1 are seven bearing walls or pillars that are critical in the support of teachers in an SBS. As I said, those roles have been changing and I trace the changes to the structures that are needed today in schools. I also discuss the implications for leaders and teachers. When mentioning both groups, leaders and teachers, instead of referring to teachers as instructional specialists and leaders as instructional leaders, I use the term lead learner, which is interchangeable; this approach defines one of the most significant changes. The results are that we turn from a focus on what students are taught to what they learn. This puts teachers, leaders, and students in the role as learners as all are learners. The leader, leadership team (a school community), and parents are expected to provide the following supports for teachers, and teachers must provide that same level of support for their students.

Pillar 1: From Leader and Teacher to Lover and Caregiver

Learning application for leaders: An SBS needs to provide a safe, wholesome, and nurturing environment for students. The fear of failure creates a need to communicate with students that their personal acceptance is not a condition of meeting high academic standards. Even though the teachers are the adults, they need those same levels of support, especially when they are expected to provide a wholesome environment for children. As I said in the previous chapter, teachers see their failure as a reflection of a tear in the child's eye. Teachers teach for reasons of the heart. The task of providing emotional support has always been one of the core reasons for leadership. Whether the leader was a tribal chief in Africa or a shaman among the Great Plains Indians, relational leadership was always a primary need.

In the modern organization, providing relational support for people within the organization has always been a very important aspect of an effective leader. During times of challenge and demoralization, a leader's supportive approach to individuals can have a positive effect to excite and soothe the emotions, while a cynical and callous attitude can become a cancerous potion creating human anxiety, rebellion, and organizational failure. Adults in the SBS are hungrily looking for emotional support and approval. This is a job that can be accomplished by the community. The support work must be done individually, authentically, and frequently to be successful. The strongest argument for providing the needed emotional support to adults and

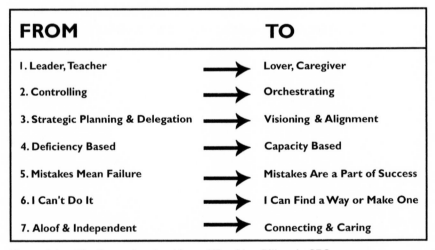

FROM	TO
1. Leader, Teacher	Lover, Caregiver
2. Controlling	Orchestrating
3. Strategic Planning & Delegation	Visioning & Alignment
4. Deficiency Based	Capacity Based
5. Mistakes Mean Failure	Mistakes Are a Part of Success
6. I Can't Do It	I Can Find a Way or Make One
7. Aloof & Independent	Connecting & Caring

Figure 3.1.   The Seven Leadership and Teaching Pillars in SBSs

students is because it models precisely what people still need in life as well. The large, powerful lessons in life are not usually taught effectively through the "point and tell" method. Unconditional love is a difficult expectation to establish through normal leadership strategies. This must become a school-wide phenomenon. Ralph Waldo Emerson once said, "What you *do* is so loud that you can't hear what they say."

Learning application for teachers: Students must know (not think) that their teacher likes them because they have been told either directly or indirectly. Students must come to know that their value as people is absolutely unrelated to their academic ability. High-performance teachers simply know how to build strong relationships with their students. Three things are essential for a teacher in an SBC: The first is to be kind. The second is to be kind. And the third is to be kind. Finally, we want this same pillar (behavior) to be true between students as well.

Pillar 2: From Controlling to Orchestrating

> Education makes people easy to lead, but difficult to drive; easy to govern, but impossible to enslave.
>
> —Peter Broughan

Learning application for leaders: Since World War II, most schools have been governed using centralized decision-making processes, primarily as a function of the Effective Schools movement and particularly as a consequence of the Nation at Risk report. That changed when suddenly decentralized decision making was deemed to be more effective. Therefore, most schools changed to a more participatory decision-making process. This, too, changed with the standards-based movement. The standards were generally superimposed on the schools by political entities believing that school participation would be adequately addressed when schools designed the curriculum to meet the standards. I learned that neither centralized nor decentralized decision making worked in the SBS. The rigid accountability of high-stakes assessment creates a level of insecurity that must be addressed through participatory decision making. Individuals who will be held most directly accountable for attaining the standards must be involved in decisions that affect their future success. The challenge for leaders is in the equity of opportunity. Neither of the most common decision-making models (centralized, decentralized) really adequately addresses the insecurity previously described. Centralized decision-making errors on the side of overcontrol and decentralized decision-making errors on the side of too little uniformity and too much expensive duplication were grossly apparent. Therefore, effective leaders used a combination of both centralized and decentralized decision-making models, which I refer to as integrated decision making. The integrated decision-making model is described in detail in chapter 4.

The nature of decision making in an SBS is proving to be kinetically dynamic for the following core reasons:

- First, the ideas come from nontraditional sources and simply must be incorporated anyway into the decision-making structure from a multiplicity of unanticipated locations.
- Second, to ensure viability, decisions must be made at a point closest to the point of implementation.
- Finally, those that are affected by a decision must be involved in the decision-making process. Involvement in decision making, while extremely important to the long-term success of the SBS, is not a direct role; rather, one must direct traffic, making sure that everyone has a stake in the outcome of the decision and is involved to their level of satisfaction.

The most accurate picture of the complex responsibility of leading integrated decision making is comparable to the director of an orchestra. The leader of an orchestra does not actually play an instrument; rather, the critically important role of the maestro is to keep all of the different musical instruments working together to complement each other. No instrument or section of instruments should dominate the sound so the final pleasing musical piece expresses the individual excellence of the musicians and their instruments by allowing the power of individuals to create a sound that is so much more than the sum of the individual instruments. This idea is presented at the conceptual level for leaders, with more detail, in the next section of this manual.

Learning application for teachers: Have you (as a teacher) ever just stopped to observe your students during the very middle of a lesson? Undoubtedly, you noticed that you were working harder than anyone else in the classroom. In my view, students in an SBS must accept more responsibility for their own education, for the same general reasons that teachers and parents should be involved in the decision-making process. At the risk of being brash, I like to say it this way: I like classrooms where more learning occurs than teaching. More effective SBCs tend to be decentralized, that is to say, they are more student-centered than teacher-directed. Students need to take more responsibility. So you say, "Fine, how can I ensure that students accept more responsibility for their own education?" Teachers are increasingly aware that their students are not motivated and that they do not care about academic success and rely on others to care for them. How can that issue be resolved? This is how.

Expect an activity regarding the move from the use of control theory to the absolute power of internal incentives. This next point may be the main vehicle to the success for which I know you strive. External control of psychology doesn't work. We have long been taught that we call such psychology extrinsic versus intrinsic motivation. External control may have been a successful approach under the traditional school program when academic success usually meant spending enough time to qualify, in spite of inadequate skills and knowledge. In the performance-based system of the SBS, however, the only variable that matters is that the student can demonstrate mastery of the standard. Most academic standards are so high and so numerous that to experience success the student simply must complete the work for themselves. External control of student motivation has typically expressed itself in a two-step approach. Punishment is used to extinguish an undesirable behavior. Rewards are used to increase the desired behavior. Students who fail to exhibit the desired behavior are punished until they modify their behavior to the one desired, at which time they are rewarded. The punishment is increased until the undesirable behavior is extinguished. Punishment hurts, of course, and consequently has a detrimental effect on the relationship between the

student and teacher. The reward is intended to increase the likelihood that the appropriate behavior will be repeated. Let us take a
good logical look at why external motivation is not effective in generating increased learning.

It is common for teachers to, caringly, intervene on behalf of the
struggling student. The teacher is motivated by a desire to lighten the
burden of the student (or to prevent the embarrassment of error), which
is entirely noble. However, the issue with this unproductive approach is
twofold:

1. Students sense that you are intervening because you do not have
   confidence that the student can do it on their own; and further,
2. Students learn someone else is responsible for their academic
   success.

I am convinced that most, if not all, experienced teachers have frequently experienced frustration when students refuse to accept responsibility for their own actions. What often makes matters worse is
that the student's parent is there to blame the cause of the concern on
almost anything but their child. The effect is devastating because students just give up and make their academic success someone else's responsibility. I am aware, of course, that making students take responsibility for their own educational successes is something in which we
have had little experience. When kids are motivated internally their
performance is at higher levels than when they are motivated exter-
nally. This is a new approach for educators, and may be the most important approach toward ensuring that all children (namely, the poor
kids of color) will meet high academic standards. When we protect a
student to prevent him or her from being embarrassed or hurt or we
apply punishments rather than let him or her take responsibility in
any given situation, it has a damaging effect on the relationship between the teacher and the student. The use of punishment to achieve
a desired behavior is not helpful in building strong and trusting relationships with children and adults alike, which are essential if people
are going to voluntarily provide the desired behavior. Schools frequently use coercion and force to achieve the desired behavior with
children. Common use does not necessarily lead to the desired change.

The focus question is, why is a threat unproductive in motivating students? To arrive at a response we must look at the work of Daniel Goleman and Abraham Maslow.

First, I look to Daniel Goleman, author of a number of books on the importance of emotional intelligence. In *Primal Leadership: Realizing the Power of Emotional Intelligence,* Goleman, McKee, and Boyatzis teach that a human is susceptible to external threat. Experienced school people have learned that threat is not necessarily productive to motivate high student achievement. According to Goleman, this is why: how a person approaches people is critically important for physiological (scientific) reasons. Happily, this phenomenon of approaching people (students) with care and concern goes back to the need of the human species to adapt to the harsh environment to survive. The system that powers this incredible nature to learn is housed in the most prehistoric part of the brain. Goleman calls it the "Open Loop nature of the limbic system." The limbic system is that portion of the brain that controls emotions. A closed-loop system, such as the circulatory system, is self-regulating by relying exclusively on sources within the body for direction. The limbic (emotional) system's open loop is the system of interest in our discussion of motivation because it relies largely on external sources to regulate itself. The open-loop system was a winning design during evolution, presumably because it allowed people to come to the emotional rescue of others. Even more importantly, the limbic system has access to its surroundings and can take the necessary actions to survive. In spite of all of the advances of modern civilization, the open-loop mechanism in the brain still affects humans the same way as in prehistoric times. The point is that people (adults and children) are quite responsive to conditions in the environment in very powerfully automatic ways. Research shows that the comforting presence of another person in a hospital's intensive care unit not only lowers the patient's blood pressure, but also lowers the secretion of fatty acids that block arteries.[7] Even more dramatically, where three or four incidents of extreme stress within a year triple the death rate of socially isolated middle-aged men, the same stressors have no impact at all on the death rate of men who cultivate close relationships.[8] The key point is that the ancient limbic system is instinctively responsive to external emotional threats or consolation.

What happens when a person confronts emotionally threatening circumstances? In an earlier volume, I attempted to summarize a view of
motivation by one of the greatest behavioral scientists in history—
Maslow's Theory of Motivation. Its central framework is that human
needs are organized into a hierarchy, with physiological needs, such as
survival, hunger, and thirst coming first, followed by progressively less
important motivators like the needs for safety, social interaction, and
ego satisfaction. To examine threat as a motivator, one must look at
Maslow's theory more deeply. Maslow theorized that each lower need
must be satisfied in a strict progression through the hierarchy. Maslow
wrote, "Once each of these needs has been satisfied, if at some time a
deficiency is detected, the individual will act to remove the deficiency."[9]

That is why threat stifles learning. If the limbic system detects a
threat, the student will remove the source of that threat. In other words,
to protect himself or herself, the student will remove the source of the
threat and become invisible to the teacher. As a consequence, the relationship is gone and with it the ability for the person to make a positive
impact. If the lesson is learned early in school, it has the potential to
have long-term consequences for the student.

Further, the capacity-based approach cannot be made to happen by
lecturing about it. People (staff, parents, and students) need to see it
in evidence. So it is with all of the basic structures. That tenet of building capacities is one of the defining differences in this book. That is, if
capacity building is good enough for the children, it must also be good
enough for the total school community.

What you do speaks so loudly that they can't hear what you say.

—Ralph Waldo Emerson

So it is with an SBS. Excellence is pervasive throughout the school,
and the district for that matter. The teachers need to align curriculum to the content standards. No less important, the leaders will
need to align the beliefs (by modeling) in the school. The limbic system can devise insurmountable barriers to learners, or create the
foundation for much enhanced potential. The creation of limiting

factors will dwarf potential. Removing limits, in the same way, enhances potential.

THE GRASSHOPPER MENTALITY

When I was a child, I would place grasshoppers in a jar with a lid. I learned a powerful lesson about human behavior from the following jar activity. In such captivity, the grasshoppers would try desperately to escape by using their powerful jumping legs to spring high against the lid. The conclusion was quite violent for the grasshoppers. The grasshoppers would continue to try to escape, initially with energy and persistence, but after repeated hurtful attempts, they would suddenly stop as if paralyzed. The grasshoppers would never try to escape again, even if I took off the lid. The grasshoppers would passively remain in captivity. Once grasshoppers know they cannot change the situation, they will never try to change it again. So, also, is it with children who feel threatened (in captivity). They make themselves invisible to avoid detection, never to try again. It has been my experience that poor children of color also become paralyzed from failure and emotional threat, and then they fall through the cracks, become invisible, and eventually drop out of school, only to struggle for a lifetime in the social system. I henceforth refer to these children as "shadow children," not in a disrespectful way, but because the term, unhappily, describes what happens to them in school. In a high-performance SBS, teachers break that pattern for the shadow kids by taking the lid off the jar right from the beginning. The massive elephant is much the same as the grasshopper when it comes to the effect of artificial restrictions. As a routine component of the elephant training process, elephant trainers in India chain young elephants to a tree. The baby elephant struggles mightily to get free of the chain, but, alas, the chain is too strong. The elephant learns of the restricting nature of the chain so well that later in the life of the elephant, its caretaker will just put a length of chain on one leg, leaving the other end unsecured. The elephant thinks it is secured in the same way as when it was young. Therefore, the elephant becomes docile and accepting of the artificial restraint of the unsecured chain. In this way the massive size and strength of the elephant is completely unrestrained and the elephant waits patiently for its caretaker to direct the daily activity.

Pillar 3: From Strategic Planning and Delegation to Visioning and Alignment

Learning application for leaders: Strategic planning assumes that someone can predict what action will need to be taken in an extremely complex environment that is perpetually changing at light-speed rates. Margaret Wheatley makes the general point in her book *Leadership and the New Science* that strategic planning is the first sign of a death rattle.[10] Delegation also assumes that someone has the divine inspiration to see precisely what has to be done and who needs to do it. I believe an SBS must have a clear, unambiguous focus on academic standards or it will fail to meet them. The most important resource in becoming a high-performance SBS is not technology, but people. Leaders must allow people to participate if they are interested in using human capital as a resource. Clear direction is the critical concern, of course, and the visioning processes create a more programmed "loose-tight" coupling, which enables for clear direction while still allowing for a myriad of unforeseen changes in the climate of change. When the purpose is clear and shared (owned), then teachers and other adults (parents) can spontaneously align the strengths of their individual commitments and beliefs with the vision. Leaders of an SBS must create an exciting, compelling vision (purpose), then step back and let the power of the focused human spirit move the school forward.

Learning application for teachers: The folly of strategic planning as applied to teaching means one assumes that someone just omnipotently knows when all students will master the targeted academic standard. Instead, use that energy to establish a community-based vision of the best that can be imagined for your classroom. When people know what the vision is, they will also be able to spontaneously align their activities in support of the vision. A good step to include in the process is to secure a commitment from every participant for what he or she may be willing to provide. It is advisable to create a signature block and with it an informal contract as to who has responsibilities for academic success. A

shared vision of academic excellence expands the challenge to other
stakeholders outside of teaching. If the transformation of the SBS is left
only to teachers, the success rate will be dramatically reduced. This
needs to be a team effort.

Pillar 4: From Deficiency Based to Capacity Based

The movement from deficiency-based to capacity-based approaches
is a primary tenet of this book. Using capacity-based approaches to leadership is especially potent because I want teachers to build on the capacities rather than the deficiencies of students. Therefore capacity-
based approaches must be modeled if they are to be used as a central
vehicle in teaching children. Think of it as emotional intelligence or
character development, at least for now. Character development is such
an important element of student success that it must be modeled by
everyone in the school. The insecure culture of an SBS requires that capacity-based, rather than deficiency-based, strategies be used. Remember, the culture of an SBS is insecure because of the rigid nature of accountability. How, then, can one make insecurity work in favor of
development and learning? In an SBS you want to work with something
that God put there in the first place—our inherent abilities and characteristics—and that is hard enough. High-performance leaders and
teachers believe in the mantra:

> People don't really change that much, anyway.
> Don't waste time trying to put in what was left out.
> Try to draw out what was left in.
> That is hard enough![11]

Consider for a moment that someone excels at something, like motivating people, empathic understanding, or selling. In my experience,
an interesting knee-jerk reaction occurs: those strengths are taken for
granted. The traditional assumption seems to be that if you want to
grow, don't waste time on working on things you are already good at;
instead, work on your weak areas so you can develop to your fullest.
That is an assumption that has been proven false to my students and

me hundreds and hundreds of times. I will explain: since 1988 I have
been teaching a graduate class on instructional leadership to administrative aspirants in Oregon using the capacity-based strategy that I discuss in this chapter. The students are exceptional in every way. They
come to a private school with higher academic standards and higher
costs because they perceive the school to be the best. That is a remarkable statement about the personal standards of students in this
field sample. The course is standards-driven and performance-based,
where each student demonstrates mastery in a classroom simulation of
a pre-conference and post-conference class with a colleague. The simulation is designed to help students master the skill of building on
strengths. During the pre-conference simulation the student is instructed to begin to help the teacher define a salient teaching strength
on which to build. The challenge to the administrator aspirants is staggering. It is deliciously amazing that very skillful students are almost
never able to help an excellent teacher identify his or her strengths in
teaching. The most significant challenge to my students was not to
keep teachers from dwelling too much on what was going well, but,
rather, it was to keep the teachers from dwelling exclusively on their
perceived weaknesses. Teachers will immediately understand this phenomenon. I was told the typical teacher is taught by the supervisor to
think about their deficiencies as the primary vehicle with which to improve. This is how I came to make this discovery, and I consequently
became completely committed to capacity-based education for all, including adults and students.

   Learning applications for leaders: For a while, long ago, I thought
that the role-playing student administrator's inability to identify a
teaching strength was indicative of a kind of professional bashfulness,
but no! It took another iteration of simulations over several years before I learned that even the very best teachers are not familiar enough
with their own teaching strengths to be able to articulate them with
confidence. For the final exam, this same pre- and post-conference
simulation strategy is used in the field with a willing school and prac-
ticing teacher. The simulation is put on videotape as the final exam intended to demonstrate student mastery of capacity-based supervision
(leadership). This activity was not designed, of course, to learn anything about teachers; rather, the tape was ostensibly about the person

role-playing the supervisor, so this finding was serendipitous. After reviewing hundreds of tapes, it became quite obvious to me that even the best teachers struggle to reveal their instructional strengths to a colleague. The inability to articulate strengths is unrelated to the existence or inexistence of instructional strengths. Rather, teachers would communicate that they simply never had thought about teaching in that way. The aforementioned reaction was nearly uniform. In my opinion, the deficiency-based (weakness) approach is not only ineffective with teachers, it also sadly establishes the expectation that the best way to help students to improve is to begin with their weaknesses. In my opinion it is completely catastrophic with regard to how we have helped teachers to grow as teachers. This observation is not intended be used to make any claims about teacher evaluation in general or to evaluate the schools' approach to evaluation. Rather, this outcome is presented as a capacity-based way for you to think about what you and the children in your school can become. This dialogue is not about anyone else but you and the children, and is written for your reflective analysis and dialogue with others and within your journal.

Consider the strength-based approach in light of the following study of effective teaching of speed reading for strength building of excellence in reading. The University of Nebraska completed a 3-year study to determine the most effective techniques for teaching speed reading. After researchers analyzed the data collected on more than 1,000 students who were tested for speed and comprehension, the results dramatically demonstrated the power of building on strengths.[12] First of all, the best teachers got the best results. The truly outstanding results, however, were a product of the best students working with the best teachers. The poor readers, however, started at 90 words per minute and made modest gains to an average of 350 words per minute. The startling outcome was that the top readers, who started at 350 words per minute, multiplied to more than 2,900 words per minute. The researchers were startled because they assumed that the poorest readers would make the greatest percentile gains, presumably because they had so much room for improvement.[13] The notion to remember and to transfer into your repertoire is that strengths are not the opposite of weaknesses, illness is not the opposite of health, success is not the opposite of failure, good is not the opposite of bad. They are not opposites; each has its own unique configuration. Somehow we have been tricked into believing that if we fix what is wrong, everything will be all right.[14] Consider other examples taken from education. Understanding why students use drugs will not lead us to understand the conditions where some students just say no. Studying why some teachers leave teaching after a relatively short period of time will not illuminate why some choose to stay for a lifetime. Studying why some children fail to read will not explain why others excel. The study of a dysfunctional family will not explain the elements of how to build a strong family. Using a weakness as the starting point for new learning or improvement has particularly negative consequences in a school. Remember your educational psychology to find out why! When one tries to help teach by starting with a student's weakness, it creates fear, intimidation, insecurity, and distrust—all of which impact heavily the learning or growing process. Let us explore this most fundamental structure of success by beginning with its application for leaders and then for teachers.

High-performance leaders focus on strengths because it is much more effective. The simple reason for staff supervision is to improve performance. Most contemporary organizations have formalized processes and detailed competencies to aid the supervisor and supervisee to improve the quality of instruction. It is not lost on teachers, however, that the deficiency-based approach to instructional improvement also helps to align with labor law contractual agreements. Sadly, the legal requirements for documentation intended for the purpose of supervision is to improve instruction, rather than to de-select a teacher. In addition, the rigid processes and competencies assume that all employees are the same, and if they are not, then they should be retrained until they are. As has been previously discussed, the "fix it" approach to leadership has been almost an obsession in the West. One of the paramount flaws of the "fix it" approach to leadership in a school is that it assumes that strengths just take care of themselves, while leaders focus on deficiencies. Ironically, that approach doesn't work for teachers or students. We have often seen coaches work with their best performer to help set the standard for the group. It is a significantly potent leadership strategy. Rather than focusing on the person with deficiencies (weaknesses), what would happen if one worked with the exceptional performers to build capacities within the school? Typically, supervisors work from formalized processes and competencies to help teachers to set clear, measurable instructional goals. Then the supervisor evaluates the teacher against the standards that were established by the instructional goals. It is hard to approach supervision differently for every person, because individualization is much more time consuming than treating each as individual the same. Using the deficiency-based supervision model leaves the supervisor with the challenge of managing the power of the human will. Ironically, teachers are expected to treat each child as an individual and work with each in such a way as to meet their individual learning needs. That type of inconsistency cannot exist if one is expecting a high-performance school. Supervisors in traditional schools focus on deficiencies or weaknesses and use critical feedback approaches to push mediocre staff to higher levels. Leaders in high-performance SBSs build on the capacities of the high-performance people by letting them set the performance standard that can pull others along. An excellent approach of the strength-based approach to leadership is voiced by Don Clifton and Paula Nelson (1996) when they write that studying strengths results in productive conclusions and studying weaknesses results in ineffective conclusions. The key point about building on strengths is nicely underscored when Clifton and Nelson state, "The study of strengths leads to the understanding of the difference between good and great." In summary, then, "There is no alchemy for weaknesess. They can be removed but they can never be transformed into strengths."[15]

What Are Strengths and Weaknesses?   Strengths are characterized by yearnings (mental telltales, often from an early age), great satisfaction, rapid learning, glimpses of excellence, and total performance of excellence. Strengths can be defined on two levels:

1. On a rudimentary level, strengths are things you do well. Those kinds of strengths are like developing the talents of others such as shooting a basketball well, being patient and understanding with friends, or having a green thumb.
2. On a more potent level, strengths are a pattern of behavior, thoughts, or feelings that produce a high degree of satisfaction or

reward and generate both psychic and financial reward. Notice the key words: behavior, thoughts, and feelings.

The definition is not limited to a specific skill.[16] According to Clifton and Nelson, a weakness is more than just a bad habit (like giving in to an urge to eat chocolate) or something you don't do very well (like keeping a tidy office or room). Rather, it is something that you do that either damages your self-image or otherwise makes your strength invisible. It is not that weaknesses should be ignored. Rather, weaknesses should be managed so the strength is free to soar to new levels of excellence.[17]

Strength-Based Teaching Is a Precondition for Excellence *Learning applications for teachers*: Students are not the same and cannot be approached with some standardized approach in mind. A "one size fits all" approach is counterproductive with children. Control therapy doesn't work for teachers any more than it does for children. As has been said, the genetic makeup of a human is such that humans cannot be forced. Rather, an individual can freely choose to improve because improvement is a primal need. Humans are amazing learners: learning from the environment is what distinguishes humans from other mammals.

New Knowledge about the Brain Can Be Used to Unlock the Potential of All Children

The subheading for this section is an amazing statement. What does or should it mean to schools? What is now known about the brain and its development and functions creates for teachers some powerful new tools that can be used with even the most challenging students. The bad news is that the students in today's public schools are more difficult to teach than ever. The good news is that while the students have been changing, so also has the understanding of the brain. This new information provides schools with the necessary tools to succeed. This may well be the most important discussion in the long history of teaching. The concepts are relatively simple, yet they challenge our assumptions about what is possible. This new knowledge will, arguably, challenge our assumptions about the potential of schools to teach all learners. I disaggregate the discussion into two parts, with an eye on what we can know and do to increase our effectiveness with all kids.

The Autonomy of the Brain and Human Potential   For teachers interested in closing the achievement gap, it must be noted that the brain is the most complicated organ in the body and the brain makes your success possible. We are interested in two points regarding the brain: (1) What is the best approach to take so all students can attain high academic standards? and (2) What can be done to enhance the potential that our students bring with them to school?

The brain has untapped potential, and this is why: the brain has approximately 100 million neurons and trillions of supporting cells—more connections than stars in the sky.[18] How then did the brain evolve and what could it mean for teachers in an SBS? The brain is the most important organ for teachers to understand because it is the key to unlocking the potential of the shadow kids. The most primitive part of the brain (shared with all species) is the brain stem surrounding the top of the spinal cord. This root of the brain regulates life functions. This primitive brain cannot be said to think or learn; rather, it is a set of preprogrammed regulators that keep the body reacting for survival.[19] It does not matter if you do or do not agree with the evolutionary explanation: the point is that from this most primitive root, the brain stem, emerged as the emotional center. Millions of years later in evolution, from these emotional areas evolved the thinking brain or the neocortex.

The Key to Student Motivation   Students are easiest to teach when they are motivated, and impossible to teach when they are not motivated. New brain research teaches us (for the first time) how to motivate our students. In the past we relied on the family to motivate the children. That is why SES played such an enormously erroneous role. It was assumed the more education the parents had, the more they would value education. If the parents valued education, it was concluded, the child would follow suit. We will learn that motivation is not necessarily a function of the educational attainment level of the parents; rather, it is a function of how the child views school in terms of threat. The deep limbic system is power-packed with functions, all of which are critical for human behavior and survival. The deep limbic system is primitive in its existence. This part of the brain is involved in setting the emotional tone. When the deep limbic system is less active, there is generally a more positive, more hopeful state of mind.[20] At first this finding surprised the nation's leading expert on brain function and potential, Dr.

Daniel Amen, and his colleagues at his clinic. Amen reports it this way: "We did not expect excessive activity in that part of the brain would correlate with solely negative feelings. The emotional shading provided by the deep limbic system is the filter through which you interpret the events of the day."[21] The limbic system is primitive and it reacts to involuntary stimulants before the thinking brain can even act. The person may be unaware of the action that is being taken as a means of protection. The person may not even realize he or she needs to act until after the limbic brain has already done so. The reaction is involuntary and reflexive, producing the fight, flight, or freeze response based on the perceived threat at hand. The following finding is central to our discussion. Amen said, "The deep limbic system colors events depending on the emotional state of mind. When one is sad (with an overactive deep limbic system), one is likely to interpret a neutral event through a negative filter. The charge one gives to certain events in their life drives one to action (such as approaching a possible mate, or consequently, it could also cause avoidance behavior such as withdrawing from someone who has hurt us in the past)."[22] If a student has been traumatized by a dramatic event like witnessing an armed robbery or being emotionally abused, the emotional component of that memory is stored in the deep limbic system of the brain. If you experience positive things, then those memories are stored as well. The more stable and positive the experiences we have, the more positive we are likely to feel; the more trauma in our lives, the more emotionally set we become in a negative way. It is also important to note that the deep limbic system affects motive and drive.[23]

Building on capacities (strengths) rather than deficiencies (weaknesses) would certainly seem to provide the student with the needed positive motivation. The consequences of using deficiency-based approaches would also seem to have a negative effect on motivation. Goleman also argues that the great blob of neurons making up the top layers of the brain is significant. Goleman suggests that "the fact that the thinking brain grew from the emotional reveals much about the relationship of thought to feeling: There was emotional brain long before there was a rational one."[24] This new neural territory added emotions to the brain's repertoire. Because that part of the brain rings and borders the brain stem, it is called the limbic system, from "limbus," the Latin word for ring. The newly developed layers of the emotional brain look roughly like a bagel.[25] It was the limbic system that refined two power-ful tools: learning and memory. These revolutionary advances allowed the human species to make much smarter choices for survival and also to fine-tune its responses to adapt to the rapidly changing environ-ment.[26] About 100 million years ago, the brain in mammals took a great leap forward. New layers of neurons (brain cells) were added to form the neocortex. The neocortex offered an extraordinary intellectual edge. *Homo sapiens*'s neocortex is so much larger than that of any other species that it has added to all that is distinctly human. The neocortex gave the human species an edge due to the neocortex's talent for strate-gizing, long-term planning, and other sophisticated mental abilities. Be-yond that, the triumphs of art, civilization, and culture are all fruits of the neocortex.[27] The key point is how this new knowledge of the brain can, for the first time, unlock the potential that was previously sacrificed to a simple lack of understanding. This reference is so important that I quote Daniel Goleman directly. Goleman concludes by arguing, "Be-cause so many of the brain's higher centers sprouted from the limbic area, the emotional brain plays a crucial role in human development. As the root from which the newer brain grew, the emotional centers are in-tertwined via a myriad of connecting circuits to all parts of the neo-cor-tex. This gives the emotional centers immense power to influence the functioning of the rest of the brain, including its centers for thought."[28]

Dr. Daniel Amen teaches that the limbic system lies near the center of the brain and sets the emotional tone as to how positive or negative you are going to be. He also teaches that the limbic system affects mo-tivation and drive. This new information helps to focus on two skill sets: (1) teaching to capacities (strengths) rather than deficiencies (weak-nesses), and (2) motivating through believing that your kids can be suc-cessful academically.

1. The limbic system provides the scientific rationale as to why build-ing on strengths is more productive than focusing on weaknesses. When weaknesses are highlighted, the limbic system most as-suredly will feel threatened, sensing an attack, which will prompt a "flight or fight" response.
2. When teachers believe in the potential of their kids, students are favorably motivated to rigorous academic work. Our expectations

set the tempo for success because the deep limbic system feels valued and safe.

It strikes me as amazing that some people naturally understand this complicated reality and its basic flight or fight response. There are, however, several significant differences being learned that give us greater knowledge and allow to us to explain what is going on in the brain. In keeping with the evidence, the scoffers are forced to reexamine their assumptions. The prehistoric limbic system is powerfully susceptible to suggestions of potential. Now we know why Henry Ford was correct in the following assertion:

> Whether you can,
> Or whether you can't,
> You are right.

Students must use their brain potential or be condemned to lose it.

What Can You Do (and When) to Enhance the Potential of Your Kids The brain starts developing slowly, then really revs up from age 3 to 5 and stays high until age 10. During these developmental years the brain develops to a maximum of 100 million neurons (brain cells) and approximately trillions of supporting cells. This phenomenal growth is magnified even further when each neuron also establishes 20,000 connections to other cells. The brain overbuilds to maximize success. Overbuilding is the same process engineers undertake when designing structures that could fall victim to the elements. When an engineer designs a bridge, the design typically exceeds expected hostile environmental conditions. For example, if a proposed bridge must routinely withstand 50-knot winds, the bridge would be designed for 100 knots. The brain growth surge is nature's way of preparing for the worst conditions before it knows what will be necessary for the survival and success of the host individual. During such incredible growth the brain uses 20 to 30% of the calories consumed (so it is vital to ensure that qualifying kids are on free or reduced lunch and breakfast).

Understanding the Sequence of Brain Growth Is a Precondition for Success The growth sequence of the brain gives teachers and students a much-desired opportunity to positively impact potential. You now know why intelligence and other elements of potential are not fixed. Potential is a function of how the brain grows, creating incredible brain capacity ostensibly to prepare for the most severe remonstration imaginable. The prehistoric limbic system was conditioned to stimulate sudden and dramatic brain growth as function of simple survival. As has been noted, the brain grows with speed until age 10 to maximize survival of the human species. The challenges of today are far different in the 21st century than they were at the time of *Pithecanthropus erectus* (primate man). We now understand that the limbic systems stimulate a receding process. The amount of the paring is determined by environmental conditions and continues until approximately age 17. To say it another way, the overbuilt brain is too much to sustain, so the limbic system stimulates paring back based on the perceived need as a child matures into adulthood. The brain chooses what to pare down based on whether it is being used or not. By establishing a kind of neural circuitry, the human species, with the open limbic system, created the amazing potential for adaptation and survival. This cell pruning is based on what a child uses; if it is used, the limbic system interprets that more synapses (connections) should be maintained. Amen said it this way: "The more they [children] learn something the more it becomes connected effecting potentation [Amen's word for potential]."[29] In other words, the more connections a child uses, the more the brain will be wired for increased potential. If, however, students don't use it, they will lose it. The "lose it" pruning begins at approximately 10 years of age and continues until the pruning is complete. The brain continues active growth until approximately age 40. In summary, then, the pruning begins at approximately age 10 and continues until the neural network is stabilized and set for the conditions at that point in time (with some variation). The events in the life are immeasurably important to the developing brain because stimulation can activate a connection that stops the pruning and enhances potential. In this way, teachers can be elated that the work that is being done in the classroom can have a direct bearing on the potential of the child. This presents teachers with a serious opportunity that could positively affect the child's personality, desire, self-image, happiness, and even, potentially, IQ. I predict that teachers will see this information as simultaneously sobering and exhilarating. The following explanation highlights the magnitude of the brain's growth and paring.

Developing capacities is a prerequisite for learning, while trying to change a child is disingenuous and undesirable. Building on capacities of students is more effective and nurturing than trying to change students. What follows is the scientific support for what many have long perceived to be the most effective approach to both students and employees alike. Have you ever met a student who had a difficult time speaking and debating publicly? For this child the mere thought of standing up in front of a group was a reason for sheer, unadulterated panic. Do you think a teacher can teach this student to thrill at, relish, and even cherish the memory of such moments? Teachers in many schools believe the answer to this question is "yes!" If you are a bit confused with how to apply these new data, then you are in the exact, correct position. In the following sections, I create a firm application for your use. Before I draw direction from the newly emerged brain science, I articulate the assumptions on which I proceed:

1. As an experienced professional educator, you are already doing everything within your grasp to help all kids be more successful.
2. It is understood that schools need to be more effective for all students.
3. As an experienced professional you have been reading and reflecting with some skepticism so far, but you still remain open to effective approaches with students even if the ideas do not represent conventional wisdom.
4. We would all feel more comfortable if the conclusions and assumptions we reached are modest, and not an idealistic stretch.

Toward a Theory of Teaching All Students Successfully   What can teachers and other educators learn from brain growth research to assist in ensuring that all students have an equal opportunity to reach high academic standards? Please be reminded that the next steps in application are based on very sound and very new evidence. Please let me explain why the scientific knowledge about the brain just exploded literally overnight. The new technologies like positron-emission tomography (PET), magnetic resonance imaging (MRI), and, maybe the most useful of them all, single photon emission computed tomography (SPECT) create clear images of the brain that allow scientists to learn what parts of the brain are at work under specified conditions. So much knowledge has been derived by such pioneers as Amen that the president and Congress termed the 1990s the decade of the brain. In fact, scientists say that the pace of their learning in neuroscience has been so great that 90% of what they now know has been learned in the last ten years.[30]

Beginning at the center of the brain at birth, a child's brain begins an incredible growth spurt, sending out thousands and thousands of signals. The neurons are trying to talk to one another, to make a connection. Imagine every person alive today, about 6.5 billion, trying to get in touch with 150,000 other people, and you will get the full scale of the complexity, and delicious vitality, of the process and also of the young mind. By the time a child reaches his or her 10th birthday, the number of successful connections is colossal—up to 15,000 synaptic connections for each of 100 billion neurons. But this is too much to sustain! Now, this is the critical opportunity where teachers must preempt the paring back and therefore enhance the development of their students. I am significantly persuaded that the time of programmed cell death provides an introspective lens into the potential of a child.

> The brain is the soul's fragile dwelling place.
>
> —William Shakespeare

In the 1990s, neuroscientists overturned more than 100 years of teaching and beliefs. As a stroke survivor, I just happened onto this new knowledge while researching the content for this book, so I am well aware of the emerging research that has incredible implications for teaching and learning. Scientists have learned that the causes of mental illness are as biological as any physical disease. Scientists have learned why the neurotransmitter dopamine calms us down and why serotonin fires us up. Scientists have learned that, contrary to what was previously believed, our memories are not stowed in one particular place but are scattered like clues on every highway and back alley of our students' brains. And we have learned how the brain grows. Given the pace of scientific discovery in this area, scientists shall surely advance our knowledge dramatically over the next several years.[31] To summarize this short discussion, by the time a child reaches puberty the number of successful connections is colossal—as many as 15,000 synaptic connections for each of the brain's 100 billion neurons. During the next 10 years or so, the brain refines and focuses its network of connections. The stronger synaptic connections become stronger still.[32] The pruning process begins at age 10 when the weaker connections wither away because they lack sufficient use. According to Amen, "What you don't use, you lose."[33] With regard to issues of poverty and their effect on pruning, there is no evidence to suggest that one SES group has either more or fewer brain connections. Each child has the same potential to make connections and to prune. There is no inherent difference between groups such as those defined by race, ethnicity, poverty, or language. Nutrition may play a factor in some cases. Some scientists are still arguing about what causes some highways to be used more frequently than others. Some argue that it is a benefit of genetic inheritance, while others claim how the child is raised is the key. Whether it is nature or nurture that defines how synaptic connections become strong is nonessential to our discussion. Our essential question, however, is, what does it mean for teaching and learning?

One thing that everyone does agree on is that by the time children reach their early teens, they have half as many synaptic connections as they had when they were 3. Scientifically, everyone agrees that the brain has carved out a unique network of connections that is completely unique to each individual. What this means scientifically is both uncertain and self-evident at the same time. It is self-evident that educators have a reason to be confident in the potential of all children to learn and grow in remarkable ways. Remember the legacy of the Coleman Report was to create a long-lasting myth about the insurmountable effect of poverty on a shadow child's ability to learn. The powerful effect of the myth of the shadow child is recognized. In the past there were powerful forces dictating the impotency of teachers. The new brain research gives teachers a reason to express hope and to begin to feel a sense of professional efficacy (potency). This opportunity is no small matter, because now teachers have a reason to confidently believe in their kids. With our new understanding of brain development, we now understand that school failure and maladjustment are not the will of God, but the lack of the will of man. For some time I have had a sobering thought: there is a spiritual premise that holds that a person cannot commit a sin if he or she is unaware. Ignorance was once a rationale for failure, but no longer. Be reminded that the paring is accomplished by the limbic system based on what is perceived to be important for the survival of the individual. Therefore, it is self-evident that the teacher should help the limbic system to clarify what is important for survival. I am strongly persuaded that what is important for survival should include not just basic academic skills, but character development as well. The concept of helping a child set priorities is certainly not new, but now we can explain what is going on in the brain of the child and make it our goal to teach goal setting to the child and to provide the necessary support, both of which are so very important. That is certainly a hopeful start. The to-do list begins with the following: the capacity-building conclusion is that teachers have current scientific evidence that students have the ability, even the need, to learn basic academic and character development skills.

Another fact that is universally supported by scientists is that when the brain is finished paring back, the child has some beautiful, smooth, resilient, traffic-free, four-lane highways. The connections are smooth and strong. In addition, the child also has some barren wastelands, where no communication makes it to the other side. The mental pathway that exists at the end of this brain development period becomes the child's filter. At this point the recurring pattern of behavior is established, as also are those characteristics that make the student unique. Allow me to say it another way. This neural circuitry and recurring pattern of behaving is what was put in or hard-wired and therefore difficult to change. It is the mental pathways that define the person's individuality. The filter defines the behavioral patterns that make the individual unique. A second key to learning is that there is no value in wishing individuality (which is hard-wired) away. Rather, teachers will want to view it as a happy confirmation that each child is unique. Attempting to rewire the hard wire of the limbic system is not only unproductive; it is unwise, because the individual will view it as a hostile act. It is a much more productive strategy to help the child understand his or her filter and then to channel it toward productive behavior. In other words, it is much more productive to build on the strengths that have been hard-wired into his or her neural circuitry, rather than focusing the child on his or her deficits. A well-traveled story helps to underscore the previous point.

The Parable of Thinking Like a Frog

There once lived a scorpion and a frog. The scorpion wanted to cross the pond but he couldn't swim because he was a scorpion. So he went up to the frog and asked, "Please, Mr. Frog, will you give me a ride on your back across the pond."

"I am inclined to say yes, Mr. Scorpion, but actually, I will have to decline. Under the circumstances, I could not protect myself if you decided to sting and kill me."

"I have no intention of stinging you," the scorpion replied, "because if I sting you and then you die I will drown, also. How dumb is that?"

The frog knew how deadly scorpions could be; nevertheless, he also appreciated the scorpion's logic. Under the threat of death, the frog thought that maybe just this once the scorpion would resist the urge to sting. So the frog agreed. The scorpion climbed onto the frog's back and they set out across the pond together. Just as they reached the middle of the pond the scorpion lost his head and stung the frog. The frog, realizing that he was dying, cried out, "Why did you sting me? I thought you just wanted a ride to the other side. Now you will die, too!"

"It is too bad, isn't it? I will just have to die," said the scorpion, as he too began to sink. "After all, I am just a scorpion. It is my nature to sting!"

Although previous wisdom encourages you to listen just like the frog, that old fable encourages you to listen differently than the frog. People can change; they must! You think to yourself that previous, conventional wisdom tells you that anyone can achieve at anything, if they simply try hard enough. So you are directed that it is your responsibility to ensure those changes. Therefore, you carefully set up the room and the lessons to control your apathetic students. You enthusiastically begin to teach all of them the skill sets to fill in the ones they lack. All of your most potent efforts go into stifling what nature provided.

We now have the science to reject this approach out of hand. We should recognize what the frog forgot, and that is that each person is an individual and must be true to his or her individual nature (like the scorpion). We must recognize that each person is wired differently; each has their own way of relating, of thinking, of solving problems. We now know that science teaches there is a limit to how much remodeling and changing will be helpful. We must appreciate that it will not help to lament these differences, and try not to muscle them into changing. Instead we must exploit the uniqueness. Help students to become more of who they already are. Great teachers see it this way: don't hurt yourself trying to put in what you think was left out. Instead try to draw out what was left in. This scientific insight is truly revolutionary, if not unconventional, even atypical. You always wanted to be a rebel, didn't you? Now is your chance!

For the astute observer this truth is monumental. It explains why the greatest teachers never quit on a student, while still recognizing that it is unrealistic to teach that any goal can be achieved through pure determination and grit. Determination and grit are very important traits, but they alone will not generate the next Einstein. It also helps to explain why a fixation on weaknesses is less than helpful. It also explains why great teachers and leaders do not treat each individual in the same exact fashion.

Many years back, I attended a coaching conference and heard one of America's most successful coaches (both college and professional), Lou Holtz, speak on his key to success. He was the first person I had ever heard trumpet the notion that "treating each person the same was not equal and therefore unequal and unfair."[34] He went on to say that some student athletes have such an extraordinary ability that the coach needed to work with them on a different level altogether, while other athletes were strong in discipline, courage, teamwork, and other important yet invisible contributions to the team. While two individuals may be, according to the coach, equally important to the success of the team, it was unfair to treat them in exactly the same way. It is readily apparent that the insight about individuality and its implications runs completely contrary to much of the conventional wisdom.

To some, this truth might appear to be overly simple. To others, however, it may seem quite complicated or complex. Actually, neither is true. Like all ideas that challenge conventional assumptions, this particular idea needs exploration by the teaching team. What does it mean for employees, for parents, for the curriculum and students? Further, what does it mean for grading, for expectations, for IQ testing, for testing, for student management, and for grouping?

The purpose of the next two chapters is to carefully examine these and other related issues. We also begin to think about the uniqueness of school in light of the science of brain growth as well as the role of the teacher, parent, student, community, and social service agencies.

Pillar 5: From Mistakes Mean Failure to Using Mistakes as the Footpath to Success

Persistence is important beyond measure; there can be no giving up in "disappointment." Only restarting the engine is acceptable. You must begin and simply adjust the course as you move along. Do not expect a straight line; rather, anticipate obstacles and curves at best. The direction is not as important as just getting started. Getting to the destination is not as important as finding joy in the fulfillment of the journey. Calvin Coolidge once observed,

> Nothing in the world can take the place of persistence.
> Talent will not; nothing is more common than
> Unsuccessful men with great talent.
> Genius will not; unrewarded genius is almost a proverb.
> Education will not; the world is full of educated derelicts.
> Persistence, determination alone is omnipotent.[35]

Pillar 6: From I Can't Do It to I Can Find a Way or Make One

Learning applications for both leaders and teachers: At least in part because children are delicate and precious, educators have been reluctant to take risks. We cannot learn and grow if we do not step out a bit. Ken Blanchard made that point very well when he said, "Why go out on a limb? Because that is where the fruit is!" My own experience has led me to say it in the following way: if you want to succeed in an SBS then you must be willing to fail more often. These comments assume that the educators in question take their vocation seriously, have developed a learning community, and, therefore, learn from their mistakes. Winston Churchill once commented,, "Success is a function of moving with undaunted enthusiasm from failure to failure!"[36]

A friend of mine works in the area of couples' counseling. He once commented that after just ten minutes into a visit he could successfully predict, with 100% accuracy, which couples would succeed in staying together. My counseling friend taught me the difference between interest and commitment. If one is interested in doing something, they do it when and if it is convenient, but when you are committed you finish the task. The obstacles are really irrelevant as compared to your commitment. My counseling friend said that those couples who said they were going to "try" always fell short with a haphazard effort, while those who said, rather, "we will," were almost always successful because their language was a tip to him as to their real intentions. Ken Blanchard says it this way: "Trying is just a noisy way of not doing something!"[37]

Winston Churchill is one of the greatest leaders in England's storied history. He looms large even in American history because Churchill emerged as the leader of the free world during World War II. In his later years, Winston Churchill delivered a speech at the English prep school he had attended as a youth. The headmaster was thrilled to have such a distinguished guest as a featured speaker. Accordingly, the headmaster took great pride in preparing an introduction that was fitting for such a distinguished individual. After the headmaster had finish his introduction, the boys in attendance leaned forward with great anticipation as Churchill approached the podium. One could almost hear the headmaster's heart beating wildly as Churchill's steely stare x-rayed the boys over the top of his reading glasses. As the crowd began to settle, Churchill, in his boomingly gruff voice, proclaimed, "Never, Never, Never, Never, Give Up!"[38] With that statement, Churchill stomped off the stage and took his seat. Many of the students were disappointed because they had expected something different. The headmaster, on the other hand, felt it was one of Churchill's finest speeches. Those simple six words summed up the grit that Churchill instilled in English people during the dark years as they suffered from almost daily Nazi air attacks.[39] At the risk of sounding overly dramatic, I believe that school people and some students in today's schools feel much the same as the traumatized people of England during the daily saturation bombing of London in 1943 and 1944. We must commit to success and never, never, never, give up.

Pillar 7: From Aloof and Independent to Connecting and Caring

Learning applications for both leaders and teachers: Throughout history leaders and great teachers alike have been viewed as strong, independent, even judgmental. These characterizations of both teachers and leaders are true, because the human species has a need to assign mystical, even evocative, images to those who are considered to be very important.

Down on earth, however, there is a no power in position, only in relationships.

Earlier we talked about the insane inflexibility of the standards and the negative effect that it is having on all of the people in the school. I have repeatedly made the point that the capacity-based approach to people is the most productive. Improvement occurs most favorably by building strong relationships. A concrete way to think about this is to consider two following domains: the relationship domain and the productivity domain. From this point forward I refer to the productivity domain as the harvest domain. To maximize improvement it is important to keep the two domains in balance. See figure 3.2. I prefer to use the word "harvest" in place of "production" because the effective teacher plants the seed and nurtures the learning process, which results in the harvest of successful students and schools. If we err, and we will err in this most complex human endeavor, we should err on the side of the human. Relationships are important because relationships generate trust. Trust is both the sun and soil; it simultaneously cultivates one to achieve and also feeds the soul. The only way to generate trust is to earn it. Trust is the direct byproduct of closeness, caring, and predictability. Trust is the lubrication that makes everything else possible. It is also the emotional glue that sustains through the taxing times of growth and learning. The bond of trust generates hope.

Leaders [teachers] are dealers in hope.

—Napoleon Bonaparte

I know that every reader has at one time looked into the eyes of students expecting to see fear and trepidation, only to see hope reflected back—with a miniscule hint of questioning. Students look to teachers and leaders for hope and help. The only possible way in which to respond is with trust building, which is the process of helping children to see a favorable future before they create it.

SUMMARY

The necessary next steps in the improvement process are already within the teacher. Teachers are the experts. No outside source can provide the

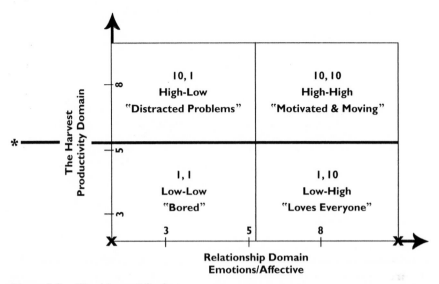

Figure 3.2.   The Harvest Scale

direction that teachers can provide because teachers understand their own strengths and the learning needs of their children.

Efficacy is a necessary first step. Each teacher must come to understand they have efficacy—that subtle yet powerful knowledge that each is potent, meaning they can make a difference in the achievement of their students. Teamwork has historically been undervalued in schools. Teamwork is a key to success because none of us is as smart as all of us together. Teamwork begins by believing in others. Professional efficacy of the teaching staff may be the single most important element in closing the achievement gap. Professional efficacy takes time and comes from the group and cannot be found in any outside source. The efficacy pattern completely revealed is to believe first in the efficacy of self, then in the efficacy of the other teachers, and finally in the effcacy of students. To build staff efficacy, meetings need to be skillfully facilitated by the staff. There are critically important meeting skills and team-building activities included in this chapter to help establish trust and professional efficacy.

Because of the intense focus on their individual classrooms, most teachers did not see the warning signs of the beginning of the demise of voter support for public schools. As a result teachers were not particularly motivated to earnestly support the reforms of the 1960s. In addition, the Department of Education (DOE) released the Coleman Report, which concluded that family SES had as much or more to do with student academic success than the school. As a consequence, there was little motivation to improve. When the Nation at Risk report was released with its inflammatory language, it came as a shock to teachers and the school community. There is no choice but to see the current political environment as a serious wake-up call. Unfortunately, the public and the politicians are completely skeptical of the schools' willingness and ability to close the achievement gap. Public schools need to demonstrate success with all students or run the risk of loosing the monopoly that public schools now enjoy. The measures to demonstrate improvement are probably too high and too numerous, while support for schools is in serious decline.

To design and implement an effective program for all students, schools must build on their capacities. Changes in the school community are happening at light speed, which is dictating a change in the relations of the key stakeholders. Understanding and responding to those transitions is an important adjustment in recognizing that public schools will respond to the current challenges with serious commitment and motivation.

To provide an insight into the transitions that are required, I have included seven "pillars" describing what is needed and why. I call the transitions pillars because the pillars are like weight-bearing walls that serve to support the standards-based classroom (SBC). In each of the seven transitions, I describe the change and then show how the given transition affects the learning of both teachers and leaders alike. One of the most important pillars is to create a safe, wholesome, and nurturing environment for all students. The atmosphere in both the school and the classroom must be facilitated rather than controlled. Long-term planning for the school community must be such that one begins with the end in mind. Learning theory on motivation and current brain understanding both strongly suggest that schools should continue their reform by building on strengths, all in terms of programs, adults, and students. In order to develop and implement a high-performance SBS, the school community needs to be willing to move away from some existing conventions. That area is new and will certainly stimulate a bit of insecurity. When that happens, teachers need to keep moving with persistence.

Teachers should not be allowed to become so discouraged that they give up. Each adult in the school needs to make a human connection with anyone who needs it.

QUESTIONS FOR DELIBERATION

1. Do you feel confident about your level of efficacy in school at the current time? On an efficacy scale of 1 to 10 (with 10 being high), rate yourself. Are you satisfied with the result? If you are not satisfied, what could you do to become more satisfied with your efficacy self-assessment?

2. Do you believe that you are a team player?

3. Please rate yourself on a scale of 1 to 10 (with 10 being high) with regard to team play. Are you satisfied with the result? If you are not satisfied with the result, what could you do improve your rating?

4. In your opinion, did public schools make good improvement progress in the post–Cold War era? If that era was before your time, please provide your thinking anyway. Why or why not?

5. How is the current era of NCLB different from all of the other reform eras? On a scale of 1 to 10 (with 10 being high), rate your level of confidence in the ability of public schools, in general, to meet the NCLB criteria. What is the rationale for your rating? Using the same rating, rate your own school's chances of meeting the NCLB criteria. Is there a discrepancy between your own school's chance and public schools' chances in general? What is your rationale for why your school-was either different than or similar to schools in general?

6. On a scale of 1 to 10 (with 10 being high), rate the relative importance of each of the seven pillars of support. What stands out in your data and why? Do you see other pillars that should have been included?

SUCCESS STRATEGIES

The Power of the Family

I have always initiated this effort by comparing the district or school to a family; over time, I worked to recruit support for the concept. A successful, broad-based strategy to build support is as follows. Begin by taking a photograph of every employee in the district or school and then create a slide show. Show the slides (or videotape) to the staff on a big screen at an annual staff event. I have always used elementary students to sing background songs that honor teaching like "Wind Beneath My Wings" by Bette Midler. I now call the picture show the family album and show it annually during our back-to-school rally. In addition, I make a point of welcoming new employees by welcoming them to the family. I do the same thing to welcome employees who have been on leave. Over the last five years I have been amazed at how frequently others have adopted the word "family." While this is a straightforward approach, the activity of having and showing a "family album" helped us to create a feeling of intimacy in a district with more than 1,000 full- and part-time school employees.

Alignment Must Come Simultaneously from Within and Without

It is important to develop intrinsic motivation in high-performance organizations. People are motivated by any number of incentives, including but not limited to money, respect, enhanced authority, and recognition. High-performance districts and schools have people who are self-starters and take the initiative. The key to developing that asset in the organization is to design intrinsic motivators. It has been said that Mahatma Ghandi said to his daughter, Indira Ghandi: There are two kinds of people in the world, those who get things done, and those who take the credit. So I want you to always be in the first group—there is less competition. Ghandi knew the important thing was to get the work done—that comes first. I realize the importance of his statement but I also know that recognition is a powerful motivator because it can help align the organization around the goals and vision. I like to call this concept "recognition density."

Recognition Density Is an Inside-Out Alignment Strategy

1. Identify the core beliefs of the district, the school, and the community.
2. Set goals to achieve those core beliefs.

3. Design solid communication strategies to create an understanding of and deep support for academic achievement as measured by the goals.
4. Whenever possible, recognize students, staff, and parents for the achievement of the academic standards.
5. Try to find ways to recognize the work of students and staff. Recognition serves as a magnet to draw the organization toward the vision.

The kind of recognition we are speaking of is intrinsic in nature. Recognize students and staff for the achievement of the academic standards. We called them student and staff all-stars. This strategy is so powerful in making change that it is almost magical. In summary, this is a powerful three-step process:

- Step 1: Publicly identify the community beliefs as important goals for the organization.
- Step 2: Annually measure progress toward the goals and report the progress, then step aside.
- Step 3: Allow the community to exert pressure to make the necessary changes to succeed in reaching the community's goals.

This three-step process requires administrators and others to step aside to ensure the recognition and affirmation fall on those who are successful in aligning the program to the organization's goals. This is a defining difference between a leader and a manager. Leaders use the core beliefs of the community in conjunction with recognition to energize the organization. Managers set goals, appoint committees, and delegate work to move forward.

NOTES

1. Gorton Carruth and Eugene Ehrlich, eds., *Giant Book of American Quotations*, (Carruth & Ehrlich Books, 1988), 30.
2. Stephen Covey, *The Seven Habits of Highly Effective People*, (New York: Simon and Schuster, 1989), 42.

3. Quoted in Covey, *Seven Habits of Highly Effective People*, 316.

4. Carruth and Ehrich, *Giant Book of American Quotations*, 104.

5. United States Department of Education, 1983, "A Nation at Risk," 5.

6. Carl Rogers, "Psychology of the Classroom," (paper presented at the Annual Meeting of the Montana Association for Supervision and Curriculum Development, Missoula, Mont., April 1969.

7. Daniel Goleman, Richard Boyatzis, and Annie McKee, *Primal Leadership: Realizing the Power of Emotional Intelligence*, (Boston: Harvard Business School Press, 2002), 6.

8. Goleman et al., *Primal Leadership: Realizing the Power of Emotional Intelligence*, 7.

9. Abraham Maslow, "Maslow's Hierarchy of Needs," *Educational Psychology Interactive*, 2004, http://chiron.valdsta.edu/whutt.col/regsy/maslow.html, [accessed 21 Feb. 2004].

10. Margaret Wheatley, *Leadership and the New Science*, (San Francisco: Barrett-Koehler Publisher, 1999).

11. Marcus Buckingham and Curt Coffman, *First Break All the Rules*, (New York: Simon and Schuster, 1999), 81.

12. Don Clifton and Paula Nelson, *Soar with Your Strengths*, (New York: Dell Publishing, 1996) 12.

13. Clifton and Nelson, *Soar with Your Strengths*, 12.

14. Clifton and Nelson, *Soar with Your Strengths*, 12.

15. Clifton and Nelson, *Soar with Your Strengths*, 13.

16. Clifton and Nelson, *Soar with Your Strengths*, 33.

17. Clifton and Nelson, *Soar with Your Strengths*, 42.

18. Daniel Amen, "Brain Science Research Matters in Mental Health," (paper presented at Meeting of Clinicians, Portland, Ore., Spring 2003), 2.

19. Goleman et al., *Primal Leadership: Realizing the Power of Emotional Intelligence*, 10.

20. Daniel Amen, M.D., *Change Your Brain, Change Your Life*, (New York: Three Rivers Press, 1998), 32.

21. Amen, *Change Your Brain, Change Your Life*, 38.

22. Amen, *Change Your Brain, Change Your Life*, 39.

23. Amen, *Change Your Brain, Change Your Life*, 40.

24. Daniel Goleman, *Emotional Intelligence: Why It Can Matter More Than IQ*, (New York: Bantam Books, 1995), 10.

25. Goleman, *Emotional Intelligence: Why It Can Matter More Than IQ*, 10.

26. Goleman, *Emotional Intelligence: Why It Can Matter More Than IQ*, 10.

27. Goleman, *Emotional Intelligence: Why It Can Matter More Than IQ*, 11.

28. Goleman, *Emotional Intelligence:Why It Matter More Than IQ*, 12.

29. Amen, "Brain Science Research Matters in Mental Health," 2.

30. Amen, "Brain Science Research Matters in Mental Health," 1.

31. Amen, "Brain Science Research Matters in Mental Health," 1.

32. Buckingham and Coffman, *First Break All the Rules*, 81.

33. Amen, "Brain Science Research Matters in Mental Health," 1.

34. Lou Houltz, "Keys to Successful Coaching," (paper presented at the annual meeting of the Montana Coaches Association, Bozeman, Mont., July 1977).

35. Ken Blanchard, *Heart of a Leader*, (Tulsa, Okla.: Honor Books, 1998), 5.

36. Quoted in John Cook, ed., *The Book of Positive Quotations*, (Minneapolis, Minn.: Fairview Press, 1987), 400.

37. Quoted in Warren Bennis and Burt Nanus, *Leaders: Strategies for Taking Charge*, (New York: Harper & Row, 1985), 45.

38. Quoted in Blanchard, *Heart of a Leader*, 48.

39. Blanchard, *Heart of a Leader*, 48.

4

THE PRODIGAL CHILD
RETURNS HOME

Nothing can more effectively contribute to the cultivation and improvement of a country, the wisdom, riches, and strength, virtue and piety, the welfare and happiness of a people, than a proper education of youth.

—Benjamin Franklin

The mediocre teacher tells, the good teacher explains. The superior teacher demonstrates. The great teacher inspires.

—William Arthur Ward

PERFORMANCE REALITIES

Why have public schools lost the support of the public (not parents)? That is a difficult question to grapple with, because when a school loses the trust and faith of an individual the circumstances is likely to be specific to that person's child. Only about 25% of the adult population has kids in school. Therefore, most of the public is forced to rely on information from parents, employees, or the press. The underlying current of the press reports and disgruntled employees is not positive. There-

fore, to present as true a response to the realities of the effectiveness of
public schools, we must look at the overall performance of schools. The
news is dark, yet it will not come as a surprise to veteran teachers or administrators. More than 25% of all students fail to graduate from high
school each year, and in many major cities, half of all poor and minority
students routinely drop out of school with poor skills, few job prospects,
and limited opportunities in life.[1] According to the National Assessment
of Educational Progress (NAEP), the outlook is not much better for
many who make it to graduation. The NAEP reports that fewer than half
of all 17-year-olds who are in school develop reading, writing, mathe-
matics, or problem-solving skills for success.[2] In spite of this evidence
suggesting that public schools are not currently performing at adequate
levels, there are reasons to hope that there is an adequate foundation on
which to build.

PERSONAL VISIONS OF EXCELLENCE ARE
THE BUILDING BLOCKS OF SUCCESS

Yes, you can be extremely confident of your ability to overcome the challenges of 21st-century life in America, because you control the critical resource to succeed. Do you realize what resource I am talking about? To
set a course for your school to follow, be in a position to predict your
school's future by creating it now. The only obstacle barring you is one of
mind. Ask the question honestly of yourself: do you really want your
school to aspire to become a high-performance SBS? If your response is
positive, then what will you personally do to support the effort to achieve
a high-performance SBS? At this time, in our journey back, I prefer that
you focus on what it will feel like to achieve a high-performance school.
Today's challenge is making these changes when schools to date have not
proven enormously successful with the student population. On balance,
however, I must note that American public schools are still the best in the
world for the students who aspire to go on to college. All legitimate organizations and groups predict that under NCLB almost 9 out of 10
schools in America will be designated as "in need of improvement."
While that is the official language, everyone knows it means failing and
consequently the schools will face some type of sanction. Such an obvi-

ously dangerous affront to one of the great institutions in this country should stimulate concerns for all public education advocates. It is beyond time for an honest look at the work that has been done in schools and the work that yet remains to be done.

WHERE FROM HERE

The discussions have been somewhat general to this point in the book. From this point forward the discussions are much more specific in nature. The Tommy Stoddard story is included here because before I outline the steps you and your school should take to regain public support, we must focus on the powerful role that teachers play in the life of a child. When a teacher gives something positive to a child it is given forever. And once a child identifies you as a teacher who cares about them, there are few limits the child will not surpass to continue in your good graces. Also, we must be reminded of the remarkable resiliency that lives in the hearts of your kids.

Three Letters from Tommy

Tommy's letter came today and now that I've read it, I will place it in my cedar chest with the other things that are important in my life.

"I wanted you to be the first to know."

I smiled as I read the words he had written and my heart swelled with a pride that I had no right to feel.

I have not seen Tommy since he was a student in my 5th grade class 15 years ago. It was early in my career, and I had only been teaching for two years.

From the first day he stepped into my classroom, I disliked Tommy. Teachers (although everyone knows differently) are not supposed to have favorites in a class, but, most especially, they are not to show dislike for a child, any child.

Nevertheless, every year there are one or two children that one cannot help but be attached to, for teachers are human, and it is human nature to like bright, pretty, intelligent people, whether they are 10 years old or 25. And sometimes—not too often, fortunately—there will be one or two students to whom the teacher just can't seem to relate.

I had thought myself quite capable of handling my personal feelings along that line until Tommy walked into my life. There wasn't a child I particularly liked that year, but Tommy was most assuredly one I disliked.

He was dirty. Not just occasionally, but all the time. His hair hung low over his ears, and he actually had to hold it out of his eyes as he wrote his papers in class. (And this was before it was fashionable to do so!) Too, he had a peculiar odor about him which I could never identify.

His physical faults were many, and his intellect left a lot to be desired. By the end of the first week I knew he was hopelessly behind the others. Not only was he behind, he was just plain slow! I began to withdraw from him immediately.

Any teacher will tell you that it's more of a pleasure to teach a bright child. It is definitely more rewarding for one's ego. But any teacher worth her credentials can channel work to the bright child, keeping him challenged and learning, while she puts her major effort on the slower ones. Any teacher can do this. Most teachers do it, but I didn't, not that year.

In fact, I concentrated on my best students and let the others follow along as best they could. Ashamed as I am to admit it, I took perverse pleasure in using my red pen, and each time I came to Tommy's papers, the cross marks (and there were many) were always a little larger and a little redder than necessary.

"Poor work!" I would write with a flourish.

While I did not actually ridicule the boy, my attitude was obviously quite apparent to the class, for he quickly became the class "goat," the outcast—the unlovable and the unloved.

He knew I didn't like him, but he didn't know why. Nor did I know—then or now—why I felt such an intense dislike for him. All I know is that he was a little boy no one cared about, and I made no effort on his behalf.

The days rolled by. We made it through the Fall Festival and the Thanksgiving holidays, and I continued marking happily with my red pen.

As the Christmas holidays approached, I knew that Tommy would never catch up in time to be promoted to the sixth-grade level. He would be a repeater.

To justify myself, I went to his cumulative folder from time to time. He had very low grades for the first four years, but no grade failure. How he had made it, I didn't know. I closed my mind to the personal remarks.

First grade: Tommy shows promise by work and attitude, but has poor home situation. Second grade: Tommy could do better. Mother terminally ill. He receives little help at home. Third grade: Tommy is a pleasant boy. Helpful, but too serious. Slow learner. Mother passed away at end of year. Fourth grade: Very slow, but well behaved. Father shows no interest.

Well, they had passed him four times, but he will certainly repeat fifth grade! Do him good! I said to myself.

And then the last day before the holiday arrived. Our little tree on the reading table sported paper and popcorn chains. Many gifts were heaped underneath, waiting for the big moment.

Teachers always get several gifts at Christmas, but mine that year seemed bigger and more elaborate than ever. There was not a student who had not brought me one. Each unwrapping brought squeals of delight, and the proud giver would receive an effusive thank you.

His gift wasn't the last one I picked up; in fact it was in the middle of the pile. Its wrapping was a brown paper bag, and he had colored Christmas trees and red bells all over it. It was stuck together with masking tape. "For Miss Jones—From Tommy" it read.

The group was completely silent and for the first time I felt conspicuous, embarrassed because they all stood watching me unwrap that gift.

As I removed the last bit of masking tape, two items fell to my desk: a gaudy rhinestone bracelet with several stones missing and a small bottle of dime-store cologne—half empty.

I could hear the snickers and whispers, and I wasn't sure I could look at Tommy.

"Isn't this lovely?" I asked, placing the bracelet on my wrist. "Tommy, would you help me fasten it?"

He smiled shyly as he fixed the clasp, and I held up my wrist for all of them to admire.

There were a few hesitant oohs and ahhs, but as I dabbed the cologne behind my ears, all the little girls lined up for a dab behind their ears.

I continued to open gifts until I reached the bottom of the pile. We ate our refreshments, and the bell rang.

The children filed out with shouts of "See you next year!" and "Merry Christmas!" but Tommy waited at his desk.

When they had all left, he walked toward me, clutching his gift and books to his chest.

"You smell just like my mom," he said softly. "Her bracelet looks real pretty on you, too. I'm glad you liked it."

He left quickly. I locked the door, sat down at my desk, and wept, resolving to make up to Tommy what I had deliberately deprived him of— a teacher who cared.

I stayed every afternoon with Tommy from the end of the Christmas holidays until the last day of school. Sometimes we worked together. Sometimes he worked alone while I drew up lesson plans or graded papers.

Slowly but surely he caught up with the rest of the class. Gradually there was a definite upward curve in his grades.

He did not have to repeat the fifth grade. In fact, his final averages were among the highest in the class, and although I knew he would be moving out of the state when school was out, I was not worried about him. Tommy had reached a level that would stand him in good stead the following year, no matter where he went. He had enjoyed a measure of success, and as we were taught in our teacher training courses, "success builds success."

I did not hear from Tommy until seven years later, when his first letter appeared in my mailbox.

Dear Miss Jones,
I just wanted you to be the first to know, I will be graduating second in my class next month.
Very truly yours
Tommy Stoddard

I sent him a card of congratulations and a small package, a pen and pencil gift set. I wondered what he would do after graduation.
Four years later, Tommy's second letter came.

Dear Miss Jones,
I wanted you to be the first to know. I was just informed that I'll be graduating first in my class. The university has not been easy, but I liked it.
Very truly yours,
Tommy Stoddard

I sent him a good pair of sterling silver monogrammed cuff links and a card, so proud of him I could burst!
And now today…Tommy's third letter.

Dear Miss Jones,
I wanted you to be the first to know. As of today I am Thomas M. Stoddard, M.D. How about that!!??
I'm going to be married in July, the 27th, to be exact. I wanted to ask if you could come and sit where Mom would sit if she were here. I'll have no family there as Dad died last year.
Very truly yours,
Tommy Stoddard

I'm not sure what kind of gift one sends to a doctor on completion of medical school and state boards. Maybe I'll just wait and take a wedding gift, but the note can't wait.

Dear Tom,
Congratulations! You made it, and you did it yourself! In spite of those like me and not because of us, this day has come for you.
God bless you. I'll be at the wedding with bells on!
Susan Dee Jones
(Betsy Arrison, personal communication, 2003)

This was a story that was circulated via e-mail as one of those forwards we all get from time to time. I've changed the names of both from the original just in case there is some truth to the story.

In the beginning God created man. Do you agree? No, that is wrong. In the beginning, God created the heavens and the earth. Then He created space, and God named the dry ground "land" and the water "seas." Then God created light, day and night, the seasons. Then God had the land burst forth with every kind of grass and seed-bearing plant. Then God proceeded to create seeds, plants, forests, birds, and animals, and ultimately He considered and created all of the things His most important creations (man and woman) would need to survive and prosper. The point being made is not whether you agree or disagree with this description of creation. The point is, where do we start to close the achievement gap? Where else can we start but at the beginning? We need to begin with consummate preparation while understanding that the processes and partnerships discussed in detail herein will succeed only if we take the time to build a strong foundation under our road to success. There are four distinct phases to this journey and that journey will take time, patience, and composure. This will be a long, slow journey with shared lessons and learning, tears and trying. This is a new reform effort. Some in government have already written us off as a failure waiting for an excuse.

DO TODAY'S TEACHERS HAVE THE SKILLS TO TEACH THE SHADOW CHILD?

The answer may startle you if you have been AYP'd like everyone else. The answer is absolutely yes, teachers have the technical know-how but lack the resources and are applying conventional assumptions that are faulty (as pointed out in the previous chapter). We know more about teaching than we have ever known before. I have tried to make it perfectly clear that the public and the politicians are much less than satisfied with contemporary public schools. Therefore, one might inaccurately conclude that today's teachers are simply not skilled enough to close the achievement gap when, in fact, it is a lack of support and resources that impact their ability to create the desired environment for their students. As shown in the story about Tommy Stoddard, an individual teacher can and does have a profound effect on student learning even in schools that are relatively ineffective. It is critically important to recognize that up-to-date research (Marzano, Pickering, and Pollock, and others) has shown us that a teacher's actions in the classroom have twice the impact on student achievement as school policies regarding curriculum, assessment, staff collegiality, and community involvement. A teacher's actions have twice the impact on a student as other respected supports for academic achievement. It is unnecessary to substantiate the effect of excellent teaching further because the work we now have is irrefutable.[3] Given that research, it would be less than intelligent if I went deeply into the technology of teaching (e.g., correct strategies and techniques, effective pedagogy) for the duration of this book because clearly that need has been met. The purpose of this book is not to review, clarify, and contribute to what is already a keen part of the skill set of high-performance teachers. Robert Marzano, who is one of the most respected scholars at the Mid-Continent Regional Educational Laboratory (McREL) in Denver, is the lead author of a book entitled *Classroom Instruction That Works*, which describes, in detail, research-based strategies that work.[4] Beyond Marzano's work, Charlotte Danielson has created a framework for excellence in teaching that is likewise so complete it leaves little, if any, room for substantive additions. Danielson's work was derived from a large-scale Educational Testing Service (ETS) project to provide a teaching framework for state and local agencies to use for making teacher licensing decisions. Regarding the completeness of her work, Danielson writes, "The framework for teaching described in this book [*Enhancing Professional Practice: A Framework for Teaching*] identifies those aspects of teachers' responsibilities that have been documented through empirical studies and theoretical research as promoting improved learning."[5] It would not serve a useful purpose to reiterate those compendiums of teaching excellence. I am persuaded that your years of experience provide you with several tools on which you should immediately continue to build. This book, therefore, necessarily moves beyond the essentials of pedagogy. The first significant strength you possess is your very strong subject-area knowledge. And the second is the knowledge you have of your students' learning needs. Most importantly, you have the ability to build lasting and strong relationships with your students. Be reminded that the limbic system reflexively evaluates stimuli as either positive or negative and responds accordingly. I believe teachers need to take that truism into account when working with all students. Further, I believe that the treatment of teachers and other adults in the school community should be consistent with our expectations for student treatment. Therefore, I build on your strengths by making the assumption that you have what you need by way of the technology of teaching. I explore the schools' existing capacities in two steps: youth development and academic development.

The last decade has witnessed a growing call for measurable school reform. The impetus for the reforms can be traced to the "back to the basics" movement of the 1970s. The movement led to an emphasis on low-level functioning skills and also the proliferation of minimum competency tests. The reform movement beginning in the 1990s and continuing today, however, is different because it is characterized by measurable and sophisticated educational goals and higher standards.

This new emphasis grew out of the 1991 Education Summit held in Charlottesville, Virginia. President George H. W. Bush and the nation's state governors presented America 2000. The proposal set ambitious national goals targeted for the year 2000. America 2000 called for the development of the world's best schools, schools that would enable our students to meet world-class academic standards. In response, national subject area associations as well as commissioned groups at the local level began, for the first time, the development of national curriculum standards. During the early part of the 1990s nearly every state in the union began to develop academic standards. By the middle of the decade, many, if not most, states and academic associations had developed rigorous academic standards. The focus on outcomes signaled in a new era of educational reform in America. It was out of this beginning that the standards-based movement (SBM) was off and running.

What Is Standards-Based Reform and How Is It Different from the Traditional Curriculum?

In the standards-based school (SBS) system, each school is expected to demonstrate high academic standards through performance-based assessments. In a traditional system, promotion or graduation is often based on seat time or the number of credits earned rather than a demonstrated level of competence as measured against a clearly stated academic standard. In other words, student academic success in an SBS is measured by academic achievement, not time or credit accumulation. In an SBS the first step is for teachers to determine what they want students to know or do, then they design the curriculum down from that academic target called a standard.

The Difference between an SBS and a Conventional School

I have observed several differences in my 34 years of work in public schools. As I discuss the differences between the two systems, I am simply amazed that the conventional model was ever embraced in the first place. Because teaching is a very autonomous and independent endeavor, there is no universally acceptable description of all of the variations of the conventional system. Therefore my descriptions remain at the conceptual level.

In a traditional classroom teachers teach until students reach some mysterious saturation point. Once that saturation point is reached, teachers spend time reviewing the important content that will appear on the test. Generally speaking, the important content is revealed at the conclusion of the unit, rather than at the beginning. The students who reach this arcane saturation point are deemed ready for the summary exam. When the students have completed the test, they have also exhausted the time allotted for that unit so the teachers move on to more content. The class moves on in spite of whether it demonstrated understanding or mastery of the previous unit.

A few students attain excellent levels of achievement. Other students are not nearly as proficient and others are completely unsuccessful. No matter, all students move on. This procedure is not the teacher's fault, because schools were originally organized for efficiency (under the principles of scientific management) like the assembly line. Typically, that meant that the whole class was compelled to slow down to accommodate the learners who were struggling.

Clear academic standards are important especially for the academically diverse student. Simply said, shadow kids have a better chance at success when they clearly understand the academic expectation. Sunshine students also experience benefits because they do not need to wait for others. When they demonstrate mastery they move on as fast as their ability and resources allow. When standards are made clear to students and their parents, students find a way to meet them. Make no mistake about it, the academic standards are high. Once, I invited members of a Rotary club to experience the eighth-grade math test, and I am sure you can anticipate how well they did.

Some students may not achieve the academic standards immediately, but they will in time, especially after the barrier is broken.

Defining the Standards-Based School (SBS)

In an SBS, it is common practice for teachers to reach agreement on the content standards and make them available to students before instruction begins. In a conventional system, students tease out what they need to remember as they advance through the curriculum. As a result the identification of the academic standards becomes a guessing game for students. Not immediately revealing the academic expectations (standards) to students causes confusion and anxiety for the students. Revealing academic expectations before instruction begins provides a subtle yet powerful strength for both students and teachers. When students clearly understand what the academic expectations are, they are less confused and less anxious. Clear expectations increase the likelihood that students will meet them. Reaching clear agreement on standards, even before the curriculum is designed, is a strength for teachers as well. In an SBS, teachers work closely together to achieve the same high academic standards. Therefore, teachers are not solely responsible for the standards. In addition the teamwork serves to reduce some of the teacher isolation that was previously mentioned. In summary, there are two main differences in an SBS: (1) curriculum content standards are developed in conjunction with other teachers and clearly made known to students and their parents before instruction begins and (2) student mastery is determined through performance-based assessments at a specific point in time. Many of the initial decisions that imposed standards on schools were political decisions made at the state level. The standards-based decisions were frequently made in total isolation or with the transparent involvement of teachers, administrators, parents, students, and, last but not least, taxpayers. With such little discerning input from voices in the field, the politicians had no way of knowing that their system was based on two gravely erroneous assumptions. The first false assumption was there is a level playing field. The second false assumption was that the public would happily increase taxes to pay for a system that clearly exceeded the limits and expectations of the conventional school system. The playing field is not level. I will say it another way: all students do not come to school equally ready to learn, nor do all students learn at the same rate or in the same way. The students who do not come to school ready to learn are the children we have been referring to as academically diverse learners in this book. These particular students (whatever they are called) soon see the school as threatening and hostile. Because of the rigorous standards the academically diverse students feel as if they have let their families, friends, and selves down, and it is painfully humiliating. High academic standards are injurious, not because they are high, but rather because they are pursued by looking for deficiencies, first of the students, then of our teachers, then of the families. Standards are problematic because the playing field is not level. The conventional question is, what has to be fixed to ensure academic success for all kids?

The "fix it," or deficiency-based, approach to improvement is entirely inconsistent with the scientific realities of the open limbic system. The word "open" in brain function context means that the limbic system (in this case) takes its stimulus instantaneously and directly from the environment. Please be reminded that the limbic system is a primitive part of the brain that when stimulated generates an instantaneous, involuntary reflexive reaction. The reaction happens so fast that the thinking brain does not have time to respond. The science of brain function research (completely new since 1990) is important to teachers because they can more accurately predict a student's reaction to certain stimuli. For instance, when threatened or traumatized, the limbic system involuntarily and instantly generates feelings of fight, flight, or freeze.

Conversely, however, the limbic system also processes positive or reassuring stimuli from the environment. Happily, the emotional reaction is so positive that Amen refers to it as "limbic bonding."[6] According to Amen, the limbic system's functions are vital to life itself to such a degree that it has an effect on the physiology of a person. For example, Stanford University psychiatrist David Spiegel demonstrated that the survival rate for women with breast cancer who were in a support group was greater than for those who were not in a support group.[7] Amen states, "Negative people present unnecessary obstacles for you to overcome because you have to push your will to succeed over their doubts, objections, and cynicism. Spending time with people who believe you'll never really amount to anything will dampen your enthusiasm for pursuing your goals and make it difficult to move though life. On the other hand, people who instill confidence in you with a can do attitude and whose spirits are uplifting will help breathe life into your palms and dreams. Spend time with people who enhance the quality of your limbic system rather than those who cause it to be inflamed."[8] Others refer to the limbic bonding response as "resonance." In terms of brain function research, resonance means that people's emotional centers are in sync.[9] Other words that resonate with the term resonance are positive, resounding, and vibrant. Seldom, if ever, does someone ask the question, what are the talents or strengths of these children (or teachers, or parents, or schools, or communities) and how can that talent be used to ensure success? I refuse to focus our attention on the results that occur when the open limbic system feels negative stimulus; I will only say that long-lasting consequences are possible. Rather, envision what could be done if every child in your school received the kind of support necessary to generate limbic bonding. Suffice it to say that the power of limbic bonding has the potential to create successful schools that previously were identified as being in need of improvement. The comprehensive use of this teaching tool has unparalleled potential for the school that can harness its majesty! I conclude this section by reporting the scientific results of a study published in the *Journal of the American Medical Association* in 1997 by researcher Michael Resnick, Ph.D., and colleagues at the University of Minnesota. They "concluded that the degree of connection (limbic bonding) that teenagers feel with parents and teachers is the most important determinant of whether they will engage in risky sexual activity, substance abuse, violence, or suicidal behavior."[10]

> The significant problems we face cannot be solved at the same level of thinking we were at when we created them.

> —Albert Einstein

The Intellectually Honest Need to Challenge the Conventional Assumptions about Teaching and Learning

I reiterate the scientific brain function research because it challenges conventional wisdom regarding how to help students achieve high academic standards in school. Teachers have been taught to have a "fix it" mentality when approaching instruction. In application, teachers pre-test students to find out where the knowledge and skill gaps exist. Armed with the gaps or deficiencies, caring teachers dutifully move forward trying to fill the gaps. All the while, they are assuming that when all the gaps are filled, the students will meet high academic standards. Is that assumption really valid? Consider that public schools are defined by academic diversity, and some of the highest academic standards, coupled with some of the world's poorest children. In answer to the valid assumption question, it may be possible to argue that deficiency-based teaching was moderately successful when students were homogeneous. Happily, for America, the day of affluent, white homogeneity is gone and with it the conventional wisdom around the use of deficiency-based instruction.

Let me be direct. The consequences of threat and trauma were relatively unknown until just recently. The most recent cautions grew out of a theoretical framework developed out of a school of thinking called humanistic psychology. A relatively small number of scholars voiced a minority report on the consequences of threat. One of the most articulate (Arthur Combs) summarized our current dilemma well when he wrote, "Whether a child feels challenged or threatened it is not a question of how it looks to his teacher—it's a question of how it looks to him. . . . Our problem, then, becomes one of finding ways of challenging people without threatening them. Again I ask *what kind of a world could we create if we really put our mind to the*

problem of finding ways of challenging without threatening children
[italics added]?"[11] The question was so complex that it has been largely
ignored. With the recent emergence of brain function research, it is
clear that we have a scientific basis on which to build. The failure of
public schools in the past is somewhat excusable, because we didn't
know. That excuse no longer exists.

When Combs posed his question regarding challenge without threat
there was no scientific evidence to suggest that he should be taken seriously. Although some of us did seriously move in that direction, the effort was sporadic and widely resisted because it was contrary to "conventional wisdom" (ignorance).

Challenge without Threat: The Secret to Success

The key to the success of the public school system is to find a way to
challenge students without threatening them. Our challenge is to put
our minds to the task of finding ways to do this. Students experience
emotional threats and trauma, and those threats vastly reduce the ability of a student to learn and grow. When a school tends to focus on deficiencies of the academically diverse learner, it generates fear, which
the open limbic system perceives as threatening and unsafe (emotionally). The perceived threat (as safe as it might seem to the teacher), in
turn, generates an inflamed limbic reaction defined by flight, fight, or
freeze. Many of the children who come to school not ready to learn
come from poor families of non-European decent. Again, I use the term
"shadow kid" to define the disadvantaged student to whom I refer. I use
the term not in a derogatory sense, but because in my opinion, it more
clearly defines how the school fails with these children. In my opinion,
"shadow kid" defines what happens when schools generate intimidation
and fear. The shadow child slowly retracts from public attention, becomes invisible, then falls through the cracks, eventually failing to finish
what becomes an incredibly destructive and disillusioning process. The
use of terms like "academically diverse," or "disadvantaged," suggest
that the student is somehow the source of school failure. Nothing could
be less true, because in an SBS, when a student fails to achieve academic rigor every support system of that child shares in the responsibility for the potentially wasted talent.

I agree with Marcus Buckingham and Curt Coffman when they write that "school should be a focused hunt for the child's areas of greatest potential. . . . Unfortunately the school is so preoccupied with the transfer of knowledge and filling skill gaps that developing areas of natural talent is disregarded."[12] President L. B. Johnson said it this way: "We just must not, and we cannot afford the real waste that comes from the neglect of a single child."[13]

How Can Your School Really Implement Such Changes?

If you are feeling a little overwhelmed do not be concerned because the steps are easy from here. Please, just break all of this down to just a few simple steps. Your school is unique so what might be appropriate for another location may not fit your needs. This is not intended to be a standardized approach for schools. Rather, I want you to approach this improvement plan by using the same capacity-based approaches suggested for students. The criteria I suggest you use in selecting the components of your school improvement plan (SIP) are those strategies that are natural extensions of your existing strengths. I am most strongly persuaded that the focus question of your SIP should be: What kind of school and world will we create when we learn how to challenge our students without threatening them? Therefore, I offer a menu of options for your consideration.

1. Decide what to do based on "fit" for your school.
2. Learn how to do it!
3. Create a consensus decision on how to proceed with what you learn.
4. After you know what and how, decide what a success would look like. Consider it your vision of excellence, the best that can be imagined in an appropriate period of time for your school and the task at hand.
5. Develop a process to evaluate if you successfully bridged the gap between what was and what was preferred.
6. Based on the evaluation of effort and the collective deepening understanding, generate a second, or a third, or a fourth, iteration of your school improvement plan.

Continue the process until you are finally satisfied with your results. Please notice that I do not suggest that you set high expectations because it is not necessary. I know that you already do the following: (1) expect too much of yourself, and (2) are already working at peak capacity to close the achievement gap. Let us continue to think about the big conceptual issues.

Conceptual Options Are an Investment in Success   The research on youth development is extremely positive and quite consistent with our focus question of challenge without threat. The research points out that the success of young people is not just a matter of chance or genes. Rather, the most up-to-date research tells us that parents, schools, peers, and communities can make a big difference in providing the conditions where young people will thrive. What are the steps to create these conditions?

1. Surround youth with positive influences. Parents have the most influence, of course. Schools and peers come second. Neighborhoods and significant community members also have a significant role to play in establishing a vision of success for youth.
2. Build abundant strengths into the lives of young people. The more strengths there are, the more readily the school can choose one and begin to build on it. This may be the best way of challenging without threatening youth.
3. Support young people with rich resources. This is critically important in cultivating the garden for growth. Please do not become discouraged if rich resources are not immediately forthcoming. Remember your success will stimulate increased support over time, which I predict will crescendo beyond any reasonable expectation. This activity may be something that will capture the imagination of community leaders.
4. Support parents. Be reminded that some parents are shouldering the parenting alone plus working a couple of jobs just to pay the rent and put food on the table. Eventually, of course, schools will be more successful with parental support and involvement. Please be reminded that schools will need to earn, of course, that type of commitment because the parents you need most are the least able to provide traditional support for the school, at least in the very beginning.

5. Create positive peer influence. Peers (whether they are friends, schoolmates, or neighbors) can also have a positive influence. Other young people can significantly enhance the feeling of well-being, crime- and drug-free lifestyles, academic success, recreational and sporting involvement, and how much young people express their talents and safety at school. This is done largely by expressing positive behaviors and values that other young people, even if they did not demonstrate them before, begin to emulate.

This is all you! Schools can have a positive impact in both how you are organized, and (more importantly) how staff relate to their students. Academic and behavioral outcomes are better when there are high expectations for learning and behavior. And that is true under the conventional system. All students must be treated with positive regard, warmth, and support. This is especially important for the academically diverse student who may be under considerable stress from worries about measuring up, personal health, family poverty, or violence.

Involve young people in constructive activities outside of school. Participation in out-of-school activities is a significant protection, although not as strong as families. Young people who participate in extracurricular activities, whether at school or elsewhere, tend to stay longer in school, show less antisocial behavior and drug use, attend school more often, show better attitudes about sex, and have better academic and career success.

Efforts to date to close the achievement gap have been largely unsuccessful. I am persuaded that the lack of success expresses a failure to recognize a penetratingly deep social issue that is reflected in the school. Social injustice and stratification are issues that must be addressed within the community and then supported at school—at least until schools are effective. The Institute for Urban and Minority Education has created a series of principles that bridge the gap between educational differences and social conflict. I am strongly convinced that America needs to move forward on this issue, but I am equally reluctant to make it a menu option for your SIP. The reason is unrelated to the issue at hand. The standards are so tough that if schools don't focus on the standards, their students will fail to meet them. It is important to place a high priority on establishing your SIP team and following the guidelines below. Your team could help other organizations and agencies to support you in the following ways. The state and district should:

1. Develop and implement educational goals that reflect the desires and needs of the community.
2. Involve teachers in the development of rigorous standards from which curriculum can be designed (at the local level).
3. Develop and implement high professional standards for all staff.
4. Make research-based instructional programs with demonstrated success available for use in schools.
5. Make an investment of time, training, and materials in the human capital of the school community.
6. Provide high-quality preschool, parent education programs, and social service resources within the school community.

At the policy level, the school organization should:

1. Support full desegregation of all school classes, programs, and extracurricular activities.
2. Support smaller classes, preferably 18 or fewer students per class at the primary level, 30 or fewer at the secondary school level (grades 6 to 12).
3. Build a secondary school schedule that gives teachers a maximum of 150 students apiece (daily).
4. Create intimacy for students, such as student advisories, within the schedule.
5. Demand more of each student.
6. End dumbed-down tracks and courses. Expand advanced placement (AP) and international baccalaureate (IB) programs for all students.
7. Help kids make course choices and have parents sign off with a commitment to match their students' effort at all levels.
8. Create schedules that get teachers talking.
9. Captivate students with real-world lessons.
10. Equitably group white students and students of color, in proportion to their numbers, in high-ability classes and in higher tracks in the primary grades, and college preparatory classes at the secondary school level.

11. Create programs that teach real-world lessons such as professional-technical programs at the secondary level and career development at the primary level.

Clear Flexible Goals How are standards and grades different? As you plan your school's way back, you will eventually want support from your community, plus you want that support to grow from trust. It is not too early to think about grades and their impact on credibility. Grading is an extremely imprecise method of reporting to parents. Most educators and non-educators assume that grades are precise indicators of what students know and can do. Additionally, it is assumed that current grading practices are the result of careful study of the most effective ways of reporting achievement and progress. That assumption is a terrible error, which is not lost on either students or the school community.

Actually, current grading practices were developed in a rather arbitrary way. For example, as early as 1913, researcher E. I. Finkelstein sounded the alarm regarding the subjectivity of grades. Finkelstein noted, "When we consider the practically universal use in all educational institutions of a system of marks . . . to indicate scholastic attainment of pupils or students in these institutions . . . we can be astonished at the blind faith that has been felt in the reliability of the marking system. School administrators have been using with confidence an absolutely uncelebrated instrument . . . variability in the marks given for the same subject by different instructors is so great as frequently to work real injustice to the students."[14] The reliability of this archaic system did not initially come under direct scrutiny. While somehow everyone just knew and cordially accepted the reality that an "A" from Mr. Smith was a tougher "A" to achieve than an "A" from Mr. Blue. Grade inflation began to become a recurring issue that has grown into a serious credibility issue. Some education critics argue that academic standards are better because they represent clear, measurable, performance-based student achievement. The traditional Carnegie credit or unit of study does not represent performance at all, but rather the time a student spends in class (often called seat time). Unfortunately, although the system has been in place for many years there is still little agreement as to the exact meaning of the letter grades. This point creates credibility problems with the public. The point was underscored in a nationwide study by researchers Glen Robinson and James Carver (1989) that involved more than 800 school districts randomly drawn from the 11,305 that have 300 or more students.

One of Robinson and Carver's major conclusions was that districts stress different elements in their grades. Although all districts stress academic achievement, they also stress such elements as effort, behavior, and attendance. The Robinson and Carver study was completed using the official policies of the selected districts.[15] In studies that have polled individual teachers, the variations were even greater. In summary, grades given by one teacher may mean something entirely different than those given by another teacher. That kind of inconsistency causes significant credibility problems, especially in a global information age that is increasingly more scientifically and technologically literate. Moreover, unreliable grading procedures, perhaps the most compelling argument for moving away from the traditional school toward clearly identified standards, represent the degree to which school improvement efforts have emphasized processes over outcomes. In fact, I remember incorrectly observing as a young school improvement consultant in the early 1970s that school improvement was a process, a process of community involvement and shared decision making. Processes are, of course, soft on measurable learning outcomes. In 1990, Finn described this shift in perspective in terms of an emerging concept of education: "Under the old . . . paradigm . . . education was thought of as a process . . . of hope" rather than measurable outcomes.[16]

The Alchemy of Personal Student Responsibility Precedes Student Success   Who gets left behind and why? Is it the student that is ignorant, lazy, or shy, or the child with a learning disability? The children who are left behind are not just those students who fit the aforementioned labels. Can schools educate all students to meet high academic standards? The answer is clearly yes. Even with a more diverse student population, schools are better able than ever before to close the achievement gap. You can successfully close the achievement gap in your school if you challenge the conventional assumptions and simultaneously keep this guiding principle in mind. How can I challenge my students without threatening them?

The children who get left behind unnecessarily are children who do not meet the mold for which traditional schools were developed. The traditional school, of course, has been most successful when the student population is similar in their level of preparation and readiness for school. The traditional school is most successful when the lives of children are stable and secure, and when the school community holds the homogeneous student population accountable for high academic standards. The nature of the student population is no longer homogeneous. In fact, the students are growing more diverse every day. As the students change, the school system has to change with them. The fact is that the students in public schools today are the most diverse in history. The warning signs are clear, compelling, and everywhere. More children are being born into poverty and into single-parent families than ever before. Please note that child poverty is increasing each year. Dr. Hsien-Hen Lu of the National Center for Children in Poverty at the Joseph L. Mailman School of Public Health at Columbia University reports that "almost one in five children (18%) in the United States lives in poverty."[17] In 2002 the U.S. Census Bureau lists those families that qualify as living in poverty as those whose income is below the federal poverty level of $14,810 for a family of three.[18] It is beyond conception to state that the largest group of people living in poverty in this, the richest nation in the history of the world, are in fact children. The traditional school assumed that students were similar and therefore had the same inherent advantages, but that is false, of course. To be sure, more children of color do live in poverty. All children who suffer from poverty come to school (regardless of color) with the same disadvantages because they bring less knowledge to school with them. Poverty is on the increase. This is not a matter of intellectual horsepower but an issue of growing child poverty. Child poverty is especially tragic in light of military spending.

Researchers have gathered new evidence on the importance of the first years of life to a child's emotional and intellectual development. Unfortunately, millions of children are poor during these crucial years of development. Further, poor children under the age of 3 face a greater risk of impaired brain development due to their exposure to a number of risk factors associated with poverty.[19]

The Myth of Intelligence and the Achievement Gap

As I previously stated, success in school is not as much a matter of intelligence as it is a matter of economics. Arthur Combs wrote that intelligence itself is a function of a person's self-concept.[20] Kids who come to us from poverty are not innately less capable than those from affluence. Intelligence is a function of both genetics and the environment. Most importantly, intelligence is not fixed and it can be learned. If you doubt this, I invite you to look at J. McVicker Hunt's book *Intelligence and Experience*.[21] There is little that scientists can say with absolute certainty about the intellect. First of all, there is no consensus about what intelligence is. Jean Piaget, a noted authority, defined intelligence as either adaptive thinking or action. Other experts have offered different definitions, many centering in some way on the ability to think abstractly or to solve problems effectively. Early definitions of intelligence tended to reflect the assumption that intelligence is an innate intellectual ability, genetically determined, and, therefore, fixed at birth. The SBS must not assume that intelligence is fixed for life, because the assumption is false and I am in draconian dispute. When I was a superintendent in a standards-based district, I would make a point to visit each classroom to ask the question, "How are your students doing academically as measured by the academic standards?" Not infrequently, teachers reported that "this is a particularly slow group," referring to their students' level of intelligence. Without too much thought, the response was typical of what I was frequently told. Many of our excellent, hardworking teachers inadvertently blamed the kids for their inability to meet the standards. I have used this example because I know that our teachers were very hardworking and understood the power of unconditional love. In short, our teachers came to work early, stayed late, and loved big. Given a moment to think about that, I am very doubtful that many would have responded accordingly. The point is that with a reflexive thought, some (clearly, not all) exposed a dangerous and incorrect assumption that students with high innate intelligence had more potential to meet the standards than those with low intelligence. The reason it is such a dangerous assumption is twofold:

1. Sam Kerman, author of "Teacher Expectation and Student Achievement" (TESA), a report on teacher training programs developed in

California, warns of the negative consequences of having low expectations. Kerman's work with TESA has clearly demonstrated that teachers treat perceived high achievers differently than perceived low achievers, and you get what you expect.[22]

2. When academically diverse students ascertain that the teacher does not believe in them, Amen says, the deep limbic system "will dampen their enthusiasm for pursuing their goals."[23]

Many traditional and emerging SBSs behave as if the student is at fault when they fail to meet or exceed the standard. When students fail, the school also fails. If schools are going to get all students to high academic standards, it is significant to understand that school success is not only a matter of intelligence. The purpose of this book is to help define what kind of classroom and teacher generates successful students and show that neither student ethnicity nor innate intelligence is a factor. Assumptions to the contrary are inane.

WHAT IS INTELLIGENCE AND WHAT FACTOR DOES IT PLAY IN SCHOOL SUCCESS?

What kinds of children are most seriously affected by the achievement gap? Essentially, children who come to school poorly nourished, abused, and frightened cannot be expected to learn in the same way or at the same rate as children who do not suffer from those severe disadvantages. This truism is at the very core of the challenge of closing the achievement gap. The shadow kids often fall through the cracks, become invisible, and ultimately drop out of school. The sunshine kids who do come to school ready to learn have a significant advantage. Shadow kids are different than sunshine kids because it is frequently presumed they are less capable of meeting high academic standards. It is primarily because of the label that shadow kids are not always treated equally. That is to say that some children are likely to be treated with warm regard and "tough love," while others are not. Therefore those students who are treated with warm personal regard tend to see the standards as a challenge rather than a threat, so the deep limbic system has a strong and positive impact on the student's motivation and drive. I am strongly persuaded that this discrepancy has more to do with poor academic performance than poverty does. The shadow kid sees the challenge as a threat causing personal trauma that inflames the deep limbic system, causing the student to retreat to protect himself. The fancy term for shadow kids is low socioeconomic status (SES). A low-SES child is deemed to bring less knowledge to school than the high-SES child. Let us make it perfectly clear that the achievement gap is not function of race, ethnicity, intelligence, or poverty. Rather, the achievement gap is a function of differences, such as the student's primary language, disabilities, or even learning style. Poverty is only one of the differences that impact the achievement gap. Poverty is a viable barrier to success in school, but it can be overcome. Students from poor homes frequently face challenging circumstances that are not barriers to the sunshine child. For example, the academically diverse learner may not have a place to study, or receive proper nutrition or medical or dental care. The learner may be negatively affected by family violence or lack of adult support, or a host of other challenges that poor families face in America. These conditions, while challenging, do not necessarily dictate that shadow kids will necessarily experience school failure and eventually drop out. We have learned that poverty can be managed with warm personal regard and tough love. The obstacle of poverty and school results began in the mid 1960s with the Coleman Report. As discussed in chapter 2, the congressionally commissioned study mistakenly overplayed the negative effects of poverty on students. Until quite recently, the Department of Education inaccurately perpetuated the mistaken assumption that poverty was the primary cause of the achievement gap. The question is not one of poverty but how schools can challenge students without threatening the academically diverse learner. In my view, the students who come to school not ready to learn are not handicapped; rather, they are just different. Some are students who do not speak English fluently, others are identified as special education learners, while still others are students who live in poverty, have a unique learning style, are medically fragile or impaired, or are behaviorally disabled. The point is that many students who attend public schools are not ready to learn when they get there.

The previous discussion about barriers suggests that students in an SBS should be given an opportunity to set their own goals. It is not unreasonable to suggest that given correct incentives students may set higher goals for themselves than the schools set. Let me say more. In a traditional school it is relatively common for students to just get by, especially during the senior year or anytime they can get away with it. Contrary to popular belief, the vast majority of American high school students want much tougher academic standards and even stricter discipline in the classroom, according to a survey of 1,000 public high school students by the New York-based Public Agenda Foundation.[24] In the traditional school most American teenagers feel they are essentially "living down" low expectations placed upon them by their schools. Two-thirds of them admit they could do a far better job if they tried, according to the survey. A report on the survey, "Getting By: What American Teenagers Really Think," turns a popular perception on its head by showing that high school students are nearly as concerned as parents and teachers over falling standards and lax discipline in schools.[25] "Half of the teens in public schools today told us their schools fail to challenge them to do their best, although 96% of the students say they want to excel," states Deborah Wadsworth, executive director of the Public Agenda Foundation. "America's teenagers are crying out for help," concludes Wadsworth. "They are telling us something we should already know—that by asking less, we get less. If we ask more, on the other hand, they will respond. Perhaps teenagers are merely marking time until we adults show that we value academic achievement and civil and ethical behavior as much as we value celebrity status, athletic prowess, or financial success."[26] It is extremely challenging to teach students when they do care, and next to impossible when they don't. And that is a key consideration in an SBS. The traditional school tried to do everything for the student, and in my opinion, it had a negative effect on student interest in taking responsibility for their own success. A critically important strength of an SBS is that students can be expected to take more responsibility for their own educational success. During a recent class in teaching methods, we had a lengthy conversation about student motivation and as the class was breaking up, I heard one of the students say, "I only wish I could invent a motivation pill so I could become rich." Suddenly I realized that I had failed to make the key point to this student. The point is that students don't need a motivation pill, because they are already motivated. Humans by nature are already motivated. We are organic systems, not mechanical ones. In other words, inputs of energy, sunlight, food, water, and oxygen are transformed into outputs of behavior, including physical, emotional, and even intellectual behavior. Motivation is already available to teachers because it comes quite naturally to humans. Therefore the key is to create an environment within every classroom where students are inherently motivated to achieve the academic goals embraced by their teacher and school. This is a long journey that begins with the step of giving students more responsibility for their own education.

THE INSIDE–OUT APPROACH

The key direction in establishing a standards-based school is both interpersonal and intrapersonal. It is intrapersonal in that teachers must examine their core principles to ensure that they align with the core principles described in this book. This is internal work. The teacher must start with self, thereby modeling the correct path for the learner. Then the work becomes interpersonal, meaning it is with the student. As we convert intrapersonal work to interpersonal work I use the work alchemy. Alchemy was a medieval belief that with special powers one could convert base metals to gold. A more contemporary meaning is to transform something common into something precious. As I use the word here, alchemy is intended to mean transforming an academically diverse learner (shadow kid) into a successful student (when measured against the standards). A value is something you believe. A principle is the collection of many values. Therefore this discussion aims at principles. The principles that I share here go beyond technique. Using technique to design and establish a high-performance SBS will not work because techniques are too small and not powerful enough. The changes that I describe require an inside–out strategy. The technique would be like cramming for a test; you might pass the test but there is no real long-term knowledge.

THE ALCHEMY OF RESPONSIBILITY:
INVOLVE THE ACADEMICALLY DIVERSE LEARNER

Motivating children to learn is a challenge for all schools. Often schools do too much for their students. And in doing so, the school loses its chance to incite each individual student to action. There can be no doubt that schools seized the motivational mantle for all of the correct reasons. Schools wanted to make learning simple, enjoyable, and fun, but in the process the students' incentives have been usurped. Being motiveless, the students passively choose to take the easy way. Experienced educators know that if they want student behavior then the strategy is to reward that behavior. Behaviorists teach us that intrinsic rewards are the strongest because the behavior is reinforcing itself. On the other hand, extrinsic rewards are weaker because the rewards are not an integral part of the behavior. We hope that our students will become intrinsically motivated to meet the academic standards, but our use of compulsory attendance, grades, and other extrinsic motivators takes it out of students' hands and leaves motivation to the teacher. When teachers do too much for students academically, students are inversely motivated to attain academic success. Students will automatically delegate their academic success to the teacher, and it will not work for the academically diverse learner. Therefore, I like the phrase "classrooms where more learning occurs than teaching." In an SBS, the teacher should be more of a guide on the side than a sage on the stage. In a standards-based classroom, the organization should be decentralized, that is to say the class should be more student-centered than teacher-directed.

Everyone agrees high academic standards are good, but few educators will say they know how to ensure all students can meet the standards. The following five reasons are the basis for that statement:

1. Teachers have never been asked to reach such high goals, especially with every child.
2. Schools are not organized for the success of all students.
3. Educators are not trained in how to develop an SBS.
4. Our communities do not support children enough.
5. NCLB is a deficiency-based law.

Cultural Competence

While the texture of the world has been changing, the core principles upon which America was founded remain strong and unchanged. At the time of President Garfield's election, the United States was nothing more than a fledgling eagle with clipped wings. As America matured, the core principles were reexamined and even tested. Today more than at any other time, the United States has it in its hands to educate each child to reach high academic standards. It is not a matter of ability. It is a matter of will. Public policy, especially at the federal level, seems to strongly suggest that as a nation we do not value education enough to give it a high priority. While our leaders say we value education, we fund other priorities like the military. I cannot say if our core principles as a people are changing. What I see by way of NCLB, however, gives me little solace. The teachers cannot wait for the government, which framed NCLB, to help. We must begin to build the strongest SBSs the world has ever seen, but to do that we have to look at the achievement gap though the lens of social dominance. Gary Howard voiced it this way: "Whereas the 20th century was an era of winning access for all people who had heretofore been excluded from the full benefits of citizenship, so the 21st century must be dedicated to assuring success for the children of the same groups of people."[27]

Students of history understand that the great civilizations contribute to the universal good through enlightenment and generosity more than through the killing and destruction of war. How history will view the next several years with regard to the priorities of this great nation, I do not know. However, I am not consoled by what I see. It is obvious to observers that America's youth, along with the aged, ill, and poor, are far too frequently left without the help that this nation can surely afford. I do not know what will happen to our youth if we simply cast this generation adrift with only pithy proclamations about the importance of education and high standards. This country cannot deplete our storehouse of the vastness of human resources. Gary R. Howard, in his paper "Leadership for Equity and Diversity: Engaging Significant Passages," has said, "The achievement gap is an unhealed wound on the heart of America. We are losing the lifeblood of the diversity of future generations at a rate that is unsustainable and culturally depleting."[28] Over time, our nation has borrowed billions for war and spent a pittance in comparison on educating our youth for civility. I know that rich nations win wars while righteous nations enhance civilization. In my first book, *Love 'Em and Lead 'Em*, I wrote that never has there been a nation wealthy enough to adequately fund both war and civility at the same time. That thought reminds me of a line from an old script: "D' ye think th' colleges has much to do with the progress of the world?" asked Mr. Hennessy. "D' ye think,"said Mr. Dooley, "'tis the mill that makes the water run?"[29] It is education that makes democracies and free nations run like the waters. Are we so confident that we can stay free by forsaking what (education) got us here? I cannot point to a time when war has ever enhanced civilization. I have heard it argued, correctly, that war has saved our freedom. But, at the same time, it is education that perpetuates our freedom through understanding, character development, and tolerance. War appears to be the way in which America defends freedom, while education should be the vehicle through which our nation perpetuates our belief in honesty, generosity, compassion, spirituality, even enlightened civility. I fear Henry Ward Beecher was accurately predicting our fate when he wrote, "The ignorant classes are the dangerous classes. Ignorance is the womb of all monsters."[30] War, not education, breeds hate and ignorance. The key question is, what should be given the highest priority; what values should drive this great nation? It is clearly a moral dilemma that is devilishly difficult to resolve to the satisfaction of all. I am not stating that there is a correct answer, only that we apparently need to resolve this diffuse dilemma with more than words of paternalistic panache.

It is apparent that we repeatedly try to serve both masters, which means that those without political voice (poor children) on the battlefield of despair and disillusionment do not get the support they need. Unfortunately that political strategy works for those who have the faculties to speak with power for themselves. While voicing concern about this very dilemma Jonathan Kozol truculently portrayed the priority gap when he wrote, "One would never have thought that children in America would ever have to choose between a teacher or a playground or sufficient toilet paper. Like grain in a time of famine, the immense resources which this nation does in fact possess goes not to the child in the greatest need, but to the child of the highest bidder—the child of parents who, more frequently than not, have enjoyed the same abundance when they were schoolchildren."[31] I do not believe there is any evidence that the federal government will successfully lead schools out of this labyrinth of desperation and disillusionment.

A Call to Efficacy

It is not helpful for school supporters to look to government for help because it is a trap. We can either agonize or organize. We need to believe in ourselves. That is where we must begin, with efficacy, which is a sense that we have personal and community potency. The question is: Do we have the capacity to stop whining and start winning? Schools will never improve if left to just government or the teachers. Simply said, the key is to recruit the caring forces in our respective communities. That does not take more resources, although it would be nice to feel the support as expressed through resources. The simple fact is that resources may well get in the way of making the meaningful alliances that will ensure success. Educators must have courageous patience, because it is patience, not politics, that defines the correct direction. What does that mean? In short, it means that we already have what we need to succeed, but we must mobilize the amity forces in the community into a great educational revolution of caring and compassion.

How can capacities that our children have that spell a victory for them and also for this republic be enhanced and pursued? That is where this book comes in. This book is designed to be interactive. We will continue to enhance our understanding of the issues in order to be successful in fully educating our children and helping them to reach their intellectual capacity. The core question being pursued in this book is: What are the conditions that must be created to close the achievement gap? In addressing this question we will never lose sight of the reality that the achievement gap resulted from a process that is deep, pervasive, and multidimensional. With societal problems there is a tendency to look for quick and easy solutions. For example, much of the hope of NCLB apparently rests in school choice and simple sanctions. Not only is there significant evidence of public skepticism but penalties and leaving most school decisions to the free market are overly simplistic solutions that don't recognize the complex realities of social dominance. The key issue with NCLB then is that to rely on such single-strategy approaches will obscure the deeper complexity of both the problems and the solutions. I found the Committee for Economic Development (CED) to be on target when its members wrote, "We call for a systematic reappraisal of the way our nation prepares children to become capable adults and urge the development of a comprehensive and coordinated human investment strategy for child development and education. Our nation must take on the difficult challenge of ensuring that all children have the opportunity to develop their fullest capacity for citizenship and productive work."[32]

THE ALCHEMY OF ALIGNED PRIORITIES

During 2002, the year prior to the U.S. war with Iraq, almost every state in the union struggled to adequately fund social needs of all kinds, including education. In the northwestern portion of the United States, for instance, almost every urban district in the state of Oregon was cutting school days because of a massive budget shortfall. That was on top of salary freezes and cuts to athletics, the arts, physical education, libraries, technology, and even instructional resources. In Oregon and across this nation, expectations are on the rise for public schools, yet resources are dwindling. We cannot continue to snivel and whine while wringing our hands because the resource gap seems to ensure failure. The simple fact is that the resources that the United States does in fact possess have been earmarked for higher priorities. The dilemma is how the United States should spend the resources it surely does have.

At the public-policy level, it is a difficult dilemma. Let me point out how needed resources are currently being used. Statistics gathered from the Council for a Livable World and from the Center for Defense Information show that in May 2003 the administration asked Congress for a $3 billion increase in defense spending, raising the 2004 defense budget from $396 billion to $399 billion. Even for the richest nation in the world that is a staggering sum, especially when our children are not being educated to world-class standards. Further information gathered from the Center for Defense Information shows our largest enemies are not spending anywhere near as much on the military. For example, the U.S. military budget is more than twice the military budget of all the potential adversaries—including Iran, Iraq, Libya, North Korea, Cuba, Sudan, and Syria—combined. The American military budget is greater than the output of the combined domestic economies of more than one-third of the individual nations in the world. Do we have the capacity to fund war and civility simultaneously? If the United States does have the capacity, it certainly seems to lack the will. This is no secret.

In less than 9 months during 2001 our nation dedicated more than a trillion dollars to tax relief and another trillion to the victims of September 11, and we are well on our way to dedicating another trillion for nation building in Iraq. Would it be fair to say that the survival and success of our nation's youth demand an equal investment? Yet the resources will not be available to buy our way into school success. The resource we have is human capital. I believe that we will not adequately fund schools for at least a number of fundamental reasons: (1) a comprehensive human resource strategy is deemed too expensive; (2) we do not care enough; and (3) schools are vulnerable to take the blame. All of that can be cooked down to priorities that do not match our contemporary needs or our historical principles.

Let's review, briefly, the dilemma that exists in this country. Very recently, the United States had the opportunity to invest in civility, but we chose differently. Instead, the elected federal officials chose to increase defense spending by $3 billion. It is important to understand that cuts in military spending would not have been necessary. Without cuts, the United States' defense expenditure is still more than $300 billion, which is larger than that of our two largest enemies combined. If there was the inclination, the United States could have funded four critically important priorities that address civility. Specifically, America has the capacity to address humanity significantly, without cutting defense.

- Reduce class size in every classroom in this nation to 15 students to one teacher (it would cost $11 billion annually).
- Offer health insurance to all children in the United States without it (the cost would be $6 billion annually).
- Provide Head Start programs to all eligible children and Early Head Start to all children living in poverty for a cost of $8 billion annually.
- Make housing assistance available to one million eligible families ($5 billion).

Poverty Mandates Failure: Myth

Do students from poverty have equity of opportunity in an SBS? Is the SBS good for students? Can and do all students thrive in such an environment? Do all students have equity of opportunity in an SBS? Are there legitimate concerns about how the SBS impacts students, and what are the consequences of those concerns? What, if anything, can be done to ameliorate the consequences of the SBS? Given the considerable concern I raise regarding the impact of standards on students, why are they so important? The comprehensive answer is to develop a human investment strategy made up of five interdependent systems.

1. Job training and social service support for family members at the school site.
2. Early childhood education.
3. Social service support at the school site.
4. Economic development (school/business partnerships).
5. Standards-based education.

These enterprises are not seen as independent endeavors but rather they are intended to be viewed as interdependent initiatives available at the school site.

Equally inane and preposterous is the mistaken assumption that intelligence can be reduced to a number. Intelligence quotient (IQ) is certainly one fascinating aspect of intelligence, but it doesn't subsume all of the others. Educators need to avoid making the mistake of trying to reduce intelligence to a single number on some kind of rating scale. That would be akin to characterizing a football game in terms of just one statistic, say, the percent of passes completed. Indeed, the rate at which a team completes their offensive passes is often correlated to success, but not always, because there is a lot more to winning than just the number of passes completed.[33] In his inaugural lecture, Philip Adey, professor of cognition, science, and education at Kings College, University of London, urged policy makers to see education as an opportunity for developing general intelligence in the population. Referring to the result of several years of research, Adey proposed that the main purpose of school education for children between 5 and 14 years old should be the development of intelligence.[34] The experts continue to devote adequate research to achieving an acceptable definition of and establishing an assessment of intelligence.

Intelligence Is Not a Precondition of Success for Students—Intelligence Can Be Learned

"Intelligence is the outcome of many aspects of an individual's brain organization. . . . We may not be able to explain intelligence in all its glory, but we now know some of the elements of an explanation," quipped William H. Calvin in his decidedly exciting book entitled *How Brains Think: Evolving Intelligence Then and Now*.[35] The title suggests that intelligence can be taught. For example, there have been efforts to teach thinking skills. *Tactics for Thinking* was developed at McREL and used as a vehicle for the teaching of thinking. In fact, the teacher's manual states, "The teaching of thinking should be overt, teacher-directed, and part of regular classroom instruction. Overt instruction in thinking skills means that the students are explicitly taught processes for specific cognitive operations."[36] More recently, a spokesperson for the Department of Education at Kings College, University of London has argued that intelligence should be taught. In his inaugural address, professor Philip Adey argued that teaching thinking was to be the main purpose of education for schoolchildren between the ages of 5 and 14. In 2003, referring to several years of research, Adey proposed "that the main purpose of education . . . should be the development of intelligence."[37] I recently heard an experienced teacher say, talking about intellectual potential of children, "It is all in the genes; if the child's parents are not the sharpest stick in the wood pile it is unrealistic to expect much more from their children." I believe that it is foolhardy to shortchange an organ as complex as the brain. According to Amen, "The brain is the most complex organ in the universe. The brain has one billion neurons [brain cells], and a trillion supporting cells. Each nerve is connected to other cells by 20,000 connections. That is 1,000,000,000,000,000 connections in the brain, more connections than stars in the universe. And the brain uses only 20–30% of the calories consumed."[38]

As you should be able to see by now, the challenge is significant. Our children have a potential that is certainly poignantly potent. These children have a right to that chance, so therefore we as teachers must be dealers in hope. As can be plainly seen, this is not an overnight process. The total school community needs to take time and recruit support to set a long-term process in place. The problem is that in the race to meet high academic standards there is no finish line. Please let me tell you a story to amplify that statement.

More than 25 years ago, in September of a brand-new school year, the community I was working in generated a substantial financial gift for the school within the district that won a challenge race. Twenty-five schools participated. Schools were able to elect the person they wanted to run the race for their particular school. Put yourself in the place of the lucky person who finds out to your chagrin that you had been elected to represent your school in the race. On race day you can see from the track that most of the schools are wearing school colors and chanting some supporting cheer for their teacher runner. You, the runner, feel a bit of adrenaline pump into your system as you gently ease your way toward the front of your teacher competitors. Just when you least expect it, the gun goes off to signal the start of the race. To your surprise you feel yourself sprinting down the first straightaway and you can hear your family as well as your school family cheering you on. Just as you start into the first of two turns you feel pressure as someone attempts to pass you. But with the ring of cheers in your ears you press forward even harder. You manage to maintain a lead down the back straightaway but you can feel the runners gaining ground on you. Now you are in the final straightaway with a very slim lead but you press even harder. Now you can see the finish line and pray that you can hold on for just another instant. Suddenly you are over the finish line in first place. Before you can even begin to celebrate, you hear a voice from the public address system blast, "That was an awful fast lap for the first lap of a 26-mile marathon."

The reason I have asked you to put yourself in these teachers' running shoes is because this is very likely a description of every year. In the story it is doubtful the winner of the first lap would go on to win the 26-mile race because she or he made no attempt to pace and set a reasonable speed for a very long run. This is a long-term effort; creating a high-performance SBS is not a sprint, it is marathon. I want you to succeed with your students, so set a proper pace. When you get tired, ask for help—sit out a lap. The SBS will not succeed if it is left to just the school. The dilemma that we confront every day is that all of our children do not come to school ready to learn. We have to slow down to teach the "whole child." We must set a course for the long run and we need help to win even with the proper pace. I'm going to slow down here and be tough on politics and phony reformists who do not really take the time to understand deeply the probing and painful moral dilemma that teachers and administrators face every day. In my first book I wrote that the dilemma is this: if schools do not discipline their efforts and focus on the academic standards, their children will fail to meet them. The standards are high and seemingly impossible for children to reach when they are hungry or abused. Teachers will point out correctly that this child needs a breakfast. Frankly, it is devilishly difficult to argue the point. I have never found the courage or the rationale for such a valueless discussion. So it is with great energy and unconditional love that the staff collects food and sometimes even clothes to nurture the soul of the whole child. It is necessary work so children have a chance to meet the standards. The point I am making is that it is becoming increasingly clear that schools cannot simultaneously create a high-performance SBS and run social support services using energy and resources meant for books and instruction. When a school is seduced into doing both, fewer kids will meet the standards even while the teachers are running the marathon at breakneck speed. The choice between social services and academic achievement is a perplexing moral dilemma for teachers. But the simple fact is clear: educators do not have the training or the resources to do both. The whole community needs to help because, as discussed earlier in this chapter, the numbers of poor children are growing at astounding rates. In America, children are the largest cohort group living in poverty. Child poverty is not just an urban or minority problem. According to the National Center for Children Living in poverty, of the 5.2 million children under the age of 6 living in poverty in 1997, 60% lived outside urban areas, including 37% living in suburbs and 23% in rural communities.[39] Children living in poverty have a significantly more difficult time meeting high academic standards. It is a fundamental question of equity of opportunity because more children of color live in poverty than do Caucasian children. This is the crux of a major public-policy debate that could frame the context of America's survival as a nation and a culture. The issue is one of defining the challenges that face this great republic. As de Tocqueville once instructed, "It cannot be doubted that in the United States the instruction of people powerfully contributes to the support of the democratic Republic, and such, must always be the case . . . where the instruction enlightens the understanding not separated from the moral education that offends the heart."[40] America's diversity has historically been a powerful strength because the public school system has served to assimilate all children into a single group.

HOW DO SCHOOL-WIDE TEACHER EXPECTATIONS AFFECT STUDENTS' SUCCESS IN AN SBC?

All kids can learn but not in the same way or at the same rate. Children are not limited as much by their innate intelligence as they are by our lack of faith in their ability to achieve. Educators treat perceived low achievers differently than perceived high achievers and we get what we expect, and that is inherently unequal. Sam Kerman, in "Teacher Expectations and Student Achievement," wrote, "Extensive research shows that the intellectual development of the student is largely a response to what teachers expect and how they communicate those expectations. Interaction with students perceived to be low achievers is less motivating and less supportive than interaction with students perceived as high achievers."[41] This fact should not be considered an indictment of teachers, since the biases demonstrated in teacher-student interactions are, in most cases, unconscious. Discriminatory interactions can easily be identified between parents and their children, managers and their workers.

Few research studies in the field of education have generated as much attention and controversy as the study by Robert Rosenthal and Lenore Jacobson entitled *Pygmalion in the Classroom*. The title was taken from the following quotation from George Bernard Shaw: "The difference between a flower girl and a lady is not how she behaves but how she is treated. I shall always be a flower girl to Professor Higgins, because he always treats me as a flower girl, and always will; but I know I can be a lady to you, because you always treat me like a lady, and always will."[42] The original Pygmalion study involved giving teachers false information about the learning potential of certain students in grades 1 through 6 in a San Francisco elementary school. Teachers were told these students had been tested and found to be on the brink of a period of rapid intellectual growth; in reality, the students had been selected at random. At the end of the experimental period, the targeted students exhibited performance on IQ tests that was superior to other students of

similar ability and superior to what would have been expected of the targeted students.[43] Those results led researchers to claim that the inflated
expectations teachers held for students actually caused students to experience higher rates of intellectual growth.[44]

Few research studies have caused as much consternation among educators and researchers, and the general public, as the Pygmalion
study. Theorists argued about the validity of the psychological effects of
expectations. Researchers set up studies attempting to replicate the
findings of Rosenthal and Jacobson. In the 1970s, the popular press began to blame school failure on the low expectations of teachers. Other
more positive approaches suggested that student performance in
school would improve if teachers and parents held high expectations
for their students. The consternation about the power of expectations
ultimately led to additional studies. Some, as you might imagine, confirmed the findings of the Pygmalion study, while others did not. Mean-
while the popular press, for the most part, continued to treat the Pygmalion findings as scientific fact, casting aspersions on teachers for the
failure of some children to learn, suggesting that teachers' low expectations were either creating or sustaining the problem.[45] Whether one
is inclined to accept the findings of the Pygmalion study or not, it is
clear that many educators and parents are interested in the potential of
expectancy research. The key question in the self-fulfilling prophecy
literature (as it came to be called) remains a central focus of this book.
The question is, what is the relationship between student achievement
in an SBS and expectations? The thesis of this theory is that expectations can have a major impact on the academic success of the shadow
kid. The expectations we hold for the children that are being left behind clearly have an effect on academic performance. Every report or
study this writer has examined concluded that high expectations for
students are central characteristics of effective schools. The power of
expectations that individual teachers hold for their children is more
pronounced when the belief in student potential is expressed school-
wide. Low-achieving schools are typically found to be lacking these beliefs about human potential. Expectations are very important in developing an SBC that is effective in meeting high academic standards. If
the school is to use the full power of expectations, then there needs to
be a partnership with the home. Previous research has indicated that

adolescents are influenced by their mother's academic expectations and achievement. In a recent study the academic expectations of the mother were found to be highly correlated (positively) with academic achievement. Not surprisingly, both marijuana and cocaine use had a strong negative effect on academic achievement. In summary, expectations are 7% of the variance. Not surprisingly, "The research on academic achievement determined that a mother's expectations were significant predictors of success."[46]

As you ponder the tools given you in this book and the exercises below, consider this example for introducing a program that will effectively help to establish the trust and caring environment so needed to facilitate a child's well-being and encourage phenomenal intellectual growth. I once observed a high school in Milwaukie, Oregon, pursue such a support effort, using the positive behaviors of children and families to reach less fortunate children (those who lived in negative environments and associated with negative peers), and the results were amazing. The program was called Caring for Kids Effectively (CaKE). My hunch is that the program did more for the adults than the students. Try it; you will benefit beyond your expectations.

SUMMARY

Historically the public schools in America were among the most highly regarded in the world; nevertheless, the public withdrew their support of schools. It was post–World War II America that created the politics of school reform. During those same years, the schools attracted the most diverse student population in history. The academically diverse student has clearly floundered in public schools. The National Assessment of Educational Progress (NAEP) has reported that fewer than half of all 17-year-olds will successfully develop basic skills in reading, math, and problem solving. And much of the public dissatisfaction is related to the schools' apparent inability to educate all students to high academic levels. The gap between the successful and unsuccessful students has been identified in the media as the achievement gap. We know that no act of kindness toward a student is ever wasted. When a teacher gives something to a child it is given forever. Tommy Stoddard (the fictitious boy in the 5th-grade class 15 years prior) was just such a boy. The touching story is intended to remind us that everything is possible with all children; the caring we give children never stops giving.

For a lengthy period of time, the Department of Education perpetuated a destructive, almost inflammatory myth. The myth was supported by a massive research effort that had been funded by Congress and carried out by James Coleman. Coleman and Christopher Jenks, Coleman's colleague, argued voraciously for years (gobbling up the spirits of caring teachers) from the bully pulpit that schools had very little effect on a student's success in school. So little, in fact, that the SES of the family had more effect on a child's success in school than the school itself. The research was in error because the focus was on the effectiveness across whole schools, ignoring the great variations between teachers. That bit of history has left teachers, administrators, and communities alike believing that poor kids of color are not capable of exceptional academic work. The false bias is doubly hurtful because it exacerbates the history of social stratification already too prevalent and divisive. It is true that some children will take more time and need more help in achieving high academic standards, but they will meet them with strong, dedicated teachers.

This chapter began a deeper look into what it will take to be successful in restoring public confidence in your school. The possible options included herein represent an overarching, multidimensional options menu for consideration. These particular options are interventions that are not necessarily associated with just teachers. Therefore, the considerations herein are aimed at developing capacity in the school, students, and community. More than 20 research-based ideas are presented as options for consideration. Of that number there are only a few that should be considered not optional. The framework for the school improvement plan (SIP) is brief and should always drive how much you try to do both as a school and as individuals. The framework included for the SIP is as follows: the individual components of the SIP should be severely limited and deemed to build on the strengths of your school. Decisions should be by consensus. An evaluation of each component of the plan should coincide with the implementation of the idea and be used at specified intervals to determine if the intervention met your stated outcomes. This measure may be either objective or subjective. In this particular situation, subjective approaches work well. Most include satisfaction measures of program participants. The satisfaction criteria should be developed ahead of implementation and used to gauge effectiveness. Objectivity should be defined and stressed.

It is significant for you, your students, and your community to know that you have the knowledge and skills to facilitate the student achievement of standards. The facts are these: it should be assumed that the individual teachers in your school have a profound effect on student learning. The only obstacle is the need for additional teamwork (which the SIP should define). Therefore this book does not focus specifically on the teacher until later.

The standards-based school (SBS) grew out of growing community dissatisfaction in the 1970s and early 1980s. In an SBS, each school is expected to demonstrate high academic standards through performance-based assessments. The academic expectations are functions of school community consensus, and they are made clear to all before instruction begins. It is significant to note that there is a feeling of distrust in standards because they are bully-based. I called the standards bully-based, because teachers frequently view the standards as too high and too numerous. Further, they are superimposed from the top down by government. Finally, the standards have not been funded, and the assessments are quite rigid and deficiency based. It has been conventional in schools to try to fix what is wrong to meet the standards—be it the curriculum, the parents, or the students—and it has become problematic because it is in stark contrast to the working of the open limbic system of the brain. The open limbic system is in the primitive brain, and it was designed millions of years ago to sense threat and to take action to survive (i.e., fight, flight, or freeze) if challenged. The learning potential of school-induced trauma could not be worse. The open limbic system was also designed to produce a warm, safe, nurtured feeling, which creates willingness and a desire to learn. That reaction defines the purpose of the limbic system. That is the outcome we are seeking with the use of the following question: How can I motivate my students without threatening them? The steps that create the conditions that stimulate youth development by building on strengths are:

1. Surround youth with positive influences.
2. Build on the strengths of the youth.

3. Support youth with as many before- and after-school programs as possible.
4. Assist and support parents by involving them.
5. Engender positive peer support.
6. Use the question "How can I motivate students without threatening them?" to design your school for success.
7. Involve youth in constructive activities outside of school.
8. Design the SIP to maximize trust.

The debate about whether intelligence is a function of nurture or nature has been addressed by the science of brain development research. The scientific conclusion has been reached and it is hopeful news for teachers and parents because we now know that intelligence can be learned. All of the powerful preceding points lead to the salient conclusion: expectations are indelibly linked to academic and behavioral performance of students.

QUESTIONS FOR DELIBERATION

1. Why do diverse learners, shadow kids, see the standards as a threat?

2. What could be done in your school to ensure that any student who did not have adequate support felt supported? Do you believe this is an important question? What is your rationale?

3. Please list the five highest core beliefs you hold regarding how your school can improve.

4. Earlier in this chapter you were invited to select a limited number of activities to include in the school improvement plan for your school. List your three highest priorities and discuss the needs of the school. How do your activities address your core beliefs?

5. The power of one: what would happen if every child that needed support and couldn't get it from any other source could get that support at school?

6. What would happen if every adult in the school agreed to provide support to a shadow child in the school? The support would be in the form of an "I care" intervention, rather than academic tutoring. Can you

imagine how much the test scores would improve? Better yet, can you imagine how good the adults would feel? The achievement gap will eventually be closed, not because of the sanctions in NCLB, but rather because of the caring forces within each school—tough love has immeasurable power.

NOTES

1. Jenny Smith, *Education and Public Health: Natural Partners in Learning for Life*, (Alexandria, Va.: Association for Supervision and Curriculum Development, 2003), 4.

2. Cited in Robert J. Marzano, Debra J. Pickering, and Jane E. Pollock, *Classroom Instruction That Works*, (Alexandria, Va.: Association for Supervision and Curriculum Development, 2001), 3.

3. Marzano et al., *Classroom Instruction That Works*.

4. Marzano et al., *Classroom Instruction That Works*.

5. Charlotte Danielson, *Enhancing Professional Practice: A Framework for Teaching*, (Alexandria, Va.: Association for Supervision and Curriculum Development, 1996), 61.

6. Daniel Amen, *Change Your Brain, Change Your Life*, (New York: Three Rivers Press, 1998), 69.

7. Cited in Amen, *Change Your Brain, Change Your Life*, 69.

8. Amen, *Change Your Brain, Change Your Life*, 68–69.

9. Daniel Goleman, Richard Boyatzis, and Annie McKee, *Primal Leadership: Realizing the Power of Emotional Intelligence*, (Boston: Harvard Business School Press, 2002), 33.

10. Cited in Amen, *Change Your Brain, Change Your Life*, 69.

11. Arthur Combs, "New Concepts of Human Potential: Challenge for Teachers," in *Four Psychologies Applied to Education*, Thomas B. Roberts, ed., (New York: Schenkman Publishing Company, 1975), 302.

12. Marcus Buckingham and Curt Coffman, *Now Discover Your Strengths*, (New York: Free Press, 2001), 32.

13. Raymond V. Hand, ed., *American Quotations*, (New York: Random House, 1989), 208.

14. Quoted in Robert J. Marzano and John S. Kendall, "A Comprehensive Guide to Designing Standardized-Based Districts, School Classrooms," http://www.ascd.org/publications/books/1996marzano/1996marzanotoc.html, [accessed 9 Sept. 2002], 13.

15. Cited in Marzano and Kendall, "A Comprehensive Guide to Designing Standardized-Based Districts, School Classrooms," 14.

16. Quoted in Marzano and Kendall, "A Comprehensive Guide to Designing Standardized-Based Districts, School Classrooms," 15.

17. Hsien-Hen Lu, "Ending Childhood Poverty," National Center for Children in Poverty at the Joseph L. Mailman School of Public Health at Columbia University, http://www.nccp.org/pub_ecp02.html, [accessed 15 Aug. 2004].

18. U.S. Census Bureau, "Poverty Thresholds 2003," http://www.census.gov/hhes/poverty/threshld/thresh03.html, [accessed 15 Aug. 2004].

19. Lu, "Early Childhood Poverty: A Statistical Profile (2002)."

20. Cited in Combs, "New Concepts of Human Potential: Challenge for Teachers," in *Four Psychologies Applied to Education*, 299.

21. Combs, "New Concepts of Human Potential: Challenge for Teachers," in *Four Psychologies Applied to Education*, 300.

22. Sam Kerman, "Teacher Expectations and Student Achievement," *Kappan*, June 1979.

23. Amen, *Change Your Brain, Change Your Life*, 68.

24. Cited in Ann Scott Tyson, "Just Getting By: High Schoolers Say the Path to a Diploma is Too Easy," HBSCO HOST: *Research Databases*, 1997, http://web16.wpnet.com/citation.asp?tb=1&_ug=dbs, [accessed 18 June 2003], 1.

25. Tyson, "Just Getting By," 1.

26. Quoted in Tyson, "Just Getting By," 2.

27. Gary R. Howard, "Leadership for Equity and Diversity: Engaging Significant Passages," (paper presented at the 36th annual IDEA Fellows Program, Denver, Colo., 6 July 2003), 6.

28. Howard, "Leadership for Equity and Diversity: Engaging Significant Passages," 7.

29. Hand, ed., *American Quotations*, 204.

30. Hand, ed., *American Quotations*, 204.

31. Jonathan Kozol, *Savage Inequalities*, (New York: Crown Publishers, 1991), 79.

32. Committee for Economic Development, "Unfinished Agenda: A New Vision for Child Development and Education," in a Statement by the Research and Policy Committee, New York: 1991, 4.

33. William H. Calvin, *How Brains Think: Evolving Intelligence Then and Now*, (New York: Basic Books, a member of Perseus Books Group, 1996), 11.

34. Philip Adey, "Can Intelligence Be Taught," *Kings College, University of London*, 2003, http://www.kcl.ac.uk/phpnews/mview.php?ArtID=63, [accessed 22 Jan. 2003], 1.

35. Calvin, *How Brains Think: Evolving Intelligence Then and Now*, 10.

36. Robert Marzano and Daisey Arredondo, "Tactics for Thinking: Teachers Manual," (Aurora, Colo.: Mid-Continent Regional Educational Laboratory, 1986), 1.

37. Adey, "Can Intelligence Be Taught," *Kings College, University of London*, 1.

38. Daniel Amen, "Brain Science Research Matters in Mental Health," (paper presented at Meeting of Clinicians in Portland, Ore., March 2003), 1.

39. "High Poverty Among Young Makes Schools' Jobs Harder," *Education Week*, 2000, http://www.edweek.org/ew/ewstory.cfm?slug=04centPov.h20, [accessed 24 Dec. 2002].

40. Hand, ed., *American Quotations*, 29.

41. Kerman, "Teacher Expectations and Student Achievement," 1.

42. Quoted in Kathleen Cotton, "Expectations and Student Achievement," in *School Improvement Series*, (Portland, Ore.: Northwest Regional Educational Laboratory, 1988), 1.

43. Cotton, "Expectations and Student Achievement," in *School Improvement Series*, 1.

44. Cotton, "Expectations and Student Achievement," in *School Improvement Series*, 1.

45. Cotton, "Expectations and Student Achievement," in *School Improvement Series*, 2.

46. Tyson, "Just Getting By," 16.

5

THE COURAGE TO CARE

Courage is the capacity to confront what can be imagined.

—Leo Ralston

You take a number of small steps which you believe are right, thinking maybe tomorrow somebody will treat this as a dangerous provocation. And then you wait. If there is no reaction, you take another step: courage is only an accumulation of small steps.

—George Konrád

There has been a great deal said and written about courage, probably because one cannot face the difficult challenges in life without courage. It is absolutely awesome to know that you have one of the most, if not the most, important attributes necessary to close the achievement gap. I am relatively confident in making that statement because you are reading and studying even while your professional life at school may be anything but pleasant. The point is, whether you are new or experienced you are still teaching, and that alone is the confirmation that you have the courage to care—congratulations! Please know that I am very grateful to you, and so also will this nation be justifiably grateful to you for saving public schools (and in the process the middle class and the republic) in America.

My purpose in this book has been to remind you of how far you have already come. Now my job is to help you to see the prolific talent that you have yet to use. Hope is the anchor of the soul. As Bertrand Russell once wrote, "Extreme hopes are born of extreme misery."[1] I realize that you have suffered and through that suffering has been forged the strength of character for the next steps. While they may be small, they will be measured steps—all. Truly, even with the new research on the brain, no one really knows what is possible. Consider the following story. Jamie Castellano, special education instructor and lecturer, while giving a presentation recently on higher level thinking, started the presentation with the following riddle:

> I start with a "V" and end with a "T"
> When I talk, there's something you cannot see
> I can sound near; I can sound far,
> It takes a very good eye, from a woman or a guy
> To know what I am
> Can you tell?[2]

Well-educated adults pondered and puzzled the riddle, but in the end they remained befuddled. The adult audience was as startled as I to find that the answer to the riddle, written by a 5th-grade student with a learning disability, is ventriloquist. What is possible? Who can say? What follows is a story of hope and the goodness of kids. Importantly, never underestimate the power of your actions. With one small gesture you can change a person's life.

Hope and Efficacy

One day, when I was a freshman in high school, I saw a kid from my class walking home from school. His name was Kyle. It looked like he was carrying all of his books. I thought to myself, "Why would anyone bring home all his books on a Friday?" He must really be a nerd.

I had quite a weekend planned (parties and a football game with my friends tomorrow afternoon), so I shrugged my shoulders and went on. As I was walking, I saw a bunch of kids running toward him. They ran at him, knocking all his books out of his arms and tripping him so he landed in the dirt. His glasses went flying, and I saw them land in the grass about ten feet from him.

He looked up and I saw this terrible sadness in his eyes. My heart went out to him. So, I jogged over to him and as he crawled around looking for his glasses, I saw a tear in his eye.

As I handed him his glasses, I said, "Those guys are jerks. They really should get lives."

He looked at me and said, "Hey, thanks!" There was a big smile on his face. It was one of those smiles that showed real gratitude.

I helped him pick up his books, and asked him why I had never seen him before. He said he had gone to private school before now. I would never have hung out with a private school kid before.

We talked all the way home, and I carried some of his books. He turned out to be a pretty cool kid. I asked him if he wanted to play a little football with my friends.

He said, "Yes."

We hung out all weekend and the more I got to know Kyle, the more I liked him, and my friends thought the same of him.

Monday morning came, and there was Kyle with the huge stack of books again. I stopped him and said, "Boy, you are gonna really build some serious muscles with this pile of books every day!"

He just laughed and handed me half the books.

Over the next four years, Kyle and I became best friends. When we were seniors, we began to think about college. Kyle decided on Georgetown, and I was going to Duke. I knew that we would always be friends, that the miles would never be a problem. He was going to be a doctor, and I was going for business on a football scholarship.

Kyle was valedictorian of our class. I teased him about being a nerd. He had to prepare a speech for graduation. I was so glad it wasn't me having to get up there and speak.

On graduation day, I saw Kyle. He looked great. He was one of those guys that really found himself during high school. He filled out and actually looked good in glasses. He had more dates than I had and all the girls loved him. Boy, sometimes I was jealous.

I could see that he was nervous about his speech. So, I smacked him on the back and said, "Hey, big guy, you'll be great!"

He looked at me with one of those looks (the really grateful one) and smiled. "Thanks," he said.

As he started his speech, he cleared his throat, and began.

"Graduation is a time to thank those who helped you make it through those tough years: your parents, your teachers, your siblings, maybe a

coach, but mostly your friends. . . . I am here to tell all of you that being a friend to someone is the best gift you can give them. I am going to
tell you a story."

I just looked at my friend with disbelief as he told the story of the first
day we met. He had planned to kill himself over the weekend. He talked
of how he had cleaned out his locker so his Mom wouldn't have to do it
later and was carrying his stuff home.

He looked hard at me and gave me a little smile.

"Thankfully, I was saved. My friend saved me from doing the unspeak-
able."

I heard the gasp go through the crowd as this handsome, popular boy
told us all about his weakest moment. I saw his mom and dad looking at
me and smiling that same grateful smile. Not until that moment did I realize its depth.

*Never underestimate the power of your actions. With one small ges-
ture you can change a person's life* [author emphasis]: for better or for
worse. God puts us all in each other's lives to impact one another in
some way.[3]

THE SCHOOL IMPROVEMENT PLAN MADE EASY: MENU OF OPTIONS

As I stated previously, you have the most important attribute necessary
to begin your journey toward making an impact on students today and
in the field of education: you care. As you take the next step in this
journey you will need to begin to develop your school improvement
plan (SIP), bringing into your circle the other teachers and support
staff in your school, the leaders, the parents, and the students. The following menu of options and the activities listed in the Appendixes will
help to facilitate this transition from conventional teaching methods to
a standards-based approach.

- Select an option that makes sense (for your school): The ideas that
  have been presented in this book are only options for your consideration. They can be viewed as a menu of possibilities. Like when
  you choose from the menu at a restaurant, you will typically choose
  what is nutritionally attractive plus pick what fits your hunger

needs at the moment. The criteria I recommend are based on which options are natural extensions of your strengths. In other words, consider those options that are possible, desirable, and attainable. Now, decide and move!

- Start small and focus your work: Create a vision of excellence defined as the best that can be imagined for your school in five years. Be practical! Then select only those options that will move your school in that direction. Select those interventions that are possible, desirable, and attainable.
- Evaluate the school's progress based on academic measures: Develop an evaluation process before implementation. The assessment criteria are whether you bridge the gap between where you are and where you want to be. Is the intervention what you expected? Who is it helping? How do you know, and why?

I ask you to consider a caution. I have had the good fortune to be an administrator in extremely desirable places to work. The few vacancies that we had each year always attracted the very best, which made the selection decisions an act of pure joy. Over the years we were fortunate to hire extremely motivated and talented educators. As talented as these candidates were, I began to notice that they all made the same serious mistake early into their tenure. I am not sure why the error was so repetitive with this particular group. Maybe it was because they were too grateful for getting a chance to work with us, maybe it was just a characteristic of someone who had excelled to such a great degree, or maybe it was just the lack of self-control or the lack of powers to discriminate. The purpose of the error is not what is relevant here. What is relevant is that they all tried to do too much. Each said that it just kind of crept up quietly on them without their clear appreciation for what was happening to them. That thought and my desire for you to focus your effort reminds me of an old farm fable.

Every day the boy would carry the calf up the mountain to the pasture and down again in the evening. At first, the little calf weighed a few pounds, but each day the calf gained a pound or two—an inconsequential amount, a modest increment the boy could easily manage. As the calf continued to grow into a cow, however, the boy continued to carry it up the mountain despite its immense weight of 1,500 pounds. It was an extraordinary load, but since the boy had been carrying the calf from its infancy and because the daily increment was negligible, it became possible for the boy to carry an animal 10 times his own weight up the mountain.

Use the teamwork approach and watch out for other members of the team. Select just a few important projects and do them well. Use the following steps to guide you as you keep academic progress in mind.

1. Decide what to do that meets the school's needs the best.
2. Learn how to do it.
3. Create a consensus decision on how to proceed.
4. Once you know what and how to proceed, decide what success would look like. Determine what is your collective vision of the best that can be imagined for your school.
5. Evaluate your relative satisfaction as it relates to the results that had been anticipated. Subjective and objective satisfaction data are fine. I am well aware of the long-standing debate as to the relative merits of the two. In my experience, some of the best data were teacher judgment.
6. Use the data that you collect to regenerate (revise) the SIP at appropriate intervals (approximately 5 years).

CAPACITY-BASED CORE BELIEFS ARE A PRECONDITION OF SUCCESSES FOR EVERYTHING ELSE

The first SIP option to think deeply about is your core beliefs. As you review the four following beliefs, examine them to determine if they describe your beliefs. If they do, I am persuaded that the most difficult work of mental preparation is already complete. If so, you are now ready to fly high. The caution I would give is that, while the beliefs seem simple, they become complex in application. The challenge for you is to own the beliefs so deeply that the application is comfortable, satisfying, and natural. Core beliefs, like the soul, are invisible, yet they always illuminate the naturally correct pathway. If you wander too far off the course it will be your beliefs that help you find the proper pathway again. Much of what has been provided about people, possibility, and potential can more readily be built on the foundation of the following beliefs.

Beliefs Option

I believe in challenge without threat. That is a remarkable statement! The challenge becomes one of finding ways of challenging our students without threatening them. What kind of world and school could we create when we learn how to challenge our students without threatening them? This is a riddle that must, necessarily, be solved child by child and day by day. No doubt, we will become more proficient as time goes on but to challenge without threat is an intimately individual pathway. All things are hard before they become easier. As we said in chapter 4, this is one of those occasions where we must find a way or make one. When the great explorers set sail to the New World they did not know what they were going to find. They just sailed west and adjusted as necessary until reaching a theretofore unknown destination.

I believe in strength-based teaching. To approach our students as a learning facilitator who teaches a child how to build on their own strengths is one of the most effective ways to develop a challenging, yet nonthreatening relationship. I believe that kids should come first. There is power in moral purpose and positive discrimination. I encourage you to discriminate and make every decision based on what is good exclusively for kids. When your school is organized more for the kids than for the adults, you will have a high-performance school.

I believe in the power of positive relationships. In a standards-based school, there is no power in position, only in relationships. Relationships build trust, and trust is the lubrication that allows one to challenge without threat. Trust is also the emotional glue that sustains us as we stumble. In a manner of speaking, we are defining a kind of tough love. This is not a kind of love that is emotional or sentimental. Rather, it is the kind of caring that is expressed in the belief in our students, in a confidence in their character, and in joy in their success.

I believe in putting kids first. There is power in making kids the most important priority, which I refer to as positive discrimination. The kinetic energy that erupts by putting kids first creates a geometric doubling of possibility. Unfortunately, putting kids first has become the politically correct thing to say, often without real substance. I frequently hear educators say, "Everything in this school is about kids." With all due respect, I have observed it is almost never true. Take the school calendar, for instance. Almost every school has some type of community input process to surface community involvement in setting the annual calendar. Then, in the final analysis, vacation schedules, childcare issues, and administrative convenience are the pressures that actually drive the school calendar. If that were not true, why would we take three months off every summer? As a teacher and administrator, I would observe the expenditures of vast resources (when they were scarce to begin with) to start a new school year just to shut it down again as things were finally beginning to run smoothly. How do kids really fit into this picture? I encourage positive discrimination and making every single decision based purely on what is good for kids.

Curriculum Alignment Option

Clear academic conditions are a precondition for success in a high-performance school. Students can and will meet the academic standards if teachers, students, and their parents are clear on what the students know and should be able to do as a result of instruction. With clear written academic goals, entrance and exit requirements can be strengthened if gaps or overlaps occur in the curriculum. When the goals of the academic content are so clear that entrance and exit requirements exist between grade levels and subject areas, the conditions for more teamwork is a natural by-product. By teamwork, I mean teamwork between teachers, between home and school, and between home and work. Having clear academic goals is critically important because it takes the mystery out of school success and encourages partnerships and increased school support. It is critically important for a high-performance school to develop clear academic goals. The first step in the process is to design and implement a broad-based participatory process to align the curriculum to the content standards. Once that is achieved, every student (and adult) in every classroom should be able to learn one thing each day worth remembering for a lifetime. The planning process described herein can be used to achieve that goal.

Written Curriculum Is the Prescription for School Improvement: Strength-Based Teaching Is the Process

Curriculum Alignment: What Is It?   In an SBS, the curriculum must be performance based and standards driven. When I hear teachers talk about curriculum alignment to the community, they often dismiss its importance by saying, "That is just a fancy way of saying 'teaching to the test'!" That concern usually comes from people who are referring to a conventional school, prior to the SBS. You will remember that in the conventional school curriculum, it was customary to keep what the students needed to know a secret until the test. Frequently in the conventional system, when the students first saw the exam they also saw the academic goal for the first time. The guessing was unnecessary, unfair, and inefficient. That type of nonsensical secrecy confused nontraditional students and also contributed to the growing credibility problem. One of the key strengths of the SBS is the elimination of the secrecy around what students need to know and do to be successful in school.

The Power of a Living Curriculum   Developing a written curriculum that defines the instructional goals has inherent value in any school, but most especially in an SBS. One cannot begin to pursue becoming a high-performance school without a written curriculum. A written curriculum is a valuable road map for many reasons. The following iteration supports the need to have a written curriculum; it is not intended to be all-inclusive.

- A written curriculum establishes the base upon which the process of evaluation and revision are more effectively carried out.
- A written curriculum provides a common curriculum across all grade levels.
- A written curriculum ensures a commitment to a common understanding of student academic expectations.
- A written curriculum defines important professional growth opportunities.

- A written curriculum helps in the clarification of future budget needs.
- A written curriculum provides a basis on which the curriculum can be evaluated for meeting the academic standards.
- A written curriculum takes advantage of the best curriculum in the school.
- A written curriculum makes the academic expectations completely clear to all, thereby demystifying the connection between school-work and school success.

If the curriculum is developed, valued, and used by teachers (I call the written curriculum a living curriculum), it creates an up-to-date instructional framework through which the appropriate curriculum adjustments can be made. A written curriculum provides the basis for curriculum teamwork at powerful levels. In the conventional school, unhappily teachers, were forced to teach content in relative isolation from other teammates. The written curriculum finally gives teachers a meaningful way to work together.

It is of paramount importance that as a school community you get clear on what students are expected to know, do, and be (character development to follow) as a result of school. It is vitally important because one cannot strengthen an unwritten curriculum that is only available in the mind of individual teachers. One cannot make school-wide or system-wide curriculum changes that can make a difference if there is no consistency from classroom to classroom or school to school.

Become an Assessment Junkie

The first and most important assessment construct is that one cannot substitute accountability for responsibility. High-performance teachers must be responsible to their students and simultaneously accountable to the public. This is a deliciously delicate dance involved in balancing accountability and responsibility. We will proceed to discuss the "balance" within the three basic components of the assessment program: (1) student assessment data, which is of central importance to determine the academic progress of students; (2) program evaluation, critical to evaluate the quality of the curriculum; and (3) reporting, which establishes credibility with the important partners by reporting the results to families, community, and region or state.

Student Assessment Data   To challenge without threat makes individual student assessment tricky. Mentally picture one of your most vulnerable students as we discuss strategies for the use of individual assessment data.

- Use assessment data to determine the strengths or capacities of the student.
- The art of continuous improvement allows focus on improvement rather than the cut score.
- Publicly recognize improvement and excellence equally.
- Use assessment strategies appropriate to the learner. Not all students are proficient with a paper and pencil exam. Alternatives may include portfolios, demonstrations, expert papers, projects, and oral presentations, as well as the conventional essays and multiple choice options.
- Always celebrate results, meaning never allow a student to feel as if his or her value as a person is connected to test scores.

Program Evaluation and Data-Based Decision Making   We will use different yet similar approaches to discuss program evaluation. The most important concept is to use the data to make program improvements. I call that process data-based decision making. To use data to make decisions about program changes, the school will need a school profile. The profile would be a collection of the most important points about the school, organized into the following sections:

1. Strengths (brag points): Identify and list the strengths of the school. Consider including such things as special programs, honors, what the school is known for, and anything that puts the school in a favorable light.
2. Demographics: Include numbers of students and staff (degrees, if favorable), as well as the percentage of students in special programs, free and reduced lunch counts, attendance data, participation in after-school sponsored activities, and other data as appropriate to the demographic makeup of your school.

3. Assessment results: Attempt to compile and use three years of data. Compare the student achievement data to your school's own baseline (stress continuous progress), state and district averages, and, most importantly, other schools like yours demographically. When selecting the content for the school profile, remember that it will become the baseline for program improvement and the main vehicle through which to publicly enhance your reputation by tracking and reporting your school's journey back to community pride and support.

I suggest three data techniques that are grounded in the capacity-based belief system:

- Compare the school's results to a school that is similar demographically. The public may not be aware of it, but it takes more time and money to educate some students to high academic standards than it does others. Comparing the school to schools that are most like your school is a legitimate way to compare.
- Your school should absolutely establish a baseline and use the baseline to demonstrate improvement. Work to create a commitment to the concept of continuous improvement. This idea is the most powerful way to use capacity-based approaches to balance the challenge of test data with open limbic system threat. Over time allow the commitment to become individualized. This is important because either people improve or programs won't. Personal improvement always precedes program improvement.
- I encourage you to broaden the criteria of measuring success to areas like attendance and dropout rates; percentage of teachers certified to teach in their assigned area; parent involvement; and student discipline, including incidents of defiance, fighting, and drug possession or trafficking. I believe that the best measure of success is customer satisfaction. For example, even if a school is strong academically, but has a 4-year dropout rate of 24% (6% per year), it is unlikely the community would view this school as successful.

If the community voices strong support for academic achievement and assumes that most of the students will graduate, only to find out that most do not graduate, the community will be disappointed. If that anomaly occurs in a community that has communicated core beliefs about the importance of graduation, even though the school was doing well academically (of course, as measured by the standards), the satisfaction level would be low for parents, students, and probably staff because academic achievement was viewed as less important than the graduation rate. If you can generate an overall satisfaction rating from community, staff, and students, it frequently becomes the most important measure. A sample question could read: Do you think the school meets its academic goal? (1) never; (2) seldom; (3) sometimes; (4) most of the time; and (5) always. Comparing results across the groups is an interesting activity. Tracking the satisfaction level over time is a powerful measure of how you are doing with three very important audiences.

There are two important ways student assessment data should be used. First, the leadership team should use the student achievement data to make decisions about school goals, objectives, and activities in the school improvement plan (SIP). Second, the data is also used to measure the progress that has been made on the SIP.

Education as a Moral Purpose: Character Education I have heard the concern expressed that the standards are so high, there is little time for anything else. With that, there is also the claim that there is no time for enrichment activities or time to develop the whole child. With all due respect, I must take sharp exception to those comments. I do not believe, nor will I accept, that the school must now divorce itself from educating the whole child. Actually, in my experience the reverse has been true. High academic standards can be an impetus for developing a character education program. Character education should be aimed at traits that are universally valued in our country. The focus of the program should be identified so there is no confusion or apprehension. I believe that character education should become the basis on which schools build an SBS. The cognitive reason is just plain simple: the kids who exhibit good character do better in school academically than those who are not character driven. While it may be true that not all kids have skills and beliefs with equal certainty, all (including the adults) will be better for it. During one of our early meetings to develop a character education program one of the youth pastors made the following comment, "A rising tide lifts all boats. The program is not just for the troubled youth, but all kids benefit from these skills; they have been inoculated for life."

"Character," writes American philosophical theorist Amitai Etzioni, "is the psychological muscle that moral conduct requires."[4] In my experience, character development is at the very foundation of attaining high academic standards. The very bedrock of character is self-discipline or self-control. The keystone of character is to motivate and guide oneself, whether going on a date or a job interview, completing homework on time, paying attention in class, taking good notes, or just getting to school on time. Etzioni goes on to argue, "Schools have a central role in cultivating character inculcating self-discipline and empathy, which in turn enable true commitment to civic and moral values."[5]

Cultural Competence   With the tremendous increase in diversity that is being experienced in the school, it would seem that one should pay increased attention to commonalities that bind humankind together. Simply said, Americans need to live and advance across our differences. Without cultural competence and character development the world can be quite confusing for our children. For instance, John Goodlad wrote, "If we begin with the concept of humankind and then add the concept of diversity in addressing such democratic essentials as liberty and justice for all we embark on a slippery slope."[6] Too many students of color have not been achieving in school as well as they should (and can) for far too long. "For the 90% of educators, who grew up in predominantly white communities (in my case rural Montana), it is natural to assume that school, as it is currently constituted, works well for all students. From our assumptions of rightness, we can easily conclude that our professional judgments are correct."[7] Schools can and have been successful in meeting the challenge. When John Morefield became the principal of Hawthorne Elementary School in Seattle, Washington, the school was one of the most racially diverse and lowest income schools in the community. Nevertheless, the school assured their entering kindergarten students that they would graduate from the fifth grade with skills at or above grade level competency. Over the years the dedicated staff delivered on this promise. The approach they used is summarized in a report, "Recreating Schools for All Children." Some of the elements of the program include unity of purpose, a caring and nurturing school environment, consistent and positive discipline, a multicultural curricu-

lum, and a belief that teaching is a calling and a vocation, not just a job.[8]
As you will notice, much of the thrust of this work is a nice foundation
on which to build a program that meets the needs of all kids. Obviously,
then, any effort at multicultural development must include all to work.
It may be that you will want to add a multicultural curriculum component, and if so, consider integrating it into the character education curriculum.

A Greater Variety of Teaching Strategies

I do not focus on pedagogy (instructional technology) in this section
for several reasons. The most important of which is that if we focus on
instructional technology, I worry that we will not be able to boost our
thinking beyond the conventional model of school. Of course, we know
that kids learn in different ways and at different rates. I am sure that we
can all agree that the previous point is an important one. I do not believe, however, that teaching technology (pedagogy) is a primary concern for you. In my view, the technology of teaching in not a primary issue; it is a secondary one. That isn't to suggest that pedagogy is
unimportant. Research has made it clear that the quality of instruction
varies from classroom to classroom. The most important factor affecting
student learning is the teacher. Of course, individual teachers have a
profound influence on student learning even in schools that are relatively ineffective.[9]

The face of closing the achievement gap has many complex expres-
sions. I am strongly persuaded that the classroom is an important element to explore. I believe that our time would be spent more wisely by
focusing on several of the primary instructional elements.

The Changing Role of the Teacher   *The teacher as facilitator*: In
the first place we have to have a different picture of good teachers and of
their functions. In a standards-based school students must be given more
responsibility for their own education. You will remember observing a
class (maybe even your own) where the person who is most committed,
most motivated, and hardest working is the teacher. For the most part, students are leaning back as if to say, "Alright, teach me but it better be easy
and fun." Of course, that picture may be a reach, but not much. The challenge we have, then, is to create classrooms where more learning occurs

than teaching. The model must be decentralized. It must be more student centered than teacher directed. In the first place, unlike the conventional model of teacher as lecturer, conditioner, reinforcer, and boss, the Taoist helper or teacher is receptive rather than intrusive. I once learned that in the world of boxers, a youngster who feels himself to be good and wants to become a boxer will go to a gym and look up the at manager and say, "I would like to be a pro, and I would like to be in your stable and I'd like you to manage my work with you." In the world of boxing, what is then done, characteristically, is to try him out. The good manager will select one of his professionals and say, "Take him on in the ring. Stretch him. Let's see what he can do. Just let him show his very best. Draw him out." If it turns out that the boxer has promise, then the good manager will take that boy and train him to be, if he is Joe Dokes, a better Joe Dokes. The point is, the teacher does not start all over and say, "Forget all you've learned." This is like saying forget what kind of body you have, or forget what you are good for. The manager or teacher takes the student and builds upon his or her own talents and builds him or her up into the very best Joe Dokes–type boxer that he can possibly be.[10]

I am sensitive about moving beyond the issue of teaching pedagogy, because I do not want it to be assumed that instructional pedagogy is ignored. Simply said, the message that I want to share is, at once, more fundamental and more detailed than the models of teaching. What is true is that teachers learn how to teach (probably after graduation and in a classroom) based on how the teacher learns best, and by modeling the teacher who had the biggest impact on them when they were students. A teacher has incredible capacity to design lessons to meet the learning needs of the students. Therefore, I have passed on the urge to put all of the hopes on the teachers' pedagogy, because that issue is secondary (to come later) to the serious task at hand. In my considered judgment, many of our strongest teachers have the skills but they do not have the terms to describe what they are doing. When the time is right, teachers possess the knowledge and skills to address instructional strategy.

Teacher as executive: Albert Shanker, president of the American Federation of Teachers (AFT), wrote an article in the *New York Times* that has always amazed me as brilliant. Whenever a product is produced or a service rendered, those who tell the workers what to do, and often how to do it, are called managers. It would appear quite natural to consider teachers as managers because they function as managers. Teachers perform the same functions as managers. Teachers help students set goals, and then they supervise and evaluate their work progress in relationship to the goals. Further, teachers are responsible for the successes and failures within their classroom. Teachers even report to the corporate board (e.g., school board, PTA, Booster club). Teachers even provide periodic written reports on the progress of their students. The aforementioned functions are quite similar to the functions of a manager—with the possible exception that teachers have a more complex job and shoulder more responsibility than managers.[11]

Unfortunately, teachers see themselves as workers, not managers, a point of view that is shared by administrators and most of the public as well. Most teachers have given little thought to what managers might do that goes beyond the traditional role, because they perceive themselves to be much more of a worker than a manager. I suggest the teacher as manager should be given some serious attention. When teachers return in the fall, each could be given business cards and stationery. Proper door plaques could be made expressing the change. Teachers could be given parking passes. Teachers from all of the feeder schools could and should be given a cap and gown and expected to take a prestigious place at the graduation of their students or former students. I personally recommend that additional monetary incentives be included, along with other duties for which the individual is qualified and interested.

NOTES

1. John Cook, ed. *The Book of Positive Quotations*, (Minneapolis, Minn.: Fairview Press, 1996), 287.

2. Jamie Castellano, "Instruction in the Inclusion Classroom," (paper presented at the Annual Meeting of American Association for Supervision and Curriculum Development, Philadelphia, Penn., January 2004), 1.

3. Kris Beal, personal communication, 4 Nov. 2003.

4. Quoted in Daniel Goleman, *Emotional Intelligence: Why It Can Matter More Than IQ*, (New York: Bantam Books, 1995), 285.

5. Quoted in Goleman, *Emotional Intelligence: Why It Can Matter More Than IQ*, 286.

6. John Goodlad, "Teaching What We Hold Sacred," *Educational Leadership*, vol. 61, no. 10 (January 2002), 18–21.

7. Gary R. Howard, "Leadership for Equity and Diversity: Engaging Significant Passages," (paper presented at the 36th annual IDEA Fellows Program, Denver, Colo., July 2003), 2.

8. Howard, "Leadership for Equity and Diversity: Engaging Significant Passages," 5.

9. Robert J. Marzano, Debra J. Pickering, and Jane E. Pollock, *Classroom Instruction That Works*, (Alexandria, Va.: Association for Supervision and Curriculum Development, 2001), 3.

10. Arthur W. Combs, "New Concepts of Human Potential: Challenge for Teachers," in *Four Psychologies Applied to Education*, Thomas B. Roberts, ed., (New York: Schenkman Publishing Company, 1975), 310.

11. Cited in William Glasser, *Choice Theory in the Classroom* (Nerw York: HarperCollins, 1986), 94–95.

EPILOGUE: TEACHING—THE FINAL BALANCING ACT

Man is the only animal that laughs
And weeps, for he is the only animal
That is struck with the difference between what things are, and what
They might have been.

—William Hazlitt

Some things you can't learn from others,
You must feel the fire.

—Norman Douglas

A paradox is defined as a statement that appears to contradict itself or to be contrary to common sense. There can be little doubt that standards are good for schools because schools have improved as a result of rigorous academic standards. Nevertheless there is much in the SBM that is pregnant with paradox. The first and arguably the most paradoxical of all is the No Child Left behind (NCLB) Act. I have written a little ballad to recognize those things that just do not make sense. This sonnet is for you, my esteemed colleagues.

NCLB: The Paradoxical Precept

The No Child Left Behind Act is a paradox; it ensures student success but sorts for failure.

The NCLB has important goals, but there is no money.

The paradox of our time is that we have higher standards, but unsatisfactory schools;

A critical Government, but approving parents;

An advanced placement curriculum, but apathetic students who do not think.

We have rigorous academic standards. But no will to succeed.

We have a large number of educational leaders, but they are lost.

We have politicians with many views, but no vision.

Higher standards, yet less success.

We value character education, but condone unethical leadership.

Too many educational experts, yet no solutions.

We believe in religious freedom but not self-control;

We seek direction, yet school leaders are cut;

We require too much, but support too little.

We talk too much, and care too little.

We teach students to be considerate, yet we do not respect them.

We agonize too much, but organize too little;

Care too much, and love too little; work too hard, and play too little.

We increase our standards, yet fail to teach.

We teach higher order thinking skills, yet students can't solve everyday problems.

Children are taught to love their neighbor at school, but ridicule their friends at home.

We get too angry, and forgive others too little; give too much and take too little.

We measure too much, and affirm too little; pressure too much and love too little.

We are more and more affective and less and less effective.

We pontificate about accountability, but not humanity.

We are struggling to learn, yet we cannot teach.

We are anxious to grow, yet we cannot go.

We have taught the blind to read, yet we cannot see.

We teach children to plan their lives, yet we ourselves are out of control.

We love our kids, but not our family.

Unions demand more, but do less.

We utilize increased technology with too little touch.

We build big dreams without foundations.

We can fly at the speed of sound, yet we know not serenity.

We can travel to the moon for rocks, but not to the shelter for love.

We fight for security abroad, but do not allow oppressive ignorance in schools.

We travel the world but not our own neighborhoods.

We fight for freedom abroad, but condone economic servitude at home.

We have walked on the moon, but not our school hallways.

We value scholastic achievement, but not character development.

We force too much, and embrace too little.

Preach about schools too often, and pray for them too seldom.

We have been here before, with Mann and Dewey, yet we are still lost, in the paradox.

Nonetheless, "We shall not cease exploration, and in the end of all our exploring, will be to arrive where started, and know that place for the first time."[1]

We have discussed how stressful it is to work in the inflexible and unforgiving atmosphere of an SBS. It is clearly a paradox that we choose this work for reasons of the heart, and in the end, it is the heart that can kill us. For the past many pages, my focus has been on the question, what is best for our kids? Now, I want to conclude with the question, what is the most important thing you can do for yourself and other adults in an SBS?

George Allen reportedly told the following story to his professional football teams during critical moments in the season. "When the sun comes up on the Serengeti Plain in Africa, the gazelle knows that it must run faster than the fastest lion or it will be killed and eaten. And the lion knows that it must run faster than the slowest gazelle or it will starve to death and die. So, when the sun comes up in the morning in Africa, no matter whether you are a gazelle or a lion, you better be running."

I am worried that you will run at breakneck speed until something awful happens. Always remember that in the race to develop standards-based schools there is no finish line. Unfortunately, this is a race that is very familiar to all of us.

In February 1998, I was working as the superintendent of a medium-sized school district in Oregon. I was working hard, having fun, experiencing success, and generally just about full of myself. In the blink of an eye it went from the best of times to the worst of times. I fell victim to a stroke.

I remember the emergency medical technician telling me that I had had a stroke. I tried to think if I knew what a stroke was, but to no avail. I returned to work almost immediately, completing my therapy during the infrequent breaks in my day. I have elected to conclude this book with the most important lesson that I learned in 32 years of being an educator.

HIGH-PERFORMANCE PEOPLE AND SCHOOLS NEED TO PRACTICE BALANCE

Like many people, I was oblivious to the dangers of chronic stress. I did not imagine that I had a thing to worry about. My doctor had told me that I was healthy, so I was feeling great. I had always exercised daily, and I generally ate the correct foods; my weight was down. I was anxious and not sleeping very well. While I thought nothing of it at the time, I later learned that I was experiencing chronic stress. On a Friday morning in February, I experienced a stroke in the privacy of a public restroom. I was absolutely stunned, as was everyone else, because I looked like I was fit and healthy. Chronic stress is a killer, and no one gets away with thumbing their nose at chronic stress. I was shocked that I had such incomplete and inaccurate information on the hidden dangers of chronic stress. (It is now called the silent killer.) I have two advanced degrees and I was also trained as an army medic, yet still ignored the danger signs and it nearly killed me. I am compelled to share this story with you as a friendly precaution. This is an extremely high priority lesson for you even if you are in excellent health. There will most assuredly be those working with you that are on the verge of a near-death experience, and that is if they are lucky.

Unfortunately, it has been my experience that those of us who are the highest risk for a stress-related (work-related) medical injury are the least open to the subject. So, it is up to you to help other members on the team who choose to be blind to this terrible risk. Most of us are left to learn this lesson on our own, because few programs teach about the importance of health and balance. I did not learn of these consequences as a part of my formal schooling. I learned this important lesson through the "Earth school" (the hard way). High-performance people tend to drive too hard. They take shortcuts that can become deadly.

The point is to establish a pace at work that can be maintained over the long run. It is not acceptable for you to shortchange yourself or your family for reasons at the school. In my mind, the balance of health and wellness includes attention to mind, body, and soul. The incredible truth is that high-performance people will sometimes ignore the balance of mind, body, and soul to get more done at school. The concept of balance is a remarkably simple, yet powerful one. If our lifestyle choices decrease our joy for living while having a negative impact on our level of performance in life and in work, one must make an investment in balance. When I say balance, I mean that each of three dimensions should receive a relatively similar amount of development and attention. The three dimensions are mind, body, and soul. Let me provide you with a few starter thoughts about the balance of mind, body, and soul.

Mind

The most frequent request that I get, especially from teachers and administrators, is not related to school improvement but to balance. Teachers will frequently say to me, "I am trying to do too much. I would appreciate it if you could just help me to focus." Ironically, if one invests in balance, more quality work gets accomplished anyway. In my experience the balance of mind does not include seeking professional assistance. Rather, balance of mind is really having the discipline to recognize what is really important in your life and then to establish priorities that reflect those values. At the risk of sounding presumptuous, is it possible your family deserves more of you than you currently give them? With all due respect, it is not acceptable for you to steal time from your family to spend more time with your school family. In my humble opinion, there is simply no gain to be had when one's priorities are misaligned. In such an instance, it is my strong opinion that both families (home and school) will suffer. I would invite you to write down all of the big chunks that occupy your time, and then estimate the time spent on each per week and month. Do you see some type of sensible balance? Are you satisfied with the outcome?

Body

When I think of body I am thinking of what it takes to get and keep your body running at peak efficiency. It seems a little mundane to comment on such an elementary truth. Simple and true, yes! Nevertheless, physical fitness is most frequently overlooked. Forgive me if I review a few basic truths for us. In my experience, there are three concepts related to physical wellness:

1. A well-balanced diet is important because it provides you with the proper fuel to meet the many demands on your time.
2. Physical fitness involves two activities. The first, cardiovascular exercise, affects the health and function of the heart, lung, and circulatory system. Healthy "cardio," as the health club rats call it, involves workouts such as riding a stationary bike, walking on a treadmill or high stepper, jogging, riding a bike, speed walking or anything that gets your heart rate up.
3. The second type of physical fitnes, resistance training, increases the nervous system and muscle activity. This creates an "after burn" that can last for days.

Soul

This is a most sensitive area to address because it is very personal for everyone. It is my personal belief that every person is born with a certain void or emptiness. Throughout life there is a search to fill that void with something that satisfies. Some people, unhappily, make unhealthy choices about filling the void. They fill it with food, drugs, exercise, sex, work, or anything else that seems to give a sense of satisfaction. In the final analysis, the only thing that really fills the emptiness adequately is God. This comment is not an altar call. Rather it is an alert that spirituality is a natural need that should be addressed in a way that makes sense for you. I have made my choice. I am a Christian. The rest is up to you.

A FINAL COMMENT

The concept I have been discussing includes finding a way to balance the three domains of physical, emotional, and spiritual (see figure 6.1). I personally do not see any of these as standing alone because they are in actuality so strongly interrelated that they become synonymous.

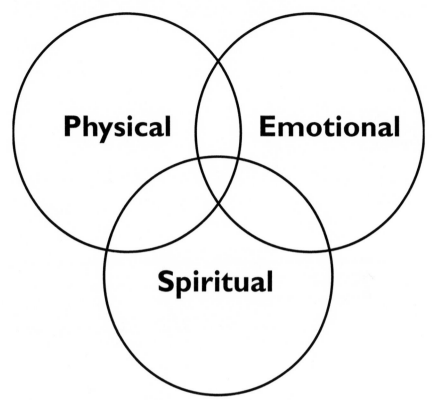

Figure 6.1.   Holistic Balance

We define school as a complex structure of dependent and inter-dependent elements whose properties are largely defined by how they function as a whole. Therefore, the school is more than the sum of its parts. In a similar way, the concept of balance unifies powerful and discretely separate entities into one whole. For example, when we see a beautiful picture on television we see a vast array of colored dots called pixels, which combine to form a pattern. If we were to focus on each individual dot, then we would see specks of color rather than the colored picture. The same is true when we listen to an orchestra. One does not hear the individual notes or instruments, but rather one hears the beautiful aural experience. The music selection and the beautiful picture on television are certainly more than the sum of the individual parts. The same is true with the concept of health and balance.

QUESTIONS OR CLARIFICATIONS

It is not unreasonable to assume that some may have questions or would like more detailed discussions. If so, I can be reached in Portland, Oregon, at (503) 247-8126 or by e-mail at superdent@msn.com.

NOTE

1. T. S. Eliot, *Collected Poems, 1909–1962*, (Orlando, Fla.: Harcourt, Brace, 1968), 208.

APPENDIX A:
DECISION BY CONSENSUS

TECHNIQUES TO FACILITATE CONSENSUS

It is possible to build relationships among the members of a face-to-face group so that decisions can be made effectively by consensus. More effective groups tend to have leaders who allow greater participation, wider initial divergence of expressed judgments, and greater acceptance of diverse decisions (see Torrance, 1975). Moreover, effective leaders have been shown to encourage minority opinions and conflict to a greater extent than less effective leaders. Coch and French (1948) have also shown that group participants with little influence over a decision usually are less likely to carry out the decision when action is required.

Stimulation of Minority

In consensual decision making, special care must be taken to uncover minority views that may not easily come to the surface. This can be done by tactfully inviting silent members to express their view. To elicit responses from others effectively, group members can use paraphrasing, summarizing, and checking the feelings of others. Sometimes someone in the group can be asked to assume the role of the minority and to express his view to the rest of the group; some members of the minority may then care to say whether the role-taker's expression was accurate.

Taking a Survey

An essential technique for obtaining a consensus is the survey. The full use of this technique involves the following steps. First, someone presents the issue clearly. Then, one or two others clarify it by restating it. Following that, everyone in turn states his reactions to the proposal.

In 1972 Gary Phillips taught Site-Based Governance Training at Battle Ground, Washington. He expounded on the use of using the survey as a tool for facilitating a consensus. Each person should be as brief as possible while still being clear, but he need not restrict himself to *yes* or *no*. He may say that he is uncertain, that he is confused and wants to hear more, that he is experiencing some pain, or he can simply say that he does not wish to talk about it. A group using the survey should not allow an individual to remain completely silent. If someone does not want to speak, he must at least say explicitly he wants to say nothing. This assures the group of bringing up to date its knowledge of every member's point of view on the question and of doing so through explicit statements, not presumptions.

CONSENSUS HANDOUT

Consensus means that:

- All participants contribute. Everyone's opinions are used and encouraged.
- Differences are viewed as helpful rather than hindering.
- Everyone can paraphrase the issue.
- Everyone has a chance to express feelings about the issue.
- Those members who continue to disagree indicate that they are willing to experiment for a prescribed period of time.
- All members share in the final decision.

Consensus does not mean that:

- A vote is unanimous.
- The result is everyone's first choice.
- Everyone agrees (only that there is enough support for the decision to be carried out).
- Conflict or resistance will be overcome immediately.

Not all decisions should be made by consensus. The most important point is that everyone agrees on how decisions are to be made.

INSTRUCTIONS FOR CONSENSUS

Consensus is a decision process of making full use of available resources and for resolving conflicts creatively. Consensus is difficult to reach, so not every ranking will meet with everyone's complete approval. Complete unanimity is not the goal—it is rarely achieved. But each individual should be able to accept the group rankings on the basis of logic and feasibility. When all group members feel this way, you have reached a consensus as defined here, and the judgment may be entered as a group decision. This means, in effect, that a single person can block the group if he or she thinks it necessary; at the same time, he or she should use this option in the best sense of reciprocity. Here are some guidelines to use in achieving consensus:

1. Avoid arguing for your own rankings. Present your position as lucidly and logically as possible, but listen to the other members' reactions and consider them carefully before you press your point.
2. Do not assume that someone must win and someone must lose when discussion reaches a stalemate. Instead, look for the next-most-acceptable alternative for all parties.
3. Do not change your mind simply to avoid conflict and to reach agreement and harmony. When agreement seems to come too quickly and easily, be suspicious. Explore the reasons and be sure everyone accepts the solution for basically similar or complimentary reasons. Yield only to positions that have objective and logically sound foundations.

4. Avoid conflict-reducing techniques such as majority vote, averages, coin flips, and bargaining. When a dissenting member finally agrees, don't feel that he or she must be rewarded by having his or her own way on some later point.
5. Differences of opinion are natural and expected. Seek them out and try to involve everyone in the decision process. Disagreements can help the group's decision because with a wide range of information and opinions, there is a greater chance that the group will hit upon more adequate solutions.

Consensus Rules

1. Everyone participates.
2. Everyone can paraphrase.
3. Everyone has a chance to express feelings.
4. Members who disagree say they will try the solution for a specified period of time.
5. All members share in the final decision.

NOTE

Reprinted by permission. Richard A. Schmuck and Philip J. Runkle, *The Handbook of Organization Development in Schools and Colleges*, 4th ed., (Prospect Heights, Ill.: Waveland Press, 1994), 310–311.

APPENDIX B: TEAM-BUILDING ACTIVITIES FOR STUDENTS AND STAFF

ACTIVITY: INTRODUCTION TO TEAM BUILDING

Outcomes:	1. Participants understand the rationale for team building.
	2. Participants establish foundation of facilitator network by beginning colleague relationships with other team members.
	3. Participants know some skill groups need to function effectively.
Time:	5–10 minutes.
Group Size:	Large group, all participants.
Materials:	None.
Directions:	1. Present the lecture below.
	2. Hold discussion to a minimum until after the first team building activity.
Reflections:	1. The trusting relationships that provide the foundation for school improvement are begun here and now.
	2. The notion of building trust or building relationships may cause some anxiety as participants wonder what is this sensitivity stuff? There is always some risk in personal exposure, but reassure as appropriate.

Mini-Lecture: The rationale for team building.

The early sessions for planning for school improvement rely heavily on small group processes. As with other programs, people often work together on important tasks without being given the opportunity to learn the skills and understandings necessary to work as a team. Typically, such group skills: (1) are left to chance; (2) cause problems and delays when they are lacking, more delays than if time were taken to develop these skills early in group settings; and (3) need development even in groups that have worked together before. Teams need the following skills if they are to function together effectively: (1) team members need to know and understand one another; they need to know who one another are; how they became the people they are; and their interests, hobbies, teaching competencies, and other information that indicates what planning team members can contribute to school improvement in their schools, (2) team members need to understand value differences and similarities, values that might influence school improvement, typically focused on such topics as feelings about kids, the importance of discipline in school, grading and evaluation techniques, instructional strategies, how people learn, and the appropriate objectives for learning, and (3) team members need to be able to solve problems together; they need to be able to make decisions about such topics as the role of parents and community in the school, the degree of responsibility the students should have for their own learning, the role of teachers in the school, how decisions should be made in the school, how to deal with problem learners, how materials should be selected and evaluated, how to use time in a school day, and appropriate goals for the school. Team members must know why cooperation and working toward consensus are important. Team members must learn to effectively use two-way communication. Team members must trust fellow members' motives and abilities and learn to be open and honest. Team members must see differences as strengths.

ACTIVITY: GETTING TO KNOW YOU

Outcomes: 1. Participants know one another better.
                2. Participants are more aware of the need to listen to one another.

3. Participants are more aware of values present in the group.

4. Facilitator has evidence of comfort level of participants.

5. Facilitator has evidence of group skills and experienced participants.

Time: 50–60 minutes.

Group Size: Small, 5–8 participants per group.

Materials: One watch per group.

Directions:
1. Facilitator discusses rational and goals of the activity.

2. Facilitator explains that each member will have 5 minutes to tell their group about themselves, highlighting (a) what helped to make them who they are; and (b) their reasons for attending.

3. Facilitator models process by going first.

4. Facilitator then directs participants to take 2 minutes to write things they want to include in their talk. (This frees the participants to listen, minimizes mental rehearsing.)

5. Facilitator reminds participants to select a timekeeper, emphasizes importance of observing time limits, as participants begin.

6. Facilitator leads group discussion of reactions, learnings. Key questions:
   - What were your reactions as you listened to others? As you talked about yourself?
   - Why is this important?
   - How else might we get acquainted?
   - What did you learn or relearn from this?
   - What strengths did you discover in others?

Reflections:
1. Before asking participants to talk about themselves, you may want to suggest a brief list of topics such as:
   - Previous work experiences.
   - Family background.
   - Travel.
   - Hobbies.
   - Current/past learning projects.

- Special events in life.
- Experience with change.
- Hopes/expectations for school improvement plan (SIP).

2. Participation should be balanced, hence the importance of timekeeping.
3. If participants don't use all their time other members may want to ask questions.
4. As you model this, try to reveal something of the real you. Don't model just career history or credential sharing.
5. Be positive.

ACTIVITY: HIGH POINTS

Outcomes: 1. Participants know more about other group members.
2. Participants continue to identify similarities and differences among members.
3. Facilitator has additional evidence of group comfort level and group skills present.
4. Facilitator has additional information about knowledge and values of participants regarding SIP.

Time: 30–40 minutes.

Group Size: Small, 5–8 participants per group.

Materials: High points worksheets.

Directions: 1. Facilitator explains goals of activity and distributes worksheets.
2. Facilitator directs participants to complete the activity in small groups by:
   - Completing worksheets individually (allow 5 minutes for this).
   - Sharing high points in groups.
   - Being careful to use no more than 4 minutes per person.
3. Facilitator leads discussion of reactions and learnings.

Questions: What else did you learn about others?

How was this like or different from the previous activity?

What similarities/differences are you discovering?

What was important to you in the conduct of this? How could you do it differently?

What can one learn from this type of discussion?

Variations: Use different periods of time or different roles on the high points worksheets.

Direct participants to share only three, four, or five of the categories on their sheets.

Direct participants to reflect what was heard by repeating information to group members about themselves after all have completed the initial sharing round.

Reflections: 1. Remember that a high point is, above all, positive. It need not be especially significant to others, but it is memorable for the speaker.

2. Abraham Maslow and others claim that it is our high points that have the greatest growth-producing impact on our lives. Does your experience support this? What makes a high point anyway?

High Points

A high point is defined as any high positive experience one remembers. This experience need not be a unique or unusual experience, but it should be a peak experience to you. It should not be negative.
During the last week:

_____

_____

_____

_____

During the last two years:

_____

_____

_____

_____

Most recent fifth of my life:

_____

_____

_____

_____

Fourth fifth of my life:

_____

_____

_____

_____

Third fifth of my life:

_____

_____

_____

_____

Second fifth of my life:

_____

_____

_____

_____

First fifth of my life:

_____

_____

_____

_____

ACTIVITY: WHIP

Outcomes: 1. Facilitators focus attention of the group.
              2. Facilitators check individual emotional states.
              3. Participants know one another better.

Time: 50–60 minutes.
Group Size: Large or small.
Materials: None.
Directions: 1. Facilitator introduces activity, typically at the recon-
                  vening of a group, by presenting a sentence comple-
                  tion task and going first.
               2. Facilitator explains that participants may pass.
               3. Possible WHIP statements include:
                  • My childhood ambition was . . .
                  • A childhood success I had was . . .
                  • My favorite activities as a child were . . .
                  • My favorite teacher was . . .
                  • My favorite subject was . . .
                  • Smells I associate with childhood are . . .
                  • My favorite extracurricular activity was . . .
                  • Sounds I associate with childhood are . . .
                  • Scenes I associate with childhood are . . .
                  • An ideal vacation would be . . .
                  • An ideal sabbatical (or time of change) would be . . .
                  • An ideal evening is . . .
                  • Spring is . . .
                  • Fall is . . .
                  • Winter is . . .
                  • One wish I have is . . .
                  • One hope I have is . . .
                  • My favorite animal is . . .
                  • My favorite color is . . .
                  • My favorite car is . . .
                  • My favorite song is . . .
Reflections: 1. This is really a dual-purpose activity. It serves as a
                  warm-up or "sponge" activity and it is a quick check of
                  the condition of the group. Watch for signs of energy
                  or fatigue, eagerness or anxiety, involvement or disen-
                  gagement.
               2. This works best when kept light and quick; if someone
                  stalls for a thought, ask him to pass.

ACTIVITY: HUMAN DEVELOPMENT

Human development activities serve to build teams through honesty
and understanding.

1. Introductions.
2. Feelings or thoughts and behaviors:
   - Something that's new and good in my life.
   - One of the nicest things that ever happened to me.
   - Something I feel good and bad about at the same time.
   - Something I enjoy doing that I do well.
   - Something I like to imagine.
   - When I am myself.
   - The most significant gift ever given to me or that I ever gave to someone.
3. Dreaming:
   - Craziest dream I ever had.
   - A dream I wish was real.
   - An idea I got from a dream.
   - A dream I've had more than once.
   - Something I solved with a dream.
   - I did something in my dream that I couldn't do otherwise.
4. Values:
   - Something someone wants me to be.
   - Two things I believe in that conflict with each other.
   - When I was criticized for doing or saying something I thought was important.
   - The time I stood up for something I strongly believe in.
   - Some qualities that I look for in friends.
   - Something I can't stand.
5. Learning:
   - Something I learned that was enjoyable.
   - A time I taught something to someone else.
   - A skill I'm learning now that I didn't have a year ago.
   - A time I learned from failure.
   - Something I want to learn in the future.
   - The best class I ever took.

- I could learn better if I . . .
- Something that's getting easier all the time.

6. Communication:
   - How I got someone to pay attention to me.
   - Once when someone wouldn't listen to me.
   - A time when I really felt heard.
   - A time when I accepted someone else's feelings.
   - One of the nicest compliments I've ever received.
   - A time when listening would have kept me out of trouble.
   - Someone felt good because of what I said.

7. Trust:
   - A place where I feel safe.
   - When someone betrayed my trust.
   - Someone I learned to trust.
   - I didn't trust someone because of what someone else said.
   - A time when I wanted to be trusted.
   - Someone whose opinion I value very much.
   - I could have hurt someone's feeling but I didn't.
   - A person I feel safe with.
   - I kept a promise.

8. Friendship:
   - How I made friends and it turned out well.
   - What I like best about the person I like the most.
   - What I value in friends of the opposite sex.
   - How I handle disagreements with a friend.
   - One way I changed to be a better friend.
   - If I'm with a friend . . .
   - Things I enjoy doing with my friends away from school.

9. Perception:
   - An experience I had that caused me to see things differently.
   - A time someone tried to change my perception.
   - Something I see differently than my parents' generation sees it.
   - A time when I tried to put myself in someone else's shoes.
   - A class I took that caused me to see things differently.

10. Being a teenager:
    - The best thing about being a teenager.
    - The worst thing about being a teenager.

- A new responsibility I've assumed.
- A turning point in my life.
- A way my personality has changed for the better.
- The person I want to be in five years.
- When I feel discriminated against because of my age.
- When I go off by myself.
- Self-understanding that I've recently gained.
- When I like myself most.
- I felt uncomfortable with the me that emerged in a situation.
- How I want others to see me.

11. Winning and losing:
    - A time I won and loved it.
    - A time I won and felt bad about it.
    - A time I lost and took it hard.
    - A time I lost and felt okay about it.
    - A time I competed with myself.
    - How do you feel about competition?
    - A time I felt like a real winner.

12. Problem solving:
    - I solved a problem effectively.
    - When the easy way out made things worse or better.
    - When people try to solve each other's problems.
    - A problem I'd like suggestions for solving.

13. Decision making:
    - Looking back on a decision I made.
    - I didn't want to have to make a decision.
    - When I got (or didn't get) to share in making a decision.
    - The most difficult decision I've ever made.
    - I have good judgment.
    - I decided to change something about myself and did.

14. Success and failure:
    - They said I couldn't do something, but I could.
    - Something at which I'm getting better.
    - Something at which I'd like to succeed.
    - Something I wish I'd tried.
    - A capability I've recently discovered.

- Something I enjoy doing because it gives me a sense of accomplishment.
- I started something and finished it.

15. Accomplishments and goals:
    - Something I did (or made) that I'm proud of.
    - A project I've got going right now.
    - Something I've finished that I had a hard time starting.
    - When I get out of high school, I hope . . .
    - If I could accomplish anything I wanted, it would be . . .
    - A goal I'm sure to obtain.

16. Taking charge:
    - A time I proved I wasn't helpless.
    - A time I put off until tomorrow . . .
    - I handled a situation well that was like situations that used to upset me.
    - I got my courage up.
    - I made a plan and it worked.
    - I surprised myself when I got it done.
    - How I got what I needed.

17. Influence:
    - When one person's mood affected everyone else.
    - Someone tried to make me do something I didn't want to do.
    - When someone expected the very best of me.
    - Things I don't like conforming to.
    - When someone criticized me.
    - Someone did something for me that I really appreciated.
    - I went along with the gang.
    - I didn't know what group to go with.
    - A time when I felt pressured.

18. Assertiveness:
    - Later.

19. Feelings are facts:
    - A time I remember feeling totally alive and in touch with the world.
    - A time I was alone but not lonely.
    - My feeling label says . . .

- A time I trusted my feelings.
- A feeling of sadness I remember.
- A feeling I've had a hard time accepting.
- I told someone how I was feeling.
- A favorite feeling.
- When someone becomes jealous.
- When my anger forced me to do something.
- How my fear helped me realize a danger.
- A time I remember feeling important.

20. Reality and other realities:
    - Something I like to imagine.
    - Someone wouldn't face reality.
    - My reality was different from someone else's.
    - Something unexplainable happened.
    - What's your astrological sign?
    - What else is out there?

21. Responsibility:
    - A way I'm independent.
    - An agreement that was hard to keep.
    - My favorite excuse.
    - I didn't do something because I knew it would hurt someone.
    - I did it myself.
    - I didn't want to accept the consequences, but I did.
    - I did it because it needed to be done.

22. Sex roles:
    - Things I like about being a young man or young woman.
    - If I were a member of the opposite sex.
    - When I felt I was seen as an object.
    - As a young man or woman, I'm expected to . . .
    - As a young man or woman, I'm never expected to . . .
    - Ways I plan to be different from adults I know.
    - The kind of man or woman I want to be.

23. Parenthood:
    - One of the best times I ever spent with my parent(s).
    - Someone I know who is a good parent.
    - Something I think parents should not do.
    - The thing I look forward to most (or least) if I become a parent.

- Something my parent(s) did that I didn't appreciate at the time but now I do.
- Something I'm grateful to my parents for.
- The toughest thing about being a parent.

NOTE

Reprinted with permission of The Institute for Development of Education Activities, Inc. (IDEA).

BIBLIOGRAPHY

Adey, Philip. "Can Intelligence Be Taught?" Kings College University of London, 2001. http://www.kcl.ac.uk/phpnews/mview.php?ArtID=63 [accessed 22 Jan. 2003].

Addison, Joseph (1672–1719), English essayist. *Spectator*, no. 215 (London, 6 Nov. 1711), quoted in Robert Andrews, *Columbia Dictionary of Quotations*. New York: Columbia University Press, 1993.

Alexander, Lamar. *America 2000, An Education Strategy*. Sourcebook, Washington, D.C.: U.S. Department of Education Press, 1991.

Amen, Daniel. "Brain Science Research Matters in Mental Health." Paper presented at Meeting of Clinicians, Portland, Ore., March 2003.

———. *Change Your Brain, Change Your Life*. New York: Three Rivers Press, 1998.

Applied Research Center. "Public Schools in the United States: Some History," 2003. http://www.arc.org/erase/j_history.html [accessed 22 Nov. 2003].

Berliner, David C., and Bruce J. Biddle. *The Manufactured Crisis*. Reading, Mass.: Addison-Wesley Publishing Company, 1995.

Blanchard, Ken. *The Heart of a Leader*. Tulsa, Okla.: Honor Books, 1998.

Bracey, Gerald. "No Child Left Behind Act: A Plan for the Destruction of Public Education, Just Say No." Paper presented at the Development of Public Education (IDEA) Fellows Program, Denver, Colo., 2003.

———. "13th Bracey Report on the Condition of Public Education." *Education News*, Oct. 2003. http://www.educationnews.org/13th-bracey-report-on-the-condition.htm [accessed 11 Dec. 2003].

Buckingham, Marcus, and Curt Coffman. *First Break All the Rules*. New York: Simon and Schuster, 1999.

Buckingham, Marcus, and Donald O. Clifton. *Now Discover Your Strengths*. New York: Free Press, 2001.

Calvin, William H. *How Brains Think: Evolving Intelligence Then and Now*. New York: Basic Books, a member of Perseus Books Group, 1996.

Carruth, Gorton, and Eugene Ehrlich, eds. *The Giant Book of American Quotations*. New York: Carruth & Ehrlich Books, 1988.

Castellano, Jamie. "Instruction in the Inclusion Classroom." Paper presented at the Annual Meeting of American Association for Supervision and Curriculum Development, Philadelphia, Penn., January 2004.

Castillo, Susan. *Oregon Superintendent's Update #23*. August 28, 2003. http://www.ode.state.or.us/superintendent/update/ [accessed 9 Sept. 2003].

Celente, Gerald. *Trends 2000*. New York: Warner Books, 1997.

Clifton, Don, and Paula Nelson. *Soar with Your Strengths*. New York: Dell Publishing, 1996.

Combs, Arthur. "Concept of Human Potential and the School." Paper presented at the annual meeting of Montana's Association for Supervision and Curriculum Development, Missoula, Mont., 8 March 1978.

———. "New Concepts of Human Potential: Challenge for Teachers," in *Four Psychologies Applied to Education*. Edited by Thomas B. Roberts. New York: Schenkman Publishing Company, 1975.

Committee for Economic Development. "Unfinished Agenda: A New Vision for Child Development and Education." Presented in a Statement by the Research and Policy Committee. New York, 1991.

Cook, John, ed. *The Book of Positive Quotations*. Minneapolis, Minn.: Fairview Press, 1996.

Cotton, Kathleen. "Expectations and Student Achievement," in *School Improvement Series*. Portland, Ore: Northwest Regional Educational Laboratory, 1988.

Covey, Stephen. *The Seven Habits of Highly Effective People*. New York: Simon and Schuster, 1989.

Danielson, Charlotte. *Enhancing Professional Practice: A Framework for Teaching*. Alexandria, Va.: Association for Supervision and Curriculum Development, 1996.

Education Week, 2000. "High Poverty Among Young Makes Schools' Jobs Harder."

Ehrenreich, Barbara. *Fear of Falling: The Inner Life of the Middle Class*. New York: Pantheon, 1989.

Einstein, Albert (1879–1955), German-born U.S. physicist. Motto for the astronomy building of Junior College, Pasadena, California, quoted in Robert

Andress, *Columbia Dictionary of Quotations*. New York: Columbia University Press, 1993.

Eliot, T. S. *Collected Poems, 1909–1962*. Orlando, Fla.: Harcourt, Brace, 1963.

Facing History and Ourselves. "Teaching is a craft . . . Adolescents Are Our Future," 22 Oct. 2003. http://facinghistory.org/facing/fhao2.nsf/main/about+us [accessed 7 Nov. 2003].

Friedlander, Jordan. "History of Education in the 19th Century." Historic Documents, Abstract. http://www.bigredboots.com/map.htm [accessed 15 Oct. 2003].

Glasser, William. *Choice Theory in the Classroom*. New York: HarperCollins, 1986.

Goleman, Daniel. *Emotional Intelligence: Why It Can Matter More Than IQ*. New York: Bantam Books, 1995.

Goleman, Daniel, Richard Boyatzis, and Annie McKee. *Primal Leadership: Realizing the Power of Emotional Intelligence*. Boston: Harvard Business School Press, 2002.

Goodlad, John I. *A Place Called School*. New York: McGraw-Hill, 1984.

Goodwin, Bryon. "Digging Deeper: Where Does the Public Stand on Standards-Based Education?" Mid-Continent Regional Educational Laboratory (McREL), *Issues Brief*, July 2003. http://www.mcrel.org/topics/product Detail.asp?productID=141

Hand, Raymond V., ed. *American Quotations*. New York: Random House, 1989.

Howard, Gary R. "Leadership for Equity and Diversity: Engaging Significant Passages." Paper presented at the 36th annual IDEA Fellows Program, Denver, Colo., July 6, 2003.

"Immigration." *Microsoft Encarta Online Encyclopedia 2003*. http://Encarta .msn.com/encylopedia_761566973/immigration.html [accessed 15 Oct. 2003].

Indiana State Department of Education. "Compulsory Attendance," 1994. http://indstate.edu/iseas/cmps-atd1.html [accessed 3 Oct. 2003].

Kerman, Sam. "Teacher Expectations and Student Achievement." *Kappan*, June 1979, 1–5.

Konrád, George (b. 1933), Hungarian writer, politician. *Sunday Correspondent* (London, 15 April 1990), on surviving as a writer in Communist Hungary, quotd in Robert Andrews, *Columbia Dictionary of Quotations*. New York: Columbia University Press, 1993.

Kozol, Jonathan. *Savage Inequalities*. New York: Crown Publishers, 1991.

Lambourne, Karen, and Maxine Baca Zinn. "Education, Race, and Family: Issues for the 1990s." Working Paper No. 16, August 1993. Julian Samora Research Institute. http://jsri.msu.edu/RandS/research/wps/wp16abs.html [accessed 22 Dec. 2003].

Lu, Hsien-Hen L. "Ending Child Poverty." National Center for Children in Poverty at the Joseph L. Mailman School of Public Health at Columbia University, 2003. http://www.nccp.org/pub_ecp02.html [accessed 15 Aug. 2004].

Marzano, Robert J. and Daisey Arredondo. "Tactics for Thinking: Teachers Manual." Aurora, Colo.: Mid-Continent Regional Educational Laboratory, 1986.

Marzano, Robert J., and John S. Kendall. "A Comprehensive Guide to Designing Standardized-Based Districts, School Classrooms," 1996. http://www.ascd.org/publications/books/1996marzano/1996marzonotoc.html [accessed 9 Sept. 2002].

Marzano, Robert J., Debra J. Pickering, and Jane E. Pollock. *Classroom Instruction That Works*. Alexandria, Va.: Association for Supervision and Curriculum Development, 2001.

Maslow, Abraham. "Maslow's Hierarchy of Needs." *Educational Psychology Interactive*, 2004. http://chiron.valdsta.edu/whutt.col/regsy/Maslow.html [accessed 21 Feb. 2004].

"National Defense Education Act." *Columbia Encyclopedia*, Sixth Edition, 2001.

Oakes, Jeannie, and Amy Stuart Wells. "Detracking for High Student Achievement." *Educational Leadership* 55, Mar. 1998. http://wilsontxt.hwwilson.com/pdffull/03461/LBEI1/LZB.pdf [accessed 12 Nov. 2003].

"Public Education in the United States." *Microsoft Encarta Online Encyclopedia 2003.* http://encarta.msn.com/encyclopedia_7615714941Public_Education_in_the_United_States. . . .

Reigber, Beth Demain. Associated Press. "Edison Schools Shareholders Approve Buyout to Take Company Private," *Miami Herald*, 12 Nov. 2003. http://www.miami.com/mld/miamiherald/business/7245618.htm?1c [accessed 15 Nov. 2003].

Rogers, Carl. "Psychology of the Classroom." Paper presented at the Annual Meeting of the Montana Association for Supervision and Curriculum Development.

Rogers, Donald J. "How to Teach Fear," in *Four Psychologies Applied to Education*. Edited by Thomas B. Roberts. New York: Schenkman Publishing Company, 1975.

Smith, Jenny. *Education and Public Health: Natural Partners in Learning for Life*. Alexandria, Va.: Association for Supervision Development and Curriculum, 2003.

Snell, Lisa. "School Choice, Education Privatization: What's the Difference?" Reason Public Policy Institute, 2002. http://www.rppi.org/charterschools.html [accessed 12 Dec. 2003].

Steinhoff, Jonathon. "No Child Left Behind Inflicts Curse on Public Schools." *Oregonian*, 5 Oct. 2003.

Tyson, Ann Scott. "Just Getting By: High Schoolers Say the Path to a Diploma is Too Easy." HBSCO HOST: *Research Databases*, 1997. http://web16.wpnet .com/citation.asp?tb=1&_ug=dbs [accessed 18 June 2003].

United States Department of Education. "A Nation at Risk," 1983.

Washington, Booker T. "Democracy and Education." Address given in New York on 30 Sept. 1896. http://teachingamericanhistory.org/library/index.asp? document=57 [accessed 6 Dec. 2003].

Webster's New Riverside Dictionary, 11th Edition, revised. New York: Houghton Mifflin Company, 1996.

Wheatley, Margaret. *Leadership and the New Science*. San Francisco: Barrett-Koehler Publisher, 1999.

Woodward, Tali. "Edison's Failing Grade: Investors and School Districts Are Ditching the Country's Leading Public Education Privatizer." *Corp Watch*, 20 June 2002. http://www.corpwatch.org/issues/PID.jsp?articleid=2688 [accessed 5 Dec. 2003].

ABOUT THE AUTHOR

Tim J. Carman was born in Lewistown, Montana, September 3, 1947, the son of Edward F. and Ann L. Carman. He was married to Donna L. Freier in 1969 and Barbara May in 1989. Tim has one child, Jami Lynn.

Dr. Carman's educational background provided a strong basis with which to write this book. He graduated from Glasgow (Montana) High School in 1965 and Northern Montana State College in 1969 with a B.A. in secondary education and social studies. He went on to earn his M.A. in history at Montana State University in 1971 and an Ed.D. in curriculum and instruction in 1979.

Carman has worked at all levels in education for 32 years and is most proud of the time he has spent teaching. He started teaching physical education even before he graduated from Northern and went on to teach at Sunhaven Middle School and then at Capital High School, both in Helena, Montana. In recent years, Carman has been teaching at the graduate school level at the University of Phoenix in Tigard, Oregon, and Lewis and Clark College in Portland, Oregon. He has had the unusual experience of teaching across all grade levels from kindergarten to graduate school.

Carman has also been an administrator at nearly all levels. In order of succession, he was an assistant principal, high school principal, assistant superintendent, director of the educational administration program at

Lewis and Clark College, and both deputy superintendent and superintendent of schools in Albany, Oregon. At the public-policy level, he was an advisor for the State Board of Education in Oregon for two years and to Oregon's governor (on education issues).

This is the second book on education Carman has written since an illness forced an untimely retirement from his final position as superintendent of schools in Albany, Oregon (8,000 students and 19 schools). His first book was written for leaders just prior to the No Child Left Behind (NCLB) Act because he wanted to continue to help schools even in retirement. The NCLB Act prompted this second book. Leaders, of course, do make a difference. It is difficult to impossible to sustain a high-performance school with a mediocre principal. The quality of a school always comes down to the quality of the teachers, and that is why he wrote this book.

For many teachers, NCLB came like a thief in the night. The unfortunate sorrow with that legislation is that it seems to assume that teachers could do more to close the achievement gap than is currently being done. He is strongly persuaded that this is not the case. There may be a select few teachers somewhere who really don't care, but the vast majority of teachers in this country pour their soul into their vocation every single day.

Over the last 32 years, Carman has learned that teachers are drawn to their work for reasons of the heart. Here is just a bit more about the motivation issue. One of the first sanctions to be imposed on a school that is deemed to be "in need of improvement" is to move the struggling student to another school. From a school improvement perspective this intervention makes absolutely no sense, because that sanction is not really intended to help the student but is intended to punish the school by drawing away precious resources from struggling schools while simultaneously putting additional pressure on neighboring schools in the form of more students. Therefore, NCLB is having a negative impact on the morale of public schools in America. It is the author's goal that people see this book as one written to help the caring forces of education to successfully meet this obvious presidential attack intended to destabilize and privatize schools in America.

Tim Carman may be reached in Portland, Oregon, by phone at (503) 247-8126 (office) or e-mail at superdent@msn.com.